WRITING AS A LEARNING TOOL

STUDIES IN WRITING

VOLUME 7

Writing as a Learning Tool

Integrating Theory and Practice

Edited by

Päivi Tynjälä
University of Jyväskylä, Finland

Lucia Mason
University of Lecce, Italy

and

Kirsti Lonka
University of Helsinki, Finland

KLUWER ACADEMIC PUBLISHERS
DORDRECHT / BOSTON / LONDON

A C.I.P. Catalogue record for this book is available from the Library of Congress.

ISBN 0-7923-6877-0 (HB)
ISBN 0-7923-6914-9 (PB)

Published by Kluwer Academic Publishers,
P.O. Box 17, 3300 AA Dordrecht, The Netherlands.

Sold and distributed in North, Central and South America
by Kluwer Academic Publishers,
101 Philip Drive, Norwell, MA 02061, U.S.A.

In all other countries, sold and distributed
by Kluwer Academic Publishers,
P.O. Box 322, 3300 AH Dordrecht, The Netherlands.

Printed on acid-free paper

Printed in the Netherlands

TABLE OF CONTENTS

PROLOGUE

LITERATE MINDS; LITERATE SOCIETIES

DAVID R. OLSON

The Ontario Institute for Studies in Education, University of Toronto, Canada

'The essential innovation which writing brings is not a new mode of exchanging and storing information but a new mentality' (Roy Harris, 1986: 99).

The relation between mind and society is fundamental to many of the human sciences. The direction of influence is the problem. Does social change entail changes in mentality or do changes in mentality produce social changes? If both, how? The study of the implications of literacy provides a forum for examining this complex relationship. A literate society can be viewed as the social organization produced by minds made literate through schooling. Conversely, literate minds may be viewed as the product of participation in a literate society. What would seem to be needed is a clearer conception, on one hand, of what a literate mentality is, and on the other, of what a literate society is. I will suggest that a literate society is not to be defined by the fact that a substantial segment of the population is literate although that is an important part of it. On the other hand, neither is personal literacy assured simply by the creation of and participation in literate institutional structures. Our puzzle is how to understand each in turn and then to suggest some of their interrelationships. First, the mind.

In this day of emphasis on domain specific competencies, the notion of anything as general as a literate mentality may strike some readers as implausible. Yet writing and literacy in modern societies is so pervasive and employed in so many contexts that there may be merit in characterizing this competence in quite general terms. There is precedent for looking at general forms of competence and yet none of the standard views acknowledge the cognitive implications of writing generally as Harris suggested in the epigram that introduced this prologue.

The modular theory of mind, suggested by Chomsky (1980) but turned into an explicit theory by Fodor (1983) was advanced primarily to explain the peculiarities

D.R Olson (2001). Prologue: Literate minds; literate societes. In G. Rijlaarsdam (Series ed.) & P. Tynjälä, L. Mason & K. Lonka (Volume eds.), *Studies in Writing, Volume 7, Writing as a Learning tool: Integrating Theory and Practice, 1 – 6.© 2001.* Kluwer Academic Publishers. Printed in the Netherlands.

of language, but when generalized offered the possibility of different modes of thought, one associated with each module. The 'theory of mind' module, for example, would explain the special human competence to understand the intentional states of oneself and others. But as no one is prepared to suggest that nature is so prescient as to have anticipated the need for a specialized module for literate thought, modular theory would seem to have little to offer to the explanation of a literate mentality.

Howard Gardner's (1993) 'multiple intelligences', an updated version of Thurstone's (1938) primary mental abilities, attempts to identify modes of thought with such faculties as spatial ability, numerical ability, verbal ability and the like. Cultural activities, such as drawing and writing (Gardner & Wolf, 1993) are seen as trading on these basic abilities. However, there is no way of using this concept of abilities to address the differences between oral competence and those special competencies associated with writing and literacy. There is no space for a 'literate mentality'. Indeed, there is every chance that what we take as verbal ability is more correctly characterized as literate ability in that measures of verbal ability frequently trade on just those aspects of and orientations to knowledge that are shaped up in a literate tradition. The ability to define isolated words is a case in point; it is a literate tradition which tends to pull words apart from things.

Piaget's theory of 'formal operations' comes closest to what may be thought of as defining a literate mentality (Piaget, 1929). It is the ability to deal with abstract symbols such as words or numerals as if they were objects in their own right and then applying formal rules to those symbols to turn them into other symbols. The result is logic on the one hand and mathematics on the other. But these activities, too, would seem to be dependent at least in part on the invention of appropriate notations and algorithms for operating on them (Damerow, 1999), activities that are characteristic of distinctively literate thought.

The 'literacy hypothesis', however, differs from all of these in suggesting that knowledge in any domain is altered by constructing written representations and then operating on these representations as a means of thinking about the domain represented. Although the project of capturing the distinctive properties of thought in each domain as it takes on the resources of writing and notations is at an early stage, some features seem clear enough. First, there is a well established link between learning to read and write and 'consciousness' of such aspects of language as words, sentences and phonemes. Second, the actual practice of writing and reading, at least in some contexts, contributes to a style of thinking which is more literal and decontextualized (Olson, 1994) and, indeed, more language based. Although writing can have such effects, many writers resist the idea that there is such thing as a 'literate mentality.' Roy Harris and I seem to be the exceptions although we have allies in some older traditions.

The 'literate mentality' thesis is not a new one. The thesis began in the Enlightenment as a theory of the evolution of culture in the hands of such writers as Vico, Condorcet, Kant, Hegel, Herder and, in this century, Cassirer, who proposed that mankind had progressed through a series of stages from primitive, to totemic, to heroic, to the modern view of 'inclusive humanity' (Cassirer, 1957). In the hands of Durkheim (1948), this became a sociological theory in which social forms of organization were seen as determining psychological states. Levy-Bruhl (1923) and Vygotsky (1962), to come to our own time, cast these mentalities into psychological terms, the former with the theory of 'primitive' mentality characterized by a contextual-dependence which he described as participatory thought, the latter with the theory 'socio-historical' cognition.

The 'literate mentality' theory is of a piece with that of Vygotsky. Vygotsky (1962) discussed the effects of writing in terms of consciousness, suggesting that writing turned speech into an object of analysis and, with the collaboration of Luria, attempted to show how forms of reasoning changed when one became literate. Vygotsky's hypotheses about thinking have not fared well empirically. Scribner and Cole (1981) showed that non-literate subjects reasoned just as logically as literate ones, the differences being accounted for in terms of 'familiarity with school-like tasks.' Bernardo, *et al.* (1995) reported similar findings in a study of 5 Filipino communities. Street (1984) argued that literacy had an impact only within certain, relatively narrowly defined, social contexts. This point becomes particularly clear in the ambitious study by Doronila (1996) who studied the acquisition, use, retention and implication of adult literacy in some 11 Filipino communities. In only some contexts was there any impact from sustained literacy programs. Those in which literacy had an impact were those in which literacy became a significant part of the activities of the community, that is, in communities which developed a 'literate tradition.' Mere reading and writing seemed to have little effect.

Yet, within a literate, schooled society, writing and reading are thought to have important effects on learning. Reading gives private access to information that would otherwise be out of reach. Writing appears to allow one to gain some distance from one's own thoughts. A well known writer, Anne Morrow Lindbergh, in an interview with the biographer of Charles Lindbergh, claimed that 'Writing allows one to put ideas and feelings on a shelf', in a sense freeing oneself from the burden of entertaining them. Empirical research on writing and thinking (Klein, 1999) tends to confirm this hypothesis but the evidence tends, like that of Lindbergh's, to be anecdotal.

And now, society. Elwert (in press) has advanced the concept of 'societal literacy' to describe the kind of literacy which is embedded in the large scale institutions of a modern bureaucratic society. Law, commerce and science are all institutions in which access to and use of written documents and written procedures such as laws, contracts and wills, along with the appropriate institutions for enforcing them, are critical to the functioning of such a society. A 'literate mentality' is the specialized mode of thought required to participate in a society organized, in part, around these complex bureaucratic structures with their historical, written archival resources. Literate societies, however, can vary greatly. Medieval scholastic philosophers were highly literate, living in a literate society but one which was quite different from a modern one. Both their society and their literacy differed from ours in the ways that texts were read, understood, consulted, and composed. Modern bureaucratic societies involve yet another form of 'literate mentality' partly because institutions themselves have changed and partly because of altered conceptions of how to read, write and use written texts in specialized domains.

Even allowing for these differences one may yet talk of societal literacy. It is the formulation and implementation of explicit procedures for the ordering of activities in terms of rules, norms, formal procedures or algorithms set out in codes, documents, and manuals such as 'Rules of order', contract law, rules for interpretation and the like. Such rules of course depend upon the ability to monitor and enforce such rules. Personal honour is not enough but the entire implement of state, whether ancient empire or modern democracy, is so ordered as to carry out these rules. Power goes hand in hand with procedure but the procedure is explicit and rule governed and generally complied with.

Finally, the relations between a literate mentality and societal literacy. The mistake was, perhaps still is, the belief, common to theories of social developers, that learning to read and write in itself will generate democratic institutions, a disciplined, trained work force, and a critical mind. The parallel mistake, from the other side, is to assume that literacy is only a matter of the ability to participate in those societally literate institutions. Personal literacy is significant in two ways. First, it is significant to the extent that it buys access to literate institutions and resources. But second, it is significant in that all forms of literacy have some impact on cognition, the impact depending upon the form of the script and the ways in which it is taught, as well as the ways in which it is used (Olson, 1994). Thus, literacy comes to have an effect, not only on consciousness of language, but on the forms of argument, the explicitness of arguments, the uses of evidence, the preference for one genre rather than another if integrated into such specialized institutions as economics, law, science or literature. Formal education is the primary means of introducing learners to the competencies required by these specialized institutions.

However, even this is not enough. Although institutions are composed of individuals, the institutions themselves are altered when they become literate institutions. That is to say, institutions in a document or bureaucratic society come to function by 'the rule of law', that is, the rules of explicit procedure and formal, enforceable agreements and accountability. Institutions themselves change as they develop these procedures developing a form of 'societal literacy'. It is in the context of societal literacy that the personal literacy of individuals comes to be of major significance. A modern bureaucratic society is often scorned for its impersonal attitude and rigid procedure. 'Rules are rules' is the refrain of the unreflective. Nonetheless, a society without documented and enforceable rules, laws, contracts and agreements is neither by definition nor practice a 'literate society'. A literate society is one which is both societally literate, having in place the infrastructure for the systematic, bureaucratic management of social affairs, and personally literate, a citizenry with both the knowledge and willingness to use their literacy in those institutions as well as in their everyday lives.

To participate in such institutions, individuals, primarily through the school, learn how to read the specialized documents of those institutions, and equally importantly, learn how to write them. Each form of writing requires a special kind of analysis, structuring the relationships between ideas, relating new information to the already known, shaping texts to fit the expectations of readers working in that domain. The ability to express oneself through writing may be a somewhat generalizable skill but it is elaborated by learning to meet the requirements of the special institutions of science, literature, law and economics. In this way our personal literacy comes into contact with societal literacy.

WRITING AS A LEARNING TOOL:
AN INTRODUCTION

PÄIVI TYNJÄLÄ*, LUCIA MASON** & KIRSTI LONKA***

* University of Jyväskylä, Finland, ** University of Lecce, Italy, *** University of Helsinki, Finland

Abstract. This introductory chapter begins with a brief historical account of the writing-to-learn movement, emphasising especially the significance of the cognitive revolution for the development of both learning research and writing research. The next section considers those theories of the writing process which have had the most profound impact on writing-to-learn, theories of writing as problem solving. Further on, theories and views of learning are discussed as essential determinants of approaches to writing as a learning tool. It is emphasised that current constructivist and social constructivist views imply the use of writing activities requiring transformations of knowledge, social interaction, and collaboration, as well as the integration of writing with other forms of learning and studying.

1   A SHORT HISTORY OF WRITING-TO-LEARN

The roots of integrating writing with learning can be traced back to mainly two sources: cross-curricular writing programmes and the process writing movement (Ackerman, 1993; Young & Fulwiler, 1986). As early as in the 19th century some American universities established discipline-specific writing courses, which can be seen as kind of predecessors of the extensive Writing-Across-the-Curriculum (WAC) movement in the 1970s. However, for a long time it was typical of educational institutions and educators to consider writing merely as a means of communication, with the emphasis on the correct usage of language. (Quinn, 1995; Russell, 1990.) Thus, writing and reading were taught in isolation and apart from domain-content learning. This trend was strengthened by the fact that mother-tongue teachers and domain-content educators and researchers at the elementary, high school and college levels had no shared forum for mutual communication. Even today it seems, as Quinn (1995: 300) has put it, that reading researchers, writing specialists, domain-content specialists and learning researchers 'read different scholarly journals, follow parallel but uncoordinated research agendas, and are not familiar with research and pedagogy from each other's fields'.

In the 1970s James Britton's studies of writing at school in Britain indicated how school writing was narrowly focussed on transferring information instead of encouraging thinking and understanding. A few years later, inspired by Britton's ideas,

P. Tynjälä, L. Mason & K. Lonka (2001). Writing as a learning tool: An introduction. In: G. Rijlaarsdam (Series ed.) & P. Tynjälä, L. Mason & K. Lonka (Volume eds.), *Studies in Writing*: *Volume 7: Writing as a Learning tool: Integrating Theory and Practice, 7 –22 .© 2001.* Kluwer Academic Publishers. Printed in the Netherlands.

Janet Emig (1977) in the United States published an essay 'Writing as a Mode of Learning' (Emig, 1977), which became an inspiration for developing writing programmes known as Writing-Across-the-Curriculum (Sheridan, 1995). An essential aspect of these programmes was the idea that writing is a mode of learning as well as communication. Thus, writing should be a business of the whole school community, not only of writing teachers. The WAC programmes involved training and workshops for teachers across the disciplines about how to use writing for content-area learning and how to deal with students' writing problems. (Young & Fulwiler, 1986.) Since the mid-70s, the number of these variously named programmes (for example, writing in the disciplines, writing in the content areas, language and learning, writing-across-the-curriculum) has increased dramatically on all levels of the educational system from elementary grades to university (Herrington & Moran, 1992).

Parallel with these developments in the area of writing education, fundamental changes took place in research on learning. Thus, the history of writing-to-learn cuts across the history of different research traditions from behaviourism to the cognitive revolution and to the current constructivist and social constructivist views of learning (Quinn, 1995). At the turn of the 1980s the cognitive revolution in psychology was reflected in writing research in the replacement of former behavioural models with novel cognitive process models (*e.g.* Hayes & Flower, 1980). Further, general models of discourse emerged where both reading and writing were conceptualised as constructive processes in which the reader's or the writer's mental representations interact with social context and discursive conventions (*e.g.* Flower, 1987). Writing researchers and educators developed approaches to writing which placed emphasis on the process of writing rather than on the final product. At the same time, many researchers began to focus on writing as a tool for thinking and domain-content learning (*e.g.* Applebee, 1984; Emig, 1977; Langer, 1986; Newell, 1984; Newell & Winograd, 1989). These studies indicated that writing tasks could be successfully applied to promote student learning in different domains.

In recent years, the scope of the writing-to-learn literature has widened from experimental studies to critical reviews and meta-analyses which have paid attention to many contradictory and inconclusive findings about writing as a learning tool. Thus, there is a need to elaborate what kind of writing might enhance learning and what kind of learning can be pursued through writing. Furthermore, it is important to develop methods of assessing learning in ways that are compatible with current views of knowledge acquisition. We hope that this book will bring some clarity to the relationship between writing and learning and stimulate the development of both the theory and the practice of writing-to-learn. In the following sections we shall first describe what kind of conceptual tools research on writing processes has produced for understanding composing and the relationships between writing, thinking and learning. After that we shall examine theories of learning, going on to discuss under what conditions writing may serve learning. At the end of the chapter we shall present an outline of the book.

2   WRITING RESEARCH: WRITING AS PROBLEM-SOLVING AND AS A TOOL FOR THINKING

The impact of the cognitivist approach to writing research over the last two decades has been remarkable. It has led to a shift in the focus of investigation from the written product to the processes that shape writing. This shift has implied paying attention to the search and generation of the ideas to be put into words to create meaning as well as to the revision of the texts. Students often encounter problems in carrying out these writing processes, and these problems continue to be neglected in teaching writing at school. The emphasis on writing as a process, rather than as a product, has been investigated further to the extent that the need for innovation in teaching and assessing written discourse has become evident (Boscolo, 1995).

Within the cognitivist perspective, writing has become much more than a graphic-motor activity in that it requires thinking processes, mainly reflection, not only before and during but also after the act of writing, when the text produced is revised. As was recently pointed out by Galbraith and Torrance (1999), a good analogy summing up the essential characteristics of writing as intended by the cognitivist approach is that of writing as problem-solving, that is, writing as a goal-oriented activity to be carried out using specific procedures. This analogy is best represented in the general model developed by Hayes and Flower (1980) through an analysis of the verbal protocols employed by students engaged in writing expository texts. Their model, which has had a great impact on theoretical and applied research on writing, conceptualises writing as articulated in three main processes: *planning, translating* plans into text, and *revising*. Planning involves generating ideas by retrieving information from memory, organising these ideas, and setting goals linked with the criteria that will be used to evaluate the written product, goals which accompany the generation process and are used in revising the product. Translating plans into a text entails turning the material retrieved from memory into sentences that make up the written product. Revision is aimed at improving the quality of the text and involves reading what has been written and editing it.

According to the model of Hayes and Flower (1980), the whole writing process operates under two kinds of information: knowledge stored in long-term memory and representation of the task environment. The first kind of information includes conceptual knowledge that refers to content (topics), discourse (text structure, syntax and style), and metacognitive knowledge (the writers themselves as writers, the writing task, and the strategies available for accomplishing the writing plans). The second kind of information, that is, the representation of the task environment, includes writers' motivation to write and topic and/or audience features which affect the writing processes, the text in progress that guides the search for ideas and influences the writing plan, and the available resources.

Hayes and Flower have also hypothesised the presence of a central executive controlling the relationships between the component processes and have underlined the recursive nature of the writing process. Planning, translating and revising can occur at any moment during writing in that they are recurrent and concurrent cognitive operations rather than stages following each other in a linear progression.

According to this model, writing expertise is about the possession of a set of sophisticated problem-solving strategies (Flower & Hayes, 1980). Expert writers are able to construct a more sophisticated representation of their goals and develop and modify this representation throughout the writing process. This enables them to revise more extensively and evaluate their texts on the basis of how well they work in terms of their goals.

The developmental model of writing proposed by Bereiter and Scardamalia (1987) also emphasises problem-solving processes in effective writing. They have made the well-known distinction between the 'knowledge telling' and 'knowledge transforming' strategies of writing. The first, typically employed by children and novice writers, is a method of composition which entails writing down everything that the writer knows about the subject. Contents are retrieved on the basis of their organisation in memory and the discourse schemas stored by the writer and are then translated directly into text. Instead, knowledge transforming is a method of composition that involves taking into account a hierarchy of goals and sub-goals which determine the development of an explicit representation of rhetorical problems and the active transformation of knowledge to satisfy communicative goals. In knowledge telling, ideas appropriate to a topic are simply generated and written down, whereas in knowledge transforming contents are considered in the light of the goals that the writing process is intended to achieve. In knowledge transforming the writer pays attention not only to appropriateness but also to clarity, plausibility and effectiveness. Knowledge transforming is about solving two problems: generating ideas and adapting them to the writers' rhetorical goal, that is, the effect(s) it should have on readers. The dialogue between content problems (what to write) and rhetorical problems (how to write) seems to bring about novel thoughts and a deeper understanding of the topic (Scardamalia & Bereiter, 1991). According to Klein (1999), however, there is so far little empirical evidence that planning and revising as mere acts promote learning through writing. Nevertheless, the effect of knowledge transforming on thinking may be based on more holistic factors, such as the development of metalinguistic awareness (see Olson, this volume; Camps & Milian, 2000), genre schemata (Klein, 1999), or text-type awareness (Björk & Räisänen, 1996).

The problem-solving approach to writing has been criticised for representing writing as a controlled and rational process (for a critical review see Galbraith & Torrance, 1999). Writing can also be seen as a *spontaneous* process of generating thoughts, constructing meaning, in all, modifying and developing thinking (*e.g.* Galbraith, 1999). The generative power of writing lies in the fact that writers may produce totally new ideas during writing. Generative writing may take place without any reflection or revision. A great deal of spontaneous writing or free writing exercises are based on this generative function of writing. Free writing exercises may help the writer to overcome writer's blocks and other problems with writing by making writing less controlled (Boice, 1993). Spontaneous writing helps the writer to externalise thoughts. However, as Klein (1999) points out, simply articulating one's own prior (mis)conceptions may not help one to challenge these ideas; therefore it does not necessarily enhance learning. The practical solution, which is elaborated on later in this chapter, may lie in breaking the writing process into two parts, drafting and revising.

In a brief summary, the debate concerning the nature of writing processes is about whether the essential characteristic of expertise in writing is a matter of mastering problem-solving strategies. In this respect, the role of social and interactive factors, such as writers' familiarity with the particular genre in which they are writing and their relationship with the discourse community in which they are participating, have been pointed out (*e.g.* Nystrand, 1989). According to the socio-interactive approach, which refers to Vygotsky's theory, the composition process is a dialogue between the writer and the reader made possible by socially shared knowledge. The meaning of a text is a social construct that is negotiated between the reader and the writer through the medium of the text.

The importance of motivational aspects has also been highlighted by two main lines of research, studies of the relationship between writing and self-efficacy (*e.g.* Pajares & Johnson, 1994, 1996) and studies of the role of interest in the production of expository texts (*e.g.* Albin, Benton & Khramtsova, 1996; Benton, Corkill, Sharp, Downey, Khramtsova, 1995; Hidi & McLaren, 1990, 1991). Self-efficacy, in this context individuals' beliefs about their ability to produce certain types of texts, have been found to be predictive of writing skills, strategy use and writing performance. These social and motivational factors have been given much more attention in the revised version of Hayes and Flower's model (Hayes, 1996), in which problem-solving is considered a component of a more general 'reflection' module and the role of working memory is emphasised.

As mentioned above, the cognitivist approach sees writing as a thinking activity since it involves seeking ideas in long-term memory, selecting and organising them, and continuously monitoring their translation into text through the revision process. This conception of writing is not new. A tradition of studies from Vygotsky to Olson argues that the acquisition and use of writing are powerful factors in the development of thinking. In any case, cognitivism has given impetus to the use of writing as a tool for learning (Boscolo, 1997).

The role of writing in thinking and learning has been widely emphasised by Langer and Applebee (1987; Langer, 1986) in their seminal works. According to these authors, this role stems from several processes. Written words make it possible to reflect on the ideas which are put into words and revise them. Moreover, writers have to convey meanings independently of the context in which the written composition is generated, requiring them to be clear and consistent. Further, the different textual forms in which writing is expressed contribute to the organisation of ideas. Finally, writing is an active process through which writers can explore and make their own ideas clear to themselves.

Langer and Applebee's (1987) analysis of the effects of different writing tasks (*e.g.* note-taking, answering questions, essays) on different learning tasks (*e.g.* recall, argumentation, composition) (1987) yielded three main findings. First, all types of written response lead to better performance in learning tasks than reading without writing. The more the material to be learned is manipulated, the better it is understood and remembered and the more stable are these effects. Second, the benefits derived from in writing tasks are 'situated', that is, the writing process only involves ideas and information dealt with in the context of a specific writing activity; its effects cannot be generalised. Third, the various learning tasks differ according to the breadth of the information to be processed and the depth of its processing. Therefore, different writing tasks promote different kinds of learning (Langer & Applebee, 1987).

In more recent years there has been growing interest in studies of using writing in the service of knowledge construction in different domains (*e.g.* Ackerman, 1993; Newell & Winograd, 1989). On the one hand, research has shown that writing tasks can be successfully employed to facilitate students' thinking and domain-content learning. In particular, there have been investigations of writing to learn in science, and science educators have highlighted the potential of writing for helping students construct knowledge about science and gain insights into writing about science (*e.g.* Connolly & Vilardi, 1989; Hollyday, Yore, & Alvermann, 1994; Keys, 1999; Mason, 1998; Mason & Boscolo, 2000; Prain & Hand, 1996; Rivard, 1994; Rowell, 1997). On the other hand, it has also been pointed out that there are methodological problems involved in the research on writing to learn (Schumacher & Gradwohl-Nash, 1991) as well as some conflicting results concerning the effectiveness of writing tasks in the learning process (*e.g.* Ackerman, 1993; Geisler, 1994; Penrose, 1992; Klein, 1999).

3   LEARNING THEORIES AND WRITING AS A LEARNING TOOL

Parallel with the emergence of the socio-constructivist approach to research on learning and instruction in general and to research on writing in particular, the use of writing for domain-content learning has also begun to be investigated in connection with the context in which text production is developed. It has been argued that perceived as a learning tool, writing cannot be seen as a means of knowledge elaboration and construction independently of the meaning that writing and learning have as cultural practices of a community (*e.g.* Greene & Ackerman, 1995). It is therefore important to analyse the conceptions of learning underlying the pedagogy of writing-to-learn and the ways in which writing is being used as a part of educational practices. In the following passages we turn to these educational questions.

Originally (in Bereiter & Scardamalia, 1987), knowledge telling and knowledge transforming as different types of writing referred to cognitive processes *within* a person who is writing: A person tells or transforms his or her own ideas while writing. However, when the notions of knowledge telling and knowledge transforming are used in connection with learning they may also refer to processes in which a person tells or transforms knowledge borrowed from others or from textbooks, for example. Thus, knowledge telling and knowledge transforming may be inter-individual or social processes in learning situations. From this perspective, as forms of writing knowledge telling and knowledge transforming have an analogical conceptual pair in the field of learning. While some people consider learning a process of acquiring and increasing one's knowledge through acts of reproducing and memorising ready-made information (cf. knowledge telling), others think that learning is a constructive and creative process where a learner constructs meanings and transforms ideas, and that this process will change her thinking (cf. knowledge transforming). Lonka, Maury and Heikkilä (1997) showed that those university students who saw writing as knowledge transforming were also more likely to see learning as the active construction of knowledge. In contrast, those students who perceived learning as the intake of knowledge were likely to see writing as knowledge telling. Interestingly, the students' essay grades also correlated with the constructivist approach to learning.

Thus, students' conceptions of learning are related to the way in which they see the aim of writing. The way in which teachers and students understand and conceptualise learning and in which they understand and conceptualise writing may also affect the way in which they use writing for learning. If teachers think that teaching and learning is about transmitting and reproducing knowledge, it follows that they will design their students knowledge telling type of writing tasks. In contrast, if teachers consider learning a constructive and transformative process they probably seek to promote this process by assigning students knowledge transforming tasks, that is, tasks that do not allow them merely to reproduce knowledge from the textbooks but, instead, require them to make their own inferences and comparisons, find their own applications and examples and so on.

The view of learning that has been dominating our educational systems until quite recently has been called a knowledge transmission paradigm. According to this view, learning is reception and reproduction of information transmitted by teachers and textbooks. Given such a conception of learning, knowledge telling writing tasks seem quite appropriate. Bereiter and Scardamalia (1987) have shown that traditional school writing is, indeed, mostly based on this knowledge telling model. However, the views of learning that nowadays dominate research on learning (and are gradually gaining ground also in schools) describe learning as an active cognitive and social process instead of passive reception of information. The chapters of our book represent this conception, grounded on cognitive constructivist and social constructivist or sociocultural theories.

Cognitive constructivism (*e.g.* von Glasersfeld, 1984, 1995) approaches learning as an individual's cognitive process of constructing knowledge. Social constructivism (*e.g.* Vygotsky, 1978; Rogoff, 1990; Rogoff, Matusov, & White, 1996) places a greater emphasis on the social nature of learning. These schools of thought do not necessarily contradict each other but may, rather, be regarded as different perspectives on or approaches to learning which, actually, implicitly involve presuppositions of the other side and share some basic assumptions (see, for example, Bereiter, 1994; Cobb, 1994, 1999). Thus, both cognitive and social constructivists stress the active nature of learning although the cognitive position links this activity to the individual student's cognitive processes, whereas social constructivism connects it, rather, to participation in culturally organised practices. Similarly, both approaches emphasise the importance of social interaction in learning although there are differences in how the mechanisms of learning in interaction are explained. Further, both views share the construction metaphor describing the very nature of learning although in certain sociocultural approaches the term 'construction' is not explicitly used. For example, Rogoff's (1990, see also Rogoff *et al.*, 1996) view of learning as participation in cultural activities has been interpreted as implicitly assuming an actively constructing learner (Cobb, 1999).

Having adopted these complementary conceptions of learning as our starting points, it follows that we regard writing to learn as a means of fostering students' knowledge construction and transformation processes through cognitive stimulation and social participation of the kind that different writing tasks may provide. We acknowledge that while it may be individual processing that is the subject of investigation, these individual processes always have a social and cultural history (Vygotsky, 1978). Thus, we consider learning and writing both social and individual activities. Accordingly, we shall examine writing to learn not only from the viewpoint of developing students' cognitive structures but also as participation in the cultural discourse practices and learning that form the basis for these structures.

Recent studies of these cultural practices have shown that classroom discourse and writing activities tend to proceed independently of one another (see the chapter by Nystrand, Gamoran and Carbonaro in this volume). However, research has also indicated that when writing is to be used as a learning tool, it would be more useful to deploy it in combination and as integrated with other forms of learning and discourse, such as reading, classroom discourse and group discussions (Dysthe, 1996; Tierney, O'Flahavan, & McGinley, 1989). For example, Dysthe (1996), inspired by Bakhtin's ideas about the dialogical nature of human communication and by Vygotsky's theory about the connection between language and thinking, has investigated how meaning and understanding are created through dialogue in a 'multivoiced classroom' where writing and talking about the subject matter are the key elements. Combining forms of discourse is an authentic way to learn because it is the way in which we work in real life. For example, in many everyday situations and in real-world jobs we have to integrate different forms of communication to form opinions on important issues, to do our jobs and to learn things. And we do not learn only contents but also modes of action and social and cultural practices.

It is possible that knowledge telling and knowledge transforming should not be contrasted either. Since knowledge transforming is a complex activity which can overload working memory (Bereiter & Scardamalia, 1987), it may be wise to ease student's work through procedural facilitation by dividing the process into two stages: first idea generation (knowledge telling), only then revision and reflection (knowledge transforming). Many learning-by-writing exercises start with free writing or spontaneous writing, where idea generation is the exclusive focus. Lonka and Ahola (1995) pointed out that it is important to diagnose the quality and level of students' (mis)conceptions at the beginning of instruction. The same exercises that make a diagnosis possible, such as focussed free writing, also help students to activate their previous knowledge. Concepts and theories which appear difficult and counter-intuitive demand special attention. It is essential to make students' strategies and knowledge open to discussion and reflection by using writing. The idea of instructional scaffolding may be applied, for example, by employing learning logs (or journals), small-group discussions and some special forms of focussed free writing (Applebee & Langer, 1983). However, it is not enough to simply reveal or generate ideas. For instance, if the writing process involves multiple drafts, it is important that students are given feedback on their ideas. This feedback should concentrate not only on behaviour but also on the development of students' thinking, encouraging them to rethink and revise their initial conceptions. In this way, knowledge telling may be a beginning for knowledge transforming in the context of writing-to-learn instruction.

4   WHAT MAKES WRITING WORK FOR LEARNING?

In recent years, several studies, meta-analyses and reviews have confirmed that writing may produce positive effects on learning, but they have also revealed that the relationship between writing and learning is not simple; writing does not automatically lead to better learning outcomes than do other learning methods (see Ackerman, 1993; Geisler, 1994; Klein, 1999; Penrose, 1992; Schumacher & Gradwohl-Nash, 1991). How learning is understood in everyday schooling and conceptualised in research varies a great deal, as does the way in which writing is used for the purpose of enhancing learning. In his recent review article Klein (1999) has distinguished between four different hypotheses about writing-to-learn. The first hypothesis is related to *spontaneous idea generation*: writers spontaneously generate knowledge 'at the point of utterance' (Britton, 1982). They do not necessarily know exactly what to write when starting to write, inventing the content only as they produce the language (see Galbraith, 1992, 1999). The second hypothesis is what Klein calls a *'forward search hypothesis'*. Forward search is the process where writers review their first drafts in order to transform their ideas through operations such as drawing inferences and detecting contradictions. According to this hypothesis, writers first externalise their ideas, then reread them to develop them further. The third hypothesis about the cognitive mechanisms of writing-to-learn is a *genre hypothesis* which assumes that genre structures are used to organise text and knowledge and that different genres require different cognitive strategies. The studies based on this hypothesis have compared different genres used in writing-to-learn, such as analytic writing, personal writing, argumentation, note-taking, and answering questions, and found differences in learning outcomes. For example, tasks requiring only minimal elaboration seem to produce only verbatim recall while tasks requiring complex elaboration, such as analytic essay writing, promote understanding (*e.g.* Langer, 1986; Wiley & Voss, 1996). The fourth hypothesis, which Klein calls a *'backward search hypothesis'*, assumes that writers construct knowledge by setting rhetorical goals, generating content to address these goals, and then revising their rhetorical goals to accommodate this content. Thus, in models of writing-to-learn based on this hypothesis rhetorical and content-related problems interact. Klein mentions the problem-solving models of Flower and Hayes (1980) and Bereiter and Scardamalia (1987) as examples of such explanatory schemes.

On the basis of his critical review, Klein (1999) concludes that these hypotheses address different operations and phases of composing and that accordingly the hypotheses are compatible with and complementary to one another. Thus, it is possible that all of them are sound. However, only the genre hypothesis has been systematically tested and verified from the viewpoint of learning. Klein suggests therefore that more empirical research is still needed to assess the validity of these hypotheses.

Although Klein's analysis of the hypotheses underlying writing-to-learn is penetrating and comprehensive, it lacks one significant viewpoint, an in-depth analysis of learning theories against the background of writing-to-learn research and of their relationship to the findings gained by it. Klein does mention that prevalent writing-to-learn education can be characterised as 'constructivist', but the hypotheses or research designs in general have not been discussed in terms of their underlying views of learning in his review. The hypotheses themselves represent the cognitive position, which does not deal with the context of learning and writing or with the cultural practices in which learning and writing are embedded. Cognitive theories provide an important basis for understanding writing processes, but the picture of writing-to-learn changes considerably when writing and learning are considered not only as cognitive processes but also as social and cultural practices.

When the social nature of learning is taken into account, the scope of writing-to-learn activities widens from individual composing operations to social and collaborative knowledge building. Seen from this perspective, writing-to-learn tasks should not be regarded as pure writing activities; instead they should be integrated with social interaction and classroom discussion and other school assignments. One possible way to do so would be small groups where students could discuss their individually performed writing tasks (*e.g.* Dysthe, 1996; Lonka & Ahola, 1995; Tynjälä, 1998) or collaborative writing activities requiring students to build shared understanding of a topic under scrutiny (*e.g.* Tynjälä & Laurinen, 2000). However, studies of the effects of collaborative writing on learning are still rare as most of the published research on collaborative writing is focussed on the improvement of the writing process and writing skills rather than on that of domain-content learning (*e.g.* Dale, 1994; Flower, Wallace, Norris, & Burnett, 1994). Among the few studies suggesting the importance of collaborative writing for content learning, the research by Keys (1994, 1995) should be mentioned. She analysed this form of writing in junior high school science education and found that writing activities had positive effects on learning in a context in which thinking, reasoning and discussing were greatly valued. This approach modified the students' attitude toward learning science concepts because they recognised that the construction of plausible and shareable explanations of scientific phenomena through collaborative writing is of greater value than giving the right answer. Obliged to discuss what to write in a report, the students had to express their ideas more clearly and continuously negotiate meanings. Engaged in a process of meaningful learning, they constructed their own understanding of scientific concepts.

In sum, we suggest that writing may be a useful and effective tool for domain-content learning provided that certain conditions are met. These are: 1) Writing tasks should promote active knowledge construction. They should induce students to engage in knowledge transforming processes rather than in reproductive activities. 2) The tasks should make use of students' previous knowledge and existing conceptions of and beliefs about the topics they are studying (free writing before studying the topic). 3) The tasks should encourage students to reflect on their own experiences and conceptualise and theorise about them. 4) The tasks should involve the students in applying theories to practical situations and solving practical problems and problems of understanding. 5) The tasks should be integrated with classroom discourse and other schoolwork, such as small-group discussions and textbook reading.

It is time to reconceptualise the relation between reading, writing and learning. There is a tendency to think that we should first read and acquire knowledge, and that only then would come the time for writing. The writing-to-learn movement reverses the situation because it is not based on the metaphor of the mind as an empty container to be filled up with information. Writing is not merely revealing what has been put into the 'black box'. Students' minds are not empty containers but instead students already have beliefs, ideas, and conceptions. Students should be encouraged to generate ideas and inferences even before they know a domain well and they should be given feedback on these ideas, helping them to revise, elaborate and reflect on their ideas. This motivates students to learn more because personally meaningful questions are being activated. This is also a start for truly student-centred, participatory instruction. The act of writing itself is not the point. Writing is a tool for thinking and a tool for learning. There are other tools as well, and by integrating the use of different learning tools we may create learning environments that support students' cognitive and social knowledge-building processes.

5   OUTLINE OF THE BOOK

Studies of writing as a learning tool have been criticised for being based on practical perspectives rather than on theories of learning, leading to calls for more theory-driven research (Schumacher & Gradwohl Nash, 1991). There has been criticism also of measuring learning outcomes in a way that focuses on memorising and reproducing factual information instead of assessing learning of the kind that shows itself as changes in students' conceptions and as the development of their thinking skills (Geisler, 1994; Schumacher & Gradwohl Nash, 1991). In this book our approach to learning by writing is strongly theory-driven. Our starting point is to integrate constructivist and sociocultural theories of learning with models of writing in order to develop and analyse pedagogical applications based on these integrative models. We shall examine the process and outcomes of learning not as the reproduction of information but as the development of students' conceptual structures, metacognitive skills, reflective thinking and participation in social activities.

In this book we do not want to confine ourselves to one particular school of thought or approach to writing to learn. Instead, we would like to offer the reader an opportunity to hear different voices and look at the issue from different viewpoints. Therefore, our authors represent various disciplines and research traditions ranging from cognitive educational psychology to sociolinguistics. Each of them brings their particular point of view to the discussion.

The book addresses the impact of writing on student learning, the basic assumption being that writing may have a profound effect on thinking. Obviously, there are no literate minds without written texts. Among the most highly valued skills in our modern Western democracies is the ability to make use of written texts, that is, literacy. But what is the impact of literacy on thinking? David R. Olson has addressed this question in a very profound manner in *The world on paper. The conceptual and cognitive implications of writing and reading* (Olson, 1994). The book presents an exciting redefinition of literacy. 'Learning to read is a matter of learning to recognize the aspects represented graphically and to infer those aspects of meaning which are not represented graphically at all' (p. 272). Learning to read is therefore learning to cope with the unexpressed, using what is known as the illocutionary force of language.

It follows that the power of writing lies in bringing into consciousness those aspects of spoken language that turn language into an object of reflection, analysis, and design (Olson, 1994: 258). Without written language it would be impossible to deal with such metalevel concepts as 'assumption', 'inference', or 'conclusion'. Once a written expression has influenced our common thought (and spoken expressions) it is extremely difficult to unthink that model and see how someone not enculturated in the same way of thinking would perceive language and the world it describes.

To write is to differentiate among what is actually said and what is intended: are we believing, asserting, conforming or only desiring something? What are the facts, what is the hypothesis, and what are the conclusions? Writing forces us to think about our own thinking in terms of what is actually claimed and what is the evidence – the basic distinction in scientific thinking (Kuhn, 1989). Literacy is not only functionally oriented but, also, a social condition: 'in reading and writing texts one participates in a "textual community", a group of readers (and writers and auditors) who share a way of reading and interpreting a body of texts' (Olson, 1994: 273). When students take part in the practices of the scientific community, it is crucial that they learn the conventions and ways of thinking that are typical of that specific literate tradition.

We asked David Olson to write the prologue to this book because we wanted to put our chapters in the broader context of literacy. It is important to elaborate on the relationships among reading, writing, literacy, and society. What is the relation between personal literacy and social literacy? What is a literate society? What does it mean to think as readers and writers do – what is a 'literate mentality'? Olson's philosophical and historical essay leads us to contemplate the fundamental questions concerning the nature of literacy and the relationship between the mind and society. By examining the concepts of a 'literate mentality' and 'societal literacy' he introduces us to the discussion about the cognitive and social nature of literacy and learning. Olson demonstrates that writing may be an important form of developing conscious thinking. He suggests a definition of a literate society which includes both societal and personal literacy and their interrelationships. One does not develop a 'literate mentality' simply by being able to read and write. The uses and functions of writing in society are important factors in developing a truly literate mind, as is the emergence of metalinguistic awareness.

In her chapter Nancy Nelson turns the focus on the individual cognitive processes and the constructivist view of learning as a promising starting point for understanding the relationship between writing and learning. Adopting the constructivist perspective, she examines learning as meaning making with selective, organisational and connective dimensions. She pays particular attention to different connective processes related to writing-to-learn. She demonstrates how using writing as a learning tool involves making connections among ideas, texts, authors, and disciplines and domains. Nelson relates her discussion of the constructive nature of writing and learning to the rationales of authority and authenticity. By reading source texts and transforming knowledge for their own texts students gain authority over them and, at the same time, they participate in activities similar to those engaged in by experts and scholars representing that particular discipline.

Writing has always played an important role in university studies even if the forms and amount of writing involved in them have varied across different countries and among different cultures of higher education. The following chapter by Päivi Tynjälä focuses on the use of traditional and novel types of writing assignments in higher education. Tynjälä examines different forms of writing- to-learn in relation to recent accounts of the development of professional expertise and to current constructivist views of learning. She concludes that in order to meet the challenges raised by the constructivist conception of learning and develop important prerequisites of professional expertise, writing in higher education should focus on knowledge transformation and knowledge building instead of reproductive activities. Furthermore, she recommends integrating writing with other learning activities, such as textbook reading, group discussions and project work, as well as giving students writing tasks designed to develop their reflective and metacognitive skills.

Martin Nystrand, Adam Gamoran and William Carbonaro discuss writing and learning by introducing their ecological approach to the study of classroom learning and writing. On the basis of large-scale empirical studies, Nystrand and his colleagues describe the nature of ordinary classroom work, showing that writing and classroom discourse have rarely been integrated as a coherent learning situation. Instead, these activities are practised separately and as independent of each other. However, from the viewpoint of learning it would be more useful to construct learning environments in which writing activities, classroom discussions and individual and small-group work would support each other and serve shared goals. According to Nystrand and his colleagues, it is important in the study of student writing that writing is not treated as an isolated and autonomous form of class activities but as an integral part of the whole learning environment with its specific social relationships. Therefore they prefer to examine classroom writing in connection with other learning activities such as classroom discussion and reading. Nystrand, Gamoran and Carbonaro suggest that it is not the amount of writing but the quality of writing that is important in classroom learning. If the aim of writing tasks is to reproduce knowledge or check on reading, learning outcomes may remain superficial and reproductive as well. In contrast, a deeper elaboration and reflection on the subject studied as well as a process-oriented approach allowing revision are more likely to produce higher-level learning outcomes.

In the next chapter Pietro Boscolo and Lucia Mason describe a study in which writing tasks were used at the elementary level to promote pupils' historical and scientific understanding. Their specific question is whether experiences from learning by writing in one discipline can be transferred to another discipline. Boscolo and Mason conducted their study first in a history class and after that in a science class. Their findings suggest that transfer may indeed occur. The fifth-grade pupils were able to use writing in tasks requiring active manipulation and transformation of information, their conceptual understanding was improved by the writing tasks, and they were able to draw on the writing-to-learn scheme in both disciplines studied.

What was interesting was that the writing tasks seemed not to improve the students' performance in tests requiring simple accretion of knowledge but did promote higher-level conceptual understanding.

Brian Hand, Vaughan Prain and Larry D. Yore have studied the use of writing tasks in science classes in junior secondary school. In addition to writing tasks commonly used in school, such as note-taking, their classes involved students writing a letter and undertaking a series of assignments called Science Writing Heuristics (SWH). These tasks were designed to support students' reasoning in laboratory work, develop their understanding of the nature of science as inquiry and to facilitate students' reflection on their own epistemological beliefs and metacognitive strategies in learning science. The findings of the study indicated that a single writing task does not necessarily influence students' science achievement, but when a sequence of tasks is applied the results are more promising. The use of sequential writing-to-learn tasks facilitated especially the students' learning of higher-level science concepts. Thus, these results seem to support Boscolo and Mason's findings and also the notion presented earlier (*e.g.* Penrose, 1992; Schumacher & Gradwohl Nash, 1991) that if the aim of studying is the simple memorising of facts, writing does not necessarily offer benefits additional to those derived from other learning methods. In contrast, writing seems to be suitable for tasks which require in-depth elaboration aimed at fostering deep understanding, conceptual change, and the development of thinking skills.

Note-taking is one form of writing, and it has been investigated over the last two decades (*e.g.* Kiewra, 1988; Kiewra, DuBois, Christian, McShane, Meyerhoffer, & Roskelley, 1991; Lonka, Lindblom-Ylänne, & Maury, 1994) to study whether and in what conditions this kind of writing activity is effective. The research group of Kirsti Lonka has examined spontaneous note-taking in entrance examinations, and their findings have shown the positive effect of reading notes on students' learning. Lonka and her colleagues start from the idea that investigations of spontaneous study strategies have important practical implications because such strategies may influence learning more strongly than experimentally induced strategies (Lonka, Lindblom-Ylänne, & Maury, 1994). The strategies people use when they study for an exam may be quite different from those adopted in psychological experiments. Well-controlled experimental situations are usually new for the subjects, and normal strategies may fail precisely because the material lacks those redundancies which the usual strategies rely on. Moreover, we cannot be sure that subjects placed in experimental situations are really trying their best. Many contradictory findings in the literature on the impact of writing on learning (Klein, 1999) may be due to the problem that in many experiments subjects are asked to apply strategies they would not normally use.

In this volume, Virpi Slotte and Kirsti Lonka analyse how students' spontaneous note-taking affect their learning when preparing for an examination. They have studied a large body of students' notes in order to examine the relationship between the quality of note-taking and the quality of essay-type examination answers. Their findings indicate that the impact of note-taking on learning outcomes depends on several factors such as the type of notes taken, the nature of the writing tasks, and the writing conditions, for example whether the notes are present or absent during essay writing. A very rigorous finding both by Lonka, Lindblom-Ylänne and Maury (1994) and by Slotte and Lonka (1998; 1999) was that generative study strategies such as concept mapping or summarising content in one's own words were effective especially in tasks that called for knowledge application. Verbatim notes or taking no notes at all were not as effective. It thus appears that the act of writing notes makes a difference, but the quality of the notes is decisive. Slotte and Lonka conclude that teachers should pay attention to students' note-taking and other study strategies and to developing students' metacognitive knowledge about effective types of studying.

The recent dramatic shift from objectivist epistemology and the knowledge transmission conception of learning to constructivist, socio-constructivist and situational theories has affected also views and practices of assessment of learning. Constructivist pedagogy aims to embed assessment practices in the learning processes and to foster students' metacognitive skills by engaging them in reflective self-assessment activities. The use of portfolios is a widespread approach to novel student assessment of this kind. In her chapter Pirjo Linnakylä describes learning portfolios as selections of student work collected over a period of time demonstrating the student's learning process, progress and achievement. Portfolios usually include also the student's own reflections on his or her learning. Pieces of work selected for inclusion in a portfolio may be written documents such as essays, reports or short stories, or they may be pictures, graphics, animations, music, and so on, depending on the field and the purpose of the portfolio. However, most portfolios include at least an introduction and a self-evaluation report in the form of written documents. Thus, being an excellent tool for self-reflection (see, for example, Lukinsky, 1990) writing is at the core of the construction of a portfolio. Increasing use of portfolios represents a shift towards assessment practices based on authentic learning tasks involving writing integrated with other forms of learning. In this way portfolios may be a part of what Nystrand, Gamoran and Carbonaro in their chapter call coherent instruction.

Modern information technology has generated new kinds of learning environments and a variety of tools for supporting both writing and learning processes. The last chapter of the book by James Hartley and Päivi Tynjälä analyses the use of modern technology in the service of writing and learning. Hartley and Tynjälä discuss how technological tools may transform the nature of writing and what kind of new possibilities technology-enriched learning environments open to learners. They present some network-based learning tools that make effective use of the potentials of writing for promoting students' individual and collaborative knowledge construction processes.

When we initially shared the idea of editing this book, our intention was to give a substantial contribution to future research in a growing area of investigation by focussing on both theoretical and practical perspectives on writing serving the needs of learning. Our main purposes were to deepen the theoretical understanding of the ways in which writing can be used to stimulate and improve thinking and learning, and to bring together studies of writing to learn at different levels of the educational system and in different learning environments. As editors we feel that the volume can truly contribute to this field. We hope that by describing the state of scientific knowledge and educational practice involved in writing as a learning tool at the beginning of the new millennium the book can serve as a useful source of ideas for theory and method and thus stimulate further research.

WRITING TO LEARN

One Theory, Two Rationales

NANCY NELSON

Louisina State University, USA

Abstract: The writing-to-learn movement is supported by constructivist theory, which draws attention to the generative nature of human knowledge and communication. Writing and learning, whether viewed from a cognitive perspective, with the focus on individuals, or from a social perspective, with the focus on groups, have selective, organizational, and connective dimensions. This chapter considers four aspects of the connective dimension that have been examined in studies of writing and learning: connections among ideas, connections among texts, connections among authors, and connections across disciplines and domains. In this discussion, attention is given to the two major rationales for the writing-to-learn initiative: the authority rationale, which posits that writers gain command of a topic through written engagement with that topic, and the authenticity rationale, which maintains that, as writers gain knowledge of the subject matter of an academic discipline, they benefit from also learning the ways of writing associated with the discipline.

1   CONSTRUCTIVIST PERSPECTIVES ON LITERACY AND LEARNING

Support for the writing-to-learn movement has come from developments in constructivist theory regarding the generative nature of learning, understanding, and interpreting as well as composing. When seen through the metaphoric lens of constructivism, learning is a process of *building* knowledge, and communication (reading and listening as well as writing and speaking) is a process of *making* meaning. The constructivist orientation, with its emphasis on generation and on human agency, stands in opposition to other, quite different, epistemologies that have influenced educational practices in the past, such as the notion that knowledge is transmitted and received. The central claim of constructivism, as Bruner and Feldman (1990) have pointed out, is that learning is productive: Humans produce their knowledge and experience, and they engage in symbolic activity as symbol makers as well as symbol users. They are not 'order-preserving copy machines' having an external reality imprinted on their minds (p. 231).

N. Nelson (2001). Writing to learn: One theory, two rationales. In: G. Rijlaarsdam (Series ed.) & P. Tynjälä, L. Mason & K. Lonka (Volume eds.), *Studies in Writing, Volume 7, Writing as a Learning tool: Integrating Theory and Practice, 23– 36.*© *2001.* Kluwer Academic Publishers. Printed in the Netherlands.

The term *metatheory* applies to constructivism, since it encompasses several theoretical strands – strands that can best be differentiated according to the perspective that is taken on human agency. Are individuals viewed as the constructive agents? Or are social groups viewed as the agents? Cognitive constructivist theory, which is grounded in the work of Bartlett (1932) and Piaget (1932), presents literacy and learning as individuals' active processes of meaning making and knowledge construction. In contrast, social constructivism focuses mainly on the knowledge-making practices of groups. One of the two major sub strands of social constructivism has developed from social semiotic research (*e.g.*, Leont'ev, 1981); it focuses on collaborations of dyads or relatively small groups. The other strand of social constructivism has developed from sociology of knowledge (Berger & Luckmann, 1966); it focuses on societies or discourse communities as constructive agents. (For histories of theory and research tied to the various perspectives, see my previous treatment, Spivey, 1997.)[1]

During the late 1970s the cognitive orientation led to one major rationale for the writing-to-learn movement: Through writing about the topics they study, individuals would, it seemed, become more engaged cognitively with the material and thus achieve more command over it. This was the position taken early on by British researchers with the Schools Council Writing Across the Curriculum Project (Martin, D'Arcy, Newton, & Parker, 1976), a research initiative that did much to foster the new interest in writing and learning. This position, which might be called the *authority rationale*, was subsequently enhanced by the research emphasizing additional benefits from social engagement in partnerships or collaborative groups. Command could come through social engagement as well as cognitive engagement, and knowledge could be shared as well as owned individually (*e.g.*, Daiute, 1986). In the 1980s the social constructivist orientation associated with the sociology of knowledge led to another major rationale for writing to learn that might be called the *authenticity rationale*: Since the 'ways of knowing' of different disciplinary groups are reflected in their writing, students can develop knowledge of the culture of a discipline by writing texts that are consistent with its disciplinary discourse practices – or, put more simply, learning the *what* of a discipline should be accompanied by learning the *how* (*e.g.*, Berkenkotter, Huckin, & Ackerman, 1988). The authority and authenticity rationales are complementary, not contradictory, and some spokespeople, particularly the social theorists concerned with education at the college and university levels, offer both in making their cases for the role of writing in learning. For example, Bruffee (1984) argued that, when collaborative activity in the classroom emulates the authentic practices of an academic community, students tie the 'authority of knowledge' to the scholarly activity of people associated with the particular discipline.

Although there tend to be different emphases in, and different rationales associated with, these various forms of constructivism, all share the emphasis on construction, or building. The constructive process – whether it is composing, comprehending, or learning, whether the focus is on individuals or on groups – has three major

---

[1] *I realize these citations of my own work may be confusing. Until 1998, I used the name Nancy Nelson Spivey for my writing; since then, I have used Nancy Nelson.*

dimensions: selective, organizational, and connective. People must determine what is relevant and what is irrelevant; they must supply organization; and they must generate links between the new and the known. Although I address all three dimensions – selective, organizational, and connective – in this chapter, I give most of my attention to the connective dimension, which appears in the theoretical and pedagogical literature through a variety of connective and constructive images, ranging from webs to rubber bands.

In examining the connective dimension, I focus on four kinds of connections that can be made as students, read, write, and learn: connections among ideas, connections among texts, connections among authors, and connections across domains or disciplines. Through making these links, students gain more *authority* over the topics they study and over the texts they read, and they also begin to engage, to a greater extent, in practices that are more *authentic* for the discipline or the content area they are studying.

2 LEARNING AS MAKING CONNECTIONS AMONG IDEAS

In 1977, Emig made her well-known argument for writing as a tool of learning. In that essay, she described writing as 'originating and creating a unique verbal construct that is graphically recorded' and reading as 'creating or recreating but not originating a verbal construct that is graphically recorded' (p. 123). Applying what I have called 'the authority rationale', she claimed that writing is particularly conducive to learning, since learning entails making connections between propositions, and since, in writing, a person must not only see connections but also make them explicit for their readers through syntactic, lexical, and rhetorical means. To support that point, she cited Vygotsky's (1962) observation that writing requires 'deliberate semantics' – 'deliberate structuring of the web of meaning' (p. 100).

Two years later, Van Nostrand (1979) published another important contribution to the writing-to-learn movement. He made a similar point in this way:

> Composing consists of joining bits of information into relationships, many of which have never existed until the composer utters them. Simply by writing – that is, by composing information – you become aware of the connections you make, and you thereby know more than you knew before starting to write. In its broadest sense, knowledge is an awareness of relationships among pieces of information. . . . No matter what the subject, no matter how much you might already know about it, simply writing about that subject will cause you to gain a new awareness of how the fragments of information about that subject relate to each other. This awareness is new knowledge. (p. 178)

When the writing-to-learn movement gained momentum in the 1980s, researchers began testing its basic premise: Is learning enhanced by writing? If so, what kinds of learning are affected? Some researchers have approached their work by examining the texts that writers produce, not only for the content but also for the connections that writers signal in their compositions (*e.g.*, Durst, 1987; Newell, 1984). These connective words, marking various kinds of relations such as cause-effect, problem-solution, topic-comment, similarity, and contrast, suggest the mental relations that writers made between ideas and also the relations between parts of their discourse. If the written product is analyzed systematically, some assumptions can be made about the cognitive operations that its writer employed (cf. van Wijk & Sanders, 1999). According to Klein (1999), who has recently reviewed the writing-to-learn literature, the strongest empirical support thus far for the link between learning and composing has come from the body of research dealing with the relations that are generated in writing. Central to this type of work, which continues to be important in explorations of the learning from writing, are taxonomies of relational types, some lists including numerous specific relations (*e.g.*, Mann & Thompson, 1988; Meyer, 1985) and others offering a small set of primitive relations into which the more specific types fall (*e.g.*, Sanders, Spooren, & Noordman, 1992). These lists are reminiscent of the taxonomies of classical rhetoricians and 18th-century Scottish rhetoricians for the kinds of thought processes used in invention. The links, when generated, can be called *invented* (a term from classical rhetoric that composition specialists have long used for the generative process) or can be called *inferred* (a term for the generative process that is often used by reading specialists).

Most academic writing-to-learn tasks involve much reading as well as writing, since students are asked to read textual materials and transform them in some way to produce their own texts. For instance, if their writing is based on their reading of a single text, the students might be asked to summarize it, to critique it, or to respond to it in some other way. As I have maintained elsewhere (Spivey, 1997) and will also maintain here, these kinds of writing-to-learn acts are hybrid acts of literacy in which reading and writing processes often blend. A person writing a summary or a critique, for example, can be a reader, building meaning *from* a text written by someone else, at the same time that he or she is a writer, building meaning *for* his or her own text. In a recent on-line study of writing from reading, van den Bergh and Rijlaarsdam (1999) examined the various types of generating that occurred as students wrote argumentative essays in response to a written assignment accompanied by an informational document on the assigned topic. One type of content generation for their own essays was associated with their reading of the written assignment and the document they were given.

In reading-writing acts, a writer's 'new' text may seem to be a mix of two kinds of material: some that the writer has replicated (paraphrased or perhaps quoted) from what was read and some that he or she has added. This generated material is considered to be invented or inferred – or, if extensive, *elaborated*. For studies of hybrid acts of literacy, the 'new' text can provide a window into student learning through the choices that are made and the material that is generated.

This is the case even in summarizing – a kind of literate practice that is an authentic, conventional component of most, if not all, academic disciplines and is important in disciplinary learning. Summaries appear as separate texts as well as abstracts attached to larger works, and interconnected summaries make up the 'literature review' that may appear either as a complete informational essay or as an introduction to a longer piece, such as a proposal or a report of a study. The type of summary that has received the most attention in the discourse research (*e.g.*, Hidi & Anderson, 1986) is a rather straightforward representation of the gist of a whole text. However, not all summaries are of this type. Others, as Latour (1987) has shown, are more 'slanted' in that the author doing the summarizing portrays the author's work in a particular fashion to achieve some kind of rhetorical effect. The two types of summary might be differentiated in terms of assumption of authority; in the straight-forward type of summary, authority stays to a great extent with the original author; but in the rhetorical type of summary, the summary-writer asserts more authority over the presentation of that other author's text.

Although the major thrust of summary writing is to reduce the source text, sum-mary writers do *add* in that they make connective inferences that become more ex-plicit in the summary. They see commonalities and generate larger, more inclusive items, such as superordinate concepts that subsume smaller ones or general proposi-tions that replace more specific ones (Brown & Day, 1983; van Dijk, 1980). This connecting operation appears to be more difficult than the selective deleting that is the major operation in summarizing, but, according to Brown and Day (1983), con-necting is the key to effective summarization. A pair of related studies by Durst (1987) and Langer and Applebee (1987) has examined the kind of learning that is associated with summarizing. As might be expected, an assignment to summarize is associated with broad – comprehensive but not very detailed or specific – learning of the material covered in the total text, whereas an assignment directed at a particu-lar portion of the text is associated with elaborate learning of the subtopic addressed in that portion but not learning of the whole.

Critiquing, which is another conventional practice associated with the academic disciplines, also involves connecting the new and the known. Someone reads a text and produces an evaluative piece about it. As Mathison (1998) has pointed out, some summarizing of the text is required, but a critique must include some evalua-tive commentary. The summarized material provides the topics in topic-comment patterns that comprise the new text. Ideally, the critique also includes some supports attached to the evaluative statements. When sociologists rated the critiques that stu-dents wrote for a sociology course, Mathison found that the critiques judged most effective were those in which the student writers had interwoven evaluative com-mentary, primarily negative, with topical material, and had supported their com-ments with evidence based on discipline-specific knowledge. Their performance in critiquing can be characterized in terms of authority and authenticity. The more suc-cessful writers were asserting authority over the other author's text but also, through supplying the disciplinary support, were making a kind of connection that had a cer-tain kind of authenticity. As is customary in the discipline, they were relating the article they critiqued to the larger sociological literature. Students who used support from personal experience instead of formal knowledge of sociology were less suc-cessful in that particular writing situation, since the raters were looking for discipli-nary support. It is important to note that this study was situated in a particular con-text and that the conclusions about the kinds of support the raters favored would not necessarily extend to other situations. Certainly, even in academe, there are contexts in which personal experience would provide strong support for critical commentary. An example in literary studies might be writing a reader-response critique of a poem, short story, or other literary text.

3   LEARNING AS MAKING CONNECTIONS AMONG TEXTS

Instead of relying on only one text, writers often consult, read, or reread multiple texts written by other writers when they compose their own academic texts, and they make various transformations, which might be organizational, selective, or connective, when they integrate material from those texts. These synthesizers may be the writers of major concern to us here: students, from elementary through graduate school, who write their reports and essays in their content-area subjects or academic disciplines (cf. Rouet, Favart, Gaonac'h, & Lacroix, 1996). They may be scholars – biologists, historians, philosophers, psychologists – who contribute to knowledge in their respective disciplines. Or they may be professional writers who produce informational texts for publication. In an act of synthesis, the writer does not rely on a single authoritative source for information. Instead, he or she has several authorities, and, through originating the new text, assumes a kind of authority himself or herself. To effect the integration, writers must reorganize content, must select what seems relevant, and must signal connections among ideas for their own readers. This process can be quite generative, since the writer creates various kinds of links between previously unrelated material and across the various sources. Here I first consider the kinds of transformations performed in synthesis, and then discuss the kinds of environments for synthesis offered by texts that are hyperlinked electronically.

3.1 Discourse Synthesis

My own research has focused on acts of reading and writing in which writers use multiple texts as they create their own. The term I use for the process is discourse synthesis, (Spivey, 1984; cf. N. Nelson, in press), since a *discourse* (a verbal treatment of a subject) is produced through *synthesis* (combining and reconciling) of other discourses. The synthetic text is developed in a literate act involving reading and writing – constructing meaning *from* texts as well as constructing meaning *for* a text. Discourse synthesis, like other kinds of discourse practices, is performed in multi-layered social contexts, including classrooms, in which writers perform in accordance with their understanding of socially-established practices, genres, and conventions. My studies of discourse synthesis began with examinations of the transformations that students, college-aged and younger, made as they wrote academic reports (Spivey, 1984, 1990, 1991; Spivey & King, 1989). I was interested in the commonality and the variability across students in those transformations, and I also wanted to learn more about the kinds of transformations that were associated with various kinds of tasks. My scope has now widened to include academic writing by accomplished scholars in various disciplines and the construction of their authoring identities (N. Nelson, 1998, in press; Spivey, 1997).

In discourse synthesis, some transformations are selective. Writers give preferential attention to material that they consider relevant for their purposes and for inclusion in their own texts. Sometimes they approach texts in a top-down fashion, searching for specific kinds of information, and other times they take a more bottom-up approach, attempting to include what appears across the various sources and thus has a kind of intertextual importance (Spivey, 1984; Spivey & King, 1989).

Selections can also be affected by rhetorical factors, such as appropriateness for the persona the writer wants to project or for the audience the writer wants to reach (Cochran, 1993; Many, Fyfe, Lewis, & Mitchell, 1996). Other transformations are organizational. Writers make determinations as to what belongs with what, and they bring related material together, supplying some kind of order or arrangement. Even though the source texts signal particular kinds of organizations, writers must often dismantle the organization of those texts and fit the pieces into their own patterns.

Still other transformations – those of major emphasis here – are connective. Writers generate links of the various types mentioned above, such as cause-effect or similarity, as they integrate two or more propositions, ideas, facts, or claims. The connective transformations can result in new knowledge for the writer, but making them often takes effort. Consider the potential difficulties in integrating the following information that was available to writers in my first study, conducted 17 years ago (Spivey, 1984). Students were writing on the topic 'armadillo', and the information came from three different articles about the armadillo. One of the articles (Curtin, 1982) provided these 'facts': 'ARMADILLO. The name for 21 species of mammals of the order Edentata, a group characterized by the lack of enamel on their teeth' (p. 705). Another article (Tate, 1982) explained: 'ARMADILLO. . . is any one of a group of mammals with few or no teeth' (p. 328). And the other (Goodwin, 1983) added: 'The armadillo is not toothless as its order name, Edentata, implies; its teeth are simple, rootless pegs placed well back in its mouth' (p. 662). Writers came up with various ways of connecting the seemingly conflicting information. For instance, one writer authoritatively but simply (and successfully, according to my raters) acknowledged the contradiction with a 'however' and moved on: 'Armadillos have been given the order name Edentata (meaning toothless); however, they are not a toothless mammal. Their teeth are rootless and have no enamel on them'.

The connections students made in writing their armadillo reports accomplished various functions. Although some were linkages *within* a topic, others integrated material *across* two different topics. For example, one student generated the following connection between information about the animal's ability to burrow and the animal's reproduction: 'To protect itself, it uses its legs and claws, which are adapted for burrowing, and digs itself into a hole. This burrowing technique is also used when birth is about to take place'. Other connections were more inclusive and integrated several topics, such as the following 'topic sentence' that enabled the writer to tie together the topics of prehistoric predecessors, current species, and physical features into one discussion: 'The armadillo is an animal that has survived for many years in different forms'. Here too, one can note that inferencing entails assertion of authority over the topic – the origination of a claim.

In another study, students wrote comparisons of squids and octopuses based on two texts, one about the squid and the other about the octopus (Spivey, 1991). In these reports, the writers strove to achieve balance in content, searching for content that was parallel for the two topics of the comparison. In some cases, they indicated relevant content by writing notations (*e.g.*, 'both', 'same', 'different') in the margins about similar or contrasting attributes. Some students who developed written plans even put them in the form of matrices connecting the similarities and differences. In addition to inferences about similarities and differences, their reports signaled other kinds of inferential material, particularly with respect to information provided for one animal and not for the other. For example, both texts indicated that the animals change colors, but only the Octopus Text attributed that change to contractions in the wall of pigment cells. Some students pointed out that wall-cell contractions cause color changes for both.

Connecting seems to be particularly difficult for young writers. In my studies the younger writers have seemed quite able to make selections and to provide organization, but they have tended to leave information in a disconnected form with gaps between statements. It may be that these younger students do not have enough topical knowledge or world knowledge to make the necessary connective inferences. Or it may be a matter of authority; perhaps the students do not feel 'authorized' to make claims. Or it may also be that they do not have enough command of the written language to signal the connections they do see or have not yet developed enough awareness of audience to perceive difficulties their readers will have with their texts.

3.2   Use of Electronically Linked Texts

The points I've made thus far have been based on studies with paper texts. What about electronic forms? The new technologies make electronic sources readily available on the internet and on cd roms, and the connective dimension of discourse synthesis can become quite visible to users and observers. Users can jump from one hyperlinked text to another and can often preserve the choices that they make. Connections among texts and among parts of texts are designed to replicate or facilitate mental connections, and it is this notion of mental connections that provides the theoretical foundation for hypertext. The structure of hypertext is often likened to the structure of human memory because of its linking and branching capacities (*e.g.*, Landow & Delaney, 1991). As early as 1945 Vannevar Bush described hypertext when he speculated about a device for moving through texts in the 'world's record' that he called the 'memex' (short for 'memory extender'). As he explained, 'Any item may be caused at will to select immediately and automatically another' (p. 104). Someone could move rapidly – make connections – from the relevant portion of one text to the relevant portion of another either by following an established thread that replicated an expert's path or by creating one's own. It seems to me that Bush was suggesting a choice between two kinds of authority: following the authority associated with someone else's expertise or assuming authority oneself.

The hypertext concept was further developed by Englebart (1963) and also by Theodor Nelson (1967), who coined the term *hypertext*. In *Literary Machines* Nelson (1981) later articulated many of the assumptions of hypertext. Here he was arguing for the authenticity of the electronic environment – its foundation in scholarly practice. It is important to note that much of his attention went to the transformations that writers make in other writers' texts:

> A piece of writing – say a sheet of typed paper on the table – looks alone and independent. This is quite misleading. Solitary it may be, but it is probably also part of a literature.

By 'a literature' we do not mean anything necessarily to do with belles-lettres or leather-bound books. We mean it in the same broad sense of 'the scientific literature', or that graduate-school question, 'Have you looked at the literature?'

A literature is a system of interconnected writings. We do not offer this as our definition, but as a discovered fact. And almost all writing is part of some literature. . . .

Consider how it works in science. A genetic theorist, say, reads current writings in three journals. These refer back, explicitly, to other writings; if he chooses to question the sources, or review their meaning, he is following links as he gets the books and journals and refers to them. He may correspond with colleagues, mentioning in his letters what he has read, and receiving replies suggesting that he read other things. (Again, the letters are implicitly connected to these other writings by implicit links.) Seeking to refresh his ideas, he goes back to Darwin, and also derives inspiration from other things he reads. . . .These are linked to his work in his mind.

In his own writing he quotes and cites the things he has read. (Again, explicit links are being made.) Other readers, taking interest in his sources, read them (following his links).

Even though in every field there is an ever-changing flux of emphasis and perspective and distortion, and an ever-changing fashion in content and approach, the ongoing mechanism of written and published text furnishes a flexible vehicle for this change, continually adapting. Linkage structure between documents forms a flux of invisible threads and rubber bands that hold the thoughts together. . . .

There is no predicting the use future people will make of what is written. Any summary, any particular view, is exactly that: the perspective of a particular individual (or school of thought) at a particular time. We cannot know how things will be seen in the future. We can assume there will never be a final and definitive view of anything. . . .

There is no Final Word. There is always a new view, a new idea, a reinterpretation. Windowing hypertext offers the possibility that all writings (never mind the word 'knowledge') may be forever revised and reinterpreted by new scholars, summarizers, popularizers, anthologizers. (Ch. 2, pp. 7-8)

Hypertext provides reading environments that offer multiplicity and flexibility, as users have options for jumping from one chunk to another or from one text to another, though some environments are more constrained than others. Users can choose among preset trails or can create their own sequences by determining what they will read and in what order they will read, as Bush (1945) had predicted. In a sense, a new link can represent learning, since a mental connection has been established (Lawless & Brown, 1997). However, a navigator can face some difficulties. The freedom of some hypertext environments can be intimidating as well as empowering, since people vary in their navigational proficiency and since all paths are not equivalent for accomplishing various learning tasks (Castelli, Colazzo, & Molinari, 1998). Although it has now become quite common for courses or units of study to be created as hypertexts – with interlinked materials, such as course texts, illlustrations, extra readings, bibliographies, syllabi, assignments, students' commentaries, and even videos – there has been little documentation of the kinds of learning associated with hypertext. The few studies reviewed by Forrester (1995) suggest that use of hypertext systems can facilitate conceptual learning, especially when students can create their own hypertext structures by establishing links. This is the *authority* rationale again for students' generation of connections.

Hypertext also makes possible *writing* environments that are characterized by multiplicity and flexibility – environments that seem conducive to discourse synthesis. A hypertext author – or a team of authors, such as students in a class (cf. Wolfe, 1995) – can create an environment that might include the original texts as well as the 'new' contributions and provide hard links among them too. In this kind of constructive activity as well as others I've discussed, there is selection and organization as well as connection. A major emphasis in hypertext writing concerns these links – which links to use and where to put them. As Johnson-Eilola (1997) has explained,

> The act of linking. . . restructures the way in which concepts such as text and research are constructed. In a Lyotardian sense, writers are not valued for their creative genius so much as their ability to combine and connect information in useful ways. (p. 214).

4   LEARNING AS MAKING CONNECTIONS AMONG AUTHORS

In disciplinary discourse, particular positions are tied to individuals, and knowing *who* is often as important as knowing *what*. Because authors' names function in this way, scholars in a particular discipline can often get a good idea of what someone else is saying with a particular text simply by reading the references. For example, Bazerman (1985), in his case study of physicists reading physics, showed how author-centered and how rapid reading can be when researchers read in order to update their knowledge on topics they pursue in their own studies.

Along with making connections across texts, writers can make connections across *people* when they perform discourse synthesis. This sort of integration was demonstrated in work of Geisler (1991), who focused on the discipline of philosophy. She studied two philosophers, whom she described as participants in the 'conversation' of philosophy, as they read a number of texts on the topic of paternalism and produced their own essays. In contrast to students who performed the same task, the philosophers made more extensive use of author attribution in their own texts to define the various approaches to the topic. In fact, they even used the authors functionally to organize their papers as they summarized and critiqued those authors' texts to set up their own positions.

Students do not always have extensive knowledge of authors, but they can still make use of author attribution as they read and write – and possibly learn something by doing so. In a study I conducted with Greene, psychology students wrote papers on the topic of egocentrism from reading five research articles (Spivey & Greene, 1989; see Spivey, 1997, Chapter 6). Through their reading and writing, these students inferred connections, particularly similarities and differences, among the researchers whose texts they read, even when there was no cross citing in the articles themselves. They made those connections explicit in their own texts, and they also drew into their reports some researchers who had been cited in the articles but whose texts were not among the five they read. Some students, asserting authority over this body of work, set the researchers up into two 'camps' by saying something like this:

'On the issue of egocentrism, some psychologists support Piaget, and others oppose him'. They originated inferences about how an author would align himself or herself with respect to Piaget, even when Piaget was not even mentioned by the author. This facet of their writing relates to an aspect of disciplinary discourse that Baynham (1999) termed *the scholarly 'I'* and defined as 'taking an authoritative position with respect to the quoted other' (p. 485). The scholarly 'I' is the rhetorical use of other authors to authorize one's own claims and is thus much more than such technical matters as including source citations, paraphrasing or quoting directly, and providing references.

Connections with other authors can play an important role in a person's construction of authoring identity in a discipline. In disciplinary authorship, scholars associate themselves through their writing with other scholars with whom they seem to share something – people who write about the same topics, who cite the same folks, who do the same kind of research, who have a similar theoretical orientation. According to Scollon (1994), authorial selves are established and ownership of ideas is established through referencing the writing of others. Alignments are often marked by citations, as a person integrates other people's work into his or her own work, but these alignments can also be marked by allusions and by shared styles and genres. It seems to be the case that disciplinary authors can do much to create their own identities through their borrowings and citations – choosing their ancestors – but they cannot totally control how they are known and with whom they are associated. Other people, such as respondents reviewing manuscripts for publication, can contribute too by suggesting related readings and additional citations (cf. Reither & Vipond, 1989). And still other people contribute through the ways in which they present the authors' work in their literature reviews and through the suggestions they make for how that work should be remembered.

Much of the research into disciplinary enculturation has focused on graduate students and on stylistic matters, such as the appropriation of particular discourse features (*e.g.*, Berkenkotter, Huckin, & Ackerman, 1988). Maureen Mathison and I were interested in other aspects of identity construction, specifically the recurring topics about which students would write when they had a choice of topics and the recurring citations they might make for the same authors (Spivey & Mathison, 1997). We conducted a longitudinal study with six university students, all psychology majors, over the course of their undergraduate programs. We found that, in some cases, these students, even as undergraduates, were building bodies of work in which one of their texts for a course was related to, and grew out of, a previous one for another course. They were also repeatedly citing some authors who were doing related work. These students were not 'authors' in the sense that they were publishing their work, but they were doing some of the things that disciplinary authors do, including the making of connections with particular disciplinary scholars.

5   LEARNING AS MAKING CONNECTIONS ACROSS DISCIPLINES
AND DOMAINS

A final kind of connection to be discussed here is a curricular matter concerning disciplines and domains of knowledge. The university disciplines today are often discussed in terms of their boundaries – boundary maintenance and formation (*e.g.*, Fuller, 1991) – and boundaries are also quite apparent across the subject areas at lower levels of schooling. Even in this chapter, I have mentioned the contrasting 'ways' of the disciplines that provide one of the rationales for writing to learn. The disciplines are separated from one another by long-established external boundaries, even though some of these boundaries between disciplines are loosening through the creation of cross-disciplinary and interdisciplinary specializations, such as *cognitive science* and *cultural studies*. Internal boundaries *within* disciplines tend to be increasing as narrower and narrower subspecializations are created. The school subjects – which, as Stengel (1997) has pointed out, are only loosely tied to academic disciplines – are even more resistant to change in internal boundaries and external boundaries. For instance, the set of subjects designated as appropriate for study in the American high school remains much the same set that was established in 1894 by the Committee of Ten of the National Education Association.

Current education is characterized by compartmentalization, as students take their courses, pass their examinations, and move on to other courses. At the university level, despite a few new interdisciplinary areas, there is little emphasis on cross-disciplinary connections or even cross-course connections. This compartmentalization is partly for curricular reasons. Since courses cannot be always taken in particular sequences, students may not have all had the same prior course experience, and thus the instructor cannot count on them to have the same sorts of knowledge. At the secondary and elementary levels, there is also much compartmentalization, even when students have had similar curricular backgrounds. For instance, the experiences students have had in literature one year are not typically connected with those they have the next year.

It seems odd that our schooling emphasizes compartmentalization and boundaries, while our societies and our disciplines value originality. Originality, even within a particular discipline, often comes from seeing and creating connections across domains and connections with other disciplines and from importing ideas from another discipline into one's own. This point was made years ago by Bartlett (1958) when considering his own synthesis process as he wrote his 1932 book, *Remembering*: 'Perhaps all original ideas come from contact of subject matter with different subject matter, of people with different people' (p. 147). With respect to his own discipline, psychology, he added: 'The most important of all conditions of originality in experimental thinking is a capacity to detect overlap and agreement between groups of facts and fields of study which have not been effectively combined, and to bring these groups into experimental contact' (p. 161). This sort of originality is highly valued in academe. In one study, Ruscio (1986) found that, when asked to describe 'outstanding' members of their field, academics identified those who produce integrative work.

This sort of creative synthesis has been a major interest of McInnis (1996), who defined the term *discourse synthesis* in a somewhat different way than I have defined it. In his terminology, 'discourse' refers, in a Foucaultian way, to a bounded body of knowledge (Foucault, 1971), the signs and practices belonging to a discourse community; and the synthesis is thus the bringing together of two bodies of knowledge. The synthesis to which McInnis referred occurs at the community level in a historical process of change and eventual consensus. However, as I have argued elsewhere (N. Nelson, in press), the discourse synthesis at the community level occurs because of discourse synthesis at the individual level – individuals' reading, writing, listening, speaking, believing, knowing, sensing, and feeling. These individuals make organizational, selective, and connective transformations as they integrate material associated with the different kinds of knowledge, often represented textually. Their integrations are made subsequently by other people, whose integrations are made by other people, and so on.

As far as I know, there has not been much attention thus far to cross-disciplinary connections that students might make in their writing and learning, since most studies have focused more narrowly on discipline-specific learning or learning in a particular content area. In our longitudinal study mentioned earlier, Mathison and I had one student who generated some interesting connections between cognitive psychology – a discipline included in his synthetic specialty, cognitive science – and public policy, a discipline not included in his specialty (Spivey & Mathison, 1997). One paper he wrote was an 'original' synthesis transporting a model for information processing from cognitive psychology to public policy, a field he was considering then for his career. He assumed authority over this material and did the sort of integration that the creative synthesizers in academia might do. His synthesis, which was cross-disciplinary in nature, approximated an authentic practice in academe and in the academic disciplines – a practice in which students rarely engage.

6   CONCLUSION

In this discussion of the constructive nature of writing and learning, I've returned several times to the two writing-to-learn themes of authority and authenticity. Through performing writing-to-learn tasks, students are authorized to comment on the topics they study and also gain some familiarity with the authentic practices of their disciplines. Although the words *authority* and *authenticity* have become tied together conceptually, particularly with respect to writing to learn, they have somewhat different etymologies: *Authority*, like *author*, developed from *auctor*, the Latin word for 'originator', which itself came from the verb *augere*, to 'increase'. *Authenticity* developed from *authentes*, the Greek word for 'doer of the deed'. Attention in this chapter has been on the authoritative 'increases' that are associated with writing to learn and on the kinds of authentic 'deeds' that are accomplished when students perform disciplinary writing.

Writing to learn typically involves reading disciplinary texts, which students use as sources for their own texts. Through writing from, and writing in response to, those texts that they read, students gain authority over them and increase their own knowledge so that they can make their own contributions. And through giving students writing tasks, instructors authorize them to make their own assertions. Unfortunately, his authoritativeness on the part of students is counter to much educational experience, which is most often characterized by deferral – deferral to the authority of a single text book and deferral to the authority of an instructor or lecturer.

Although the issue of authenticity can be addressed in various ways, a major emphasis in writing-to-learn pedagogy is authenticity relative to a particular discipline, subdiscipline, or content field. Students, as constructors of meaning and knowledge and as 'doers of deeds' can perform tasks that have some similarity to those performed by disciplinary 'doers' and can thereby acquire some of the ways of knowing and ways of speaking and writing associated with that discipline and with the scholars in that discourse community.

WRITING, LEARNING AND THE DEVELOPMENT OF EXPERTISE IN HIGHER EDUCATION

PÄIVI TYNJÄLÄ

University of Jyväskylä, Finland

Abstract. This chapter combines the issue of writing to learn with recent views of the development of prerequisites of professional expertise during higher education. The knowledge-intensive or symbolic-analytic work characteristic of today's professional jobs challenges educationalists to develop instructional methods that integrate domain-content learning with practising the general skills needed in today's working life. It is argued here that constructivist and social constructivist views of learning offer promising starting points for developing instruction of this kind. Different traditional and novel forms of writing are discussed from the viewpoint of these constructivist approaches and expertise development. It is concluded that each form of student writing has different benefits. Different forms of writing and writing assignments entail different kinds of activities and thinking processes that, in turn, lead to different kinds of learning. From the perspectives of constructivism and studies of expertise, the general direction in developing writing-to-learn tasks would be moving from reproductive learning towards various reflective, metacognitive, and knowledge-building activities and integrating writing with other forms of learning and studying such as reading and group discussions.

1   PROFESSIONAL EXPERTISE AND THE AIMS OF HIGHER EDUCATION

A growing number of university graduates will find their future jobs in professions that can be characterised as representing what Robert Reich (1992) has called symbolic-analytic services. Work of this kind involves recognising, identifying and solving problems, devising plans, strategies and reports, giving presentations, negotiating, and participating in networks and teams of other experts. Thus, in addition to domain-specific knowledge, symbolic-analytic experts need personal transferable and general skills, such as critical and abstract thinking, an ability to think conceptually and holistically, and to use and produce information. Further, they must have teamwork and co-operation skills, communication skills including those of oral presentation and report writing, an ability to reflect on one's own practice, technical skills such as use of communications technology, and, above all, lifelong learning skills.

These types of general and specific skills and knowledge are widely accepted as aims of higher education in today's society (see, for example, Allan, 1996; Atkins, 1995). However, educational practices in general, and practices in higher education in particular, have been criticised for not developing these prerequisites of symbolic-

P. Tynjälä (2001). Writing, learning and the development of expertise in higher education. In: G. Rijlaarsdam (Series ed.) & P. Tynjälä, L. Mason & K. Lonka (Volume eds.), *Studies in Writing, Volume 7, Writing as a Learning tool: Integrating Theory and Practice, 37 – 56.*© 2001. Kluwer Academic Publishers. Printed in the Netherlands.

analytic work and professional expertise. It has been argued that traditional school practices differ significantly from practices and activities required in real life and in the real expert environments for which students are supposed to be prepared. As a consequence, students often acquire inert knowledge (see, for example, Bereiter & Scardamalia, 1993; Geisler, 1994; Mandl, Gruber, & Renkl, 1996; Resnick, 1987). Such knowledge can be used in instructional settings but cannot be transferred to complex problems of working life. For example, Geisler (1994) has shown that reading and writing practices in educational contexts are quite distinct from those used by experts in academic professions. The literacy practices of experts involve the creation and transformation of knowledge while the literacy practices of students involve acquiring, reproducing and demonstrating knowledge. Experts engage in knowledge transforming; students engage in knowledge telling (see, for example, Bereiter & Scardamalia, 1987; Scardamalia & Bereiter, 1991). The differences between educational cultures and the cultures of real-life experts can be seen also in other practices: Experts often work in teams, they communicate and share their knowledge with colleagues in pursuit of common aims, they search for new knowledge, apply it and transform it for novel uses. By contrast, students in schools, colleges and universities work mainly individually, are often forbidden to cooperate or share their knowledge with peers (in exams), and are encouraged to simply memorise and reproduce the knowledge they have acquired. Examinations in particular seem to function as obstacles to students to achieve deep personal understanding (*e.g.* Entwistle, 1995; Entwistle, Entwistle, & Tait, 1993).

An important challenge to today's higher education is to develop instructional practices that would integrate studying domain-specific knowledge with practising the personal transferable and generic academic skills described above. In this chapter I shall suggest that the use of writing as a learning tool can provide an important basis for fostering those skills that future experts need in the symbolic-analytic or knowledge-intensive jobs of the information society. However, this requires that we take into account what is known about the development of expert knowledge and the nature of learning and that we use writing as a tool for transforming and creating knowledge as an authentic activity. In the following section, I shall first briefly examine recent discussions of what is important in developing expert knowledge and what kind of role writing can play in it. After this I shall deal with the pedagogical implications of recent constructivist and social constructivist views of learning. The rest of the chapter analyses different forms of writing from the viewpoint of learning and the development of expertise. Although the focus of the chapter is on learning and studying in higher education, the ideas to be presented apply well on any other level of education.

2   RELATIONSHIP BETWEEN WRITING AND THE DEVELOPMENT OF EXPERT KNOWLEDGE

Expert knowledge consists of several components (see, for example, Bereiter & Scardamalia, 1993; Eteläpelto & Light, 1999). First, what we mainly learn during our education is formal and theoretical knowledge that is declarative and explicit in nature. The second constituent of expert knowledge is practical knowledge, often called procedural knowledge, that manifests itself as skills or 'knowing-how'. Practical knowledge is learnt in practical situations and is often informal and implicit (or tacit) in nature. Third, self-regulatory knowledge, involving metacognitive and reflective skills, is also an important aspect of expertise. The development of expertise is a long process during which the different elements of expert knowledge are integrated into a coherent whole, and high-level expertise demands the integration of theoretical and practical knowledge. Accordingly, from the educational viewpoint the central question is how this integration takes place. Leinhardt and others (1995) argue that true integration of these two kinds of professional knowledge is best fostered when university students transform abstract theories and formal knowledge for use in practical situations and, vice versa, employ their practical knowledge to construct principles and conceptual models. Thus, *theorising practice and particularising theory* are suggested as keys to the development of expert knowledge.

On the basis of Anderson's (1982, 1987) view of skill acquisition, Bereiter and Scardamalia (1993) emphasise the significance of *problem-solving* as a tool for pursuing the integration of expert knowledge. Much of high-level expert knowledge is informal and implicit in nature, often referred to as tacit knowledge or hidden knowledge. Knowledge of this kind arises and grows from practical experience and is manifested in an expert's actions and decisions. However, it is not easy to express in words. According to Bereiter and Scardamalia, a pivotal aspect in the development of expertise is converting formal knowledge into an expert's informal knowledge and skills, which takes place when formal knowledge is used in solving problems. Thus, formal knowledge acquired from textbooks and lectures is converted into an expert's informal knowledge by being used to solve problems of understanding. Similarly, formal knowledge is converted into skill by being used to solve practical problems, problems of procedure.

From the pedagogical viewpoint, these ideas imply that we should integrate theory and practice in student learning and arrange problem-solving tasks to promote students' expertise development. Students should systematically analyse their experiences of practice periods, for example, and conceptualise and explicate their practical knowledge. They should also have opportunities to use the theoretical knowledge they are studying for solving authentic, real-life problems. Writing can serve as a mediating tool for these purposes. Many studies have shown that writing can successfully be used as a tool for reflection and analytic thought, making implicit presuppositions and beliefs explicit and thus objects of transformation (see, for example, Ballantyne & Packer, 1995; Brown, 1998; Harrison, 1996; Lyons, 1999).

Scardamalia and Bereiter (1991) have analysed the relationship between literate expertise (reading and writing) and domain expertise. They have argued that literate expertise involves a dialectical process that serves to advance domain knowledge. They hypothesise that the knowledge transforming type of writing enhances simultaneously both writing expertise and subject-matter understanding. Accordingly, Scardamalia and Bereiter recommend that in addition to practising their domain-specific skills, experts in learned fields should continuously read and write about their special domain in order to develop their expertise. This idea can also be applied to university studies: The development of expert knowledge requires the integration of reading, writing and domain-specific practice.

3   PEDAGOGICAL IMPLICATIONS OF CONSTRUCTIVISM AND SOCIAL CONSTRUCTIVISM

The development of expertise cannot be fully understood without the concept of learning. Views and conceptions of learning have changed in a fundamental way during the last decades. Behaviourist theories have been replaced by constructivist and social constructivist positions, which offer a more promising starting point for understanding the relationship between learning, writing and the development of expertise. In this section I shall briefly examine the basic tenets of constructivism and their implications for instruction. Thereafter I shall discuss how different forms of writing practised in higher education can be considered from certain perspectives provided by constructivist thought.

Until recently, most educational practices have been grounded on an objectivist epistemology and a common-sense view of teaching and learning as knowledge transmission. An objectivist epistemology assumes that knowledge exists independently of the knower and that teaching is a matter of transmitting this knowledge from the teacher or study materials to the student. Hence, learning is seen as the reception and storage of knowledge. In this view, assessment of learning is based on quantitative measures. Learners have learned the better the more knowledge they can reproduce in tests or examinations. In the last few years, the knowledge transmission paradigm has been questioned by the constructivist epistemology, which emphasises that learning is about active construction of knowledge, not about passive reception of information. Ultimately, constructivism is not a theory of learning but, rather, an epistemological view – a theory of knowledge and knowing. Instead of being an unified outlook it is a conglomeration of diverse positions. What unites them is that individuals or social communities metaphorically describe the acquisition of knowledge as a building process in which knowledge is actively constructed.

Different branches of constructivist thought have somewhat different pedagogical implications (see, for example, Steffe & Gale, 1995). Cognitive constructivists are interested in individuals' knowledge construction processes and the development of mental models, while social constructivists, the sociocultural approach and social constructionists are more interested in social, dialogical and collaborative processes and put great emphasis on language and discourse. The interactionist view attempts to include both individual and social aspects. Because cognitive constructivism emphasises changes in individual students' knowledge structures and mental models, its pedagogical applications aim to develop tools for promoting conceptual change. By contrast, social constructivists, the sociocultural approach and situationalists have emphasised social interaction, collaboration and authentic learning tasks. Social constructionists stress discourse and the negotiation of meaning and are less interested in what is taking place in individual students' heads. In short, the most important pedagogical implications of the different constructivist and constructionist views may be summarised as follows.

Learner-centeredness. As constructivism emphasises the learner's active role in the learning process, the student's activity comes into the focus of any learning situation. What the student is doing is more important than what the teacher is doing. However, this does not mean undervaluing the teacher's input or leaving students on their own. On the contrary, the teacher' role remains important, but changes from that of a transmitter of information to a guide of students' learning process. Because the learning processes are based on the learner's previous knowledge and beliefs directing his perceptions and interpretations of new information, it is important to ground instruction on students' earlier conceptions of the phenomena to be studied (*e.g.* Vosniadou, 1994). This way students' knowledge is not only an 'end product' but also a starting point of learning.

Process orientation. Pedagogical applications of constructivism pay much attention to learners' learning processes and their meta-cognitive and self-regulative skills (Boekaerts, 1997; Vermunt, 1995; Vermunt, 1998; von Wright, 1992). It is considered important that students become aware of their learning strategies and preferences and learn to reflect on and regulate their learning processes. Students are encouraged to focus on understanding and on meaningful learning instead of simple rote learning and reproduction of information. This is supported by shifting the focus from learning detailed facts to a problem orientation. The focus is on problems rather than on categories of knowledge: not 'the heart' but 'how does the heart work?' (Bereiter & Scardamalia, 1993, 211).

Multidimensionality and diversity in learning. In education constructivist thought stimulates ideas about the importance of diversity and variety in learning situations and learning processes. First, cognitive constructivism emphasises the importance of using multiple representations of concepts and information (Feltovich, Spiro, & Coulson, 1993; Lehtinen & Repo, 1996; Spiro, Feltovich, Jacobson, & Coulson, 1995). When new information is perceived through more than one sense and processed in a variety of ways, cognitive structures become more complex and deep, involving rich associations between different elements. Second, diversity and multidimensionality can be seen as issues of the epistemological level. Social constructionism (Berger & Luckmann, 1979; Gergen 1995) presents reality as a social construction which is built in the interaction between individuals and the community. Even 'objective facts' are produced through social meaning making and negotiation. That is, they are socially constructed, not objectively discovered. It is therefore important in teaching to emphasise the relativity of knowledge and familiarise students with the various ways of producing knowledge. Although common language and culture enable us to understand things in basically the same way, people, because of their individual experiences, may attribute things different meanings. It is therefore important that different interpretations by learners are taken into account and discussed. It follows that interactive and co-operative forms of studying, in which individual interpretations and understandings meet each other, are useful ways to organise learning (*e.g.* Hendry, 1996). Third, diversity has been argued for also by the situated learning camp, although on different grounds. The theorists of situated learning emphasise that we learn not only a subject but also cultural practices – and that we learn subjects *through* cultural practices (Brown, Collins, & Duguid, 1989; Lave & Wenger, 1991; Mandl *et al.*, 1996). It is therefore important that learning situations are as authentic as possible and that the cultures of learning and studying simulate real-life situations and the cultures of working life.

Social interaction. Both cognitive constructivist (*e.g.* Piaget, 1963) and social constructivist (*e.g.* Vygotsky, 1986) thought emphasise the significance of social interaction in learning although the mechanisms of the social influence are seen differently (see, Rogoff, 1999). In Piaget's view, social interaction brings about cognitive conflict within an individual, whereas according to Vygotsky learning takes place *between* partners. In any case, social interaction has two-way effects: first, it requires an individual to externalise their thinking and, second, it makes it possible for an individual to internalise ideas presented on the social plane. Therefore, negotiating and sharing meanings through discussion and different forms of collaboration are considered essential elements of learning (Dillenbourg, 1999; Gergen, 1995).

Development of curricula and assessment. If taken seriously, constructivism has implications also for large-scale educational issues, such as curriculum design and forms of assessment. Because of the constantly developing and changing nature of knowledge, the contents of curricula cannot be strictly defined beforehand. Instead, curricula should present general aims and emphasise the development of students' metacognitive and lifelong learning skills. Constructivism also makes it necessary to develop assessment procedures that are embedded in the learning processes, focus on authentic tasks, pay attention to learners' individual orientations and foster their metacognitive skills (Biggs, 1996; Boud, 1995; Dochy & Moerkerke, 1997; Jonassen, 1991). If learning is understood as a process of knowledge construction, then also the procedures used to assess learning must be changed radically (Biggs, 1996: 353). Traditional examinations often lead students to adopt a surface approach to learning and studying and to attempt to memorise the material instead of trying to understand it (Biggs, 1996; Entwistle & Entwistle, 1992; Entwistle *et al.*, 1993). In contrast, assessment methods that emphasise the learning process itself and encourage students to engage in metacognitive and reflective activities are in harmony with the constructivist view of learning. Assessment methods of this kind are based on learning assignments rather than on separate test situations and include also self- and peer assessment and the use of portfolios (see Pirjo Linnakylä's chapter in this volume).

4   FORMS OF WRITING IN HIGHER EDUCATION FROM THE VIEWPOINT OF LEARNING

In this section I shall analyse traditional and novel forms of writing used in higher education against the background of the views of learning and the development of expert knowledge described above. I shall focus on writing and learning tasks assigned to students by teachers and tutors. Writing related to students' spontaneous study strategies, such as note-taking while preparing for examinations, will be discussed in the chapter by Virpi Slotte and Kirsti Lonka. Writing related to the use of portfolios will be considered in the chapter by Pirjo Linnakylä.

4.1 Preparing for Examinations and Writing Examination Answers

When dealing with writing examination answers we cannot focus only on the actual writing process during the examination but have to look at the whole situation of students' preparation for the examination. What kind of learning processes is taking place during the preparation? Research on student learning has shown since the seventies that students may employ different learning strategies ranging from a deep approach focusing on meaning and understanding to a surface approach involving memorising and reproduction and focusing on passing the exam (*e.g.* Biggs, 1987; Entwistle & Entwistle, 1991). Research has also shown that students often approach learning and studying in distinct ways depending on the assessment method (*e.g.* Scouller, 1998; Thomas & Bain, 1984). For example, in a study by Scouller (1998), students were more likely to employ surface approaches when facing multiple-choice examinations and deep approaches when preparing assignment essays. Students often perceive examinations, especially multiple-choice type examinations, as assessing lower levels of intellectual processing, while they perceive coursework essays as assessing higher levels of cognitive processing. However, not only multiple-choice examinations but also essay-type examination questions seem to influence students' approaches to studying. Entwistle and others (1993) have noted the worrying fact that the forthcoming examination itself may distort students' efforts to achieve personal understanding. Most of the students in their study intended to develop a narrow form of understanding aimed at answering examination questions rather than at developing a deep understanding and a personal conception of the subject matter. Thus, preparing for examinations seems to represent studying that easily leads students to memorising, rote learning, a surface approach and a reproductive orientation.

Examinations also represent highly product-oriented assessment practices. They do not focus on or give support to the actual learning processes. Examination questions themselves need not to be reproductive and answering them may require deep understanding, higher-order thinking, evaluating, analysing and synthesising knowledge. However, from the viewpoint of learning it is more useful to practise higher-order thinking skills already in the studying phase than only in the assessment phase. Although some students may develop efficient strategies of deep learning while preparing for exams, many other students may not.

Examination situations often encourage the kind of writing processes that rely mainly on a knowledge telling type of writing (see Bereiter & Scardamalia, 1987). Students have to answer examination questions by rote without access to source materials, they have limited time for writing down their answers and they often tend to reproduce knowledge as such instead of aiming at knowledge transformations and higher-order thinking. In addition, tests and examinations often arouse anxiety, which may further hamper students' thinking processes.

One problem in examinations is that they are often far removed from authentic real-life situations: employers hardly expect their employees to write documents on a pure memory basis without any source materials. Examinations do not support social interaction, sharing of meanings or collaboration either. Instead, they tend to lead to individual studying and competition. Altogether, using examinations as a basic form of assessment has many problems from the viewpoint of learning, and therefore learning researchers and educational practitioners have developed alternative forms of assessment that are better integrated into the learning process itself. Pirjo Linnakylä's chapter in this volume will describe some of them in greater detail.

4.2 Essay writing based on sources

While examinations, especially those requiring mainly factual recall, represent a reproductive outlook on learning, essay writing is more compatible with the current constructivist view. Essay writing based on sources combines three constructive activities – reading, writing and learning – to produce an unique text of the student's own with her own interpretations and conceptualisations. Essay writing is about *discourse synthesis* (Spivey, 1990; Spivey, 1997; Spivey & King, 1989): selecting, connecting and reorganising content from source texts. When composing an essay, students have no need to focus on memorising and rote learning as often is the case in preparing for examinations. Instead – as Nancy Nelson describes in more detail in her chapter – they can concentrate on understanding and making different kinds of knowledge transformations. These knowledge transformations while composing involve various kinds of reasoning operations, including questioning, hypothesising, metacommenting, using schemata, paraphrasing, citing evidence, validating and restating (McGinley, 1992). Thus, essay writing based on sources brings about higher order-thinking processes in students.

Essay writing has also some other characteristics that promote constructive rather than reproductive learning. Reading and writing for composing an essay are very learner-centred activities in which the student alternates between multiple roles of a reader of source articles, a note writer, a note reader, an essay writer and an essay reader (of her own draft). In these changing roles the student engages in 'internal collaboration' or a 'dialectic' (Tierney, O'Flahavan, & McGinley, 1989) with herself. This internal dialectic may also be extended to the collaborative planning process if essay plans and drafts are shared with other students and tutors during the writing process (see, for example, Lonka & Ahola, 1995: 356-357; Tynjälä 1998a: 178). In this way essay writing may be supported by social interaction where individuals externalise their thinking in two ways, first by writing and secondly by discussing their work with peers.

Writing seems also to be a means to promote personal understanding of the given topic. This idea has often emerged in expert writers' perceptions that their understanding of what they are writing about grows and develops in the course of writing. The notion that text production may improve knowledge and develop understanding is supported also by theories of the writing process (Galbraith, 1999; Scardamalia & Bereiter, 1991). However, the mechanisms behind this effect are not yet clear, and there are various theoretical explanations. For example, in their model of the *knowledge transforming* type of writing Bereiter and Scardamalia (1987) assume that the dialectic between rhetorical problems and content problems leads to knowledge transforming processes which, in turn, lead to improved knowledge (Scardamalia & Bereiter, 1991). Another theoretical account of the development of knowledge is Galbraith's (1999) knowledge-constituting model, which assumes that new ideas emerge in what he calls the *dispositional dialectic* between the writer's implicit disposition and the emerging text. Both the dialectics assumed by these two theories are present in essay writing, and a further third type of dialectic can also be found, the dialectic between the writer's emerging text and the source texts being used. Thus, essay writing involves at least three different dialectical relationships: 1) the dialectic between rhetoric and content, 2) the dialectic between the writer's disposition and the emerging text, and 3) the dialectic between the writer's text and the source texts. The interaction between these dialectical processes seems to generate new thoughts, ideas and insights, and in this way the student may deepen his or her understanding of the topic more profoundly than in the case of merely reading the source materials for an examination, for example. The essay is also a means to integrate the learning process and assessment. When writing an essay the student is simultaneously learning and preparing the assessment task – unlike in examinations where the learning process and the assessment situation are separated.

Altogether, essay writing seems to be an ideal tool for learning. However, studies of student learning have shown that students' conceptions of what an essay is vary a great deal, and like any other assignment essay writing may be approached on a surface or a deep level (Biggs, 1988; Hounsell, 1984; Entwistle, 1995; Penrose, 1992). How students understand what essay writing is all about seems to be related to the approaches they adopt to writing as well as to the qualitative and structural features of their essays (Campbell, Smith, & Brooker, 1998; Prosser & Webb, 1994). Students who see learning and essay writing mainly as reproductive activities are likely to adopt a surface approach and use reproductive strategies in note-taking, and in drafting and revising their texts, while students who understand learning and writing as construction and reconstruction of meanings are more likely to use more in-depth and sophisticated writing strategies and they also produce essays with a highly developed conceptual structure. Although students' approaches to essay writing may vary, in general they are more likely to employ deep learning approaches when preparing their assignment essays than when preparing for examinations (Scouller, 1998).

Students differ not only in their approaches to learning while writing an essay but also in their writing strategies. Torrance and his colleagues (Torrance, Thomas, & Robinson, 1994) have identified three distinct groups of students in terms of the strategies they used while composing an essay: 'planners', who planned extensively and made few revisions, 'revisers', who developed content and structure through extensive revision, and 'mixed strategy writers', who both planned before starting to write and revised extensively during the writing process. The planners were reported to be more productive than the revisers and the mixed strategy writers as measured in the number of words written per hour. However, Torrance and others did not examine the learning-related effects of different writing strategies, and further research is needed to investigate the relationship between essay-writing strategies, approaches to learning and writing, and learning processes and outcomes due to essay writing.

4.3   Thesis Writing and Research Tasks

Thesis writing represents the same kind of discourse synthesis and active learning as essay writing. Conducting a research project of one's own and writing a thesis is probably the most demanding assignment required of university students. Research is about creating new knowledge. It is a knowledge-building and –constructing activity which involves using existing knowledge to formulate new problems and answering these new problems by carrying out an empirical or a theoretical study. In the current constructivist view, learning is similarly seen as knowledge constructing activity very akin to the research process. At the cognitive level, creating new knowledge and coming to understand existing knowledge resemble each other as processes (Bereiter & Scardamalia, 1993: 200; Popper, 1977: 461). For this reason, research-like activities are the foundation of many recent innovations in learning (see, for example, Brown & Campione, 1996; Scardamalia & Bereiter, 1996). Instead of being passive recipients of information, in new forms of learning students are required to actively identify and recognise problems, formulate hypotheses and theories of their own, search for evidence and test their theories, and present the conclusions that they have drawn from their research. Thesis writing is a form of studying that involves all these elements. Thus, although completing a thesis or dissertation is a very traditional component of university education, at the same time it meets the challenges posed by new learning theories.

4.4   Summary Writing

Summary writing is not a common type of assignment in higher education but it may be applied, for example, in small groups or study circles as a learning task when there is an extensive amount of literature to be studied (see, for example, Tynjälä, 1998b). As in essay writing, in summary writing students' reading and writing processes are integrated, and students have to make selective transformations of the contents: They have to evaluate the content and make decisions about which elements of the texts are most essential. In the process of summarising writers use different transformational rules to decide which parts of the source text they should delete or ignore and which parts they should use for making generalisations and integrations of the content (Brown & Day, 1983; Hidi & Anderson, 1986; Kintsch & van Dijk, 1978). Making integrations and generalisations are processes through which students construct the meaning in a more active way than when they simply read a text through, leading to higher-level comprehension. Thus, summary writing can be seen as a learning task that may 'force' students to search for a deep understanding of the topic instead of engaging in rote learning and reproductive activities. However, summarisation skills seem to develop relatively late, and students inevitably need instruction and guidance in effective summarisation (Hare & Borchardt, 1984).

Radmacher and Latosi-Sawin (1995) have investigated summary writing on a university psychology course and compared the participating students' examination results with the results of those students who did not write summaries. The mean score of the final examination for the summary-writing class was significantly higher than for the class without summary writing exercises. This finding suggests that summary writing promotes text comprehension. The participating students' own assessments support this finding as they emphasised that they had found summary writing activities effective tools for both learning the course contents and for promoting their writing skills.

Summary writing tasks are usually conducted so that students have access to the source text while summarising. Kirby and Pedwell (1991) have compared this familiar type of summarisation with a less familiar task, text-absent summarisation, in which students are warned that the text will be removed after they have read it but before they start to summarise it. The results of the study indicated that the two types of summarising encourage different processes in students adopting different approaches to learning. Under text-present conditions surface learners wrote more extensive summaries whereas under text-absent conditions deep learners tended to write more extensive summaries. Text-absent summarisation also promoted recall of more difficult texts, but the benefit was confined to students who generally adopted a deep approach to learning and who had been able to produce more extensive summaries of the text in question. Thus, text-absent summarisation seems to benefit deep learners and students who have good summarisation skills.

4.5 Journal Writing

Journal writing is a form of written discourse that has gained popularity during the last few years. Journals are informal and personal writings that are used to encourage students to engage in reflective thinking and in the active elaboration of their own ideas about the subject that is being studied. One advantage of using journals in learning is that they make it possible to integrate a narrative form of discourse and content learning. (On narratives see Bruner, 1986, 1987, 1990.) Journals are excellent tools for making thinking visible and tangible and, consequently, for developing thinking and transforming ideas (see Lukinsky, 1990). In this way they enable students to engage in an internal dialogue. Although journals are personal and private texts, they can also be used as source material to promote dialogue with others in classroom discussions.

Recent literature on journal writing indicates that in educational settings journals have been used for various purposes, such as: 1) to enhance formal writing and develop writing skills; 2) as a psychological 'dumping ground'; 3) as a part of a larger project; 4) to promote self-awareness; 5) to recreate experiences, ideas, feelings and impressions; 6) to enhance the social context of the classroom, for example in group discussions; 7) to promote critical thinking, reflection and metacognitive skills; 8) to develop reflective practice; 8) to help students and teachers to get to know each other; 9) to generate dialogue between students and teachers or course feedback; and 10) to promote scientific understanding (Anson & Beach, 1995; Audet, Hickman, & Dobrynina, 1996; Commander & Smith, 1996; McCrindle & Christensen, 1995; Morrison, 1996; November, 1996.) Students may be asked to keep journals regularly, for example after each lecture or session on a course they are attending or on a weekly basis. Depending on the purposes of the course and the journal-writing, students may be asked to express their own ideas about the topics dealt with in the classroom, formulate their own theories, raise questions, criticise, reflect on their own performance and so on. Journals may also be used before a new topic is introduced to students in order to activate their previous knowledge and make them conscious of their existing conceptions of the topic. After instruction students may then examine their earlier conceptions in the light of the new information. In this way journals serve to develop students' metacognitive or reflective skills (McCrindle & Christensen, 1995; Morrison, 1996). For example, in a study by McCrindle and Christensen (1995), keeping learning journals during a university course was found to be a more effective learning method than writing scientific reports. In a learning task, the group that wrote learning journals made more use of metacognitive strategies and applied more sophisticated cognitive strategies than the group that wrote scientific reports. The journal group also expressed more sophisticated conceptions of learning and performed significantly better in the final exam than the scientific report group.

Journals are intended to provide students with an informal, personal and private channel for self-expression, reflection and learning. Accordingly, the original journals are often kept as students' private texts which are never read by the teacher. In such cases journals may be used by students as material for classroom discussions or for other written assignments that will be marked. Students may also be asked to select extracts from their journal to be included in a larger portfolio. On some courses journals may be read regularly by the teacher who may then comment on students' ideas or use them when planning further instruction.

Although journals are traditionally regarded as tools for individual and private expression, they can also serve as mediators in social interaction. For example, group discussions on difficult topics may progress better if students have first had time to think about the matter on their own and to write their thoughts down in their journals. Some educators have also had promising experiences from 'dialogue journals'. A dialogue journal is a journal used for the purpose of carrying out a discussion in written form between two persons, a student and a teacher or two students (see, Staton, Shuy, Peyton, & Reed, 1988; Anson & Beach, 1995: 65-79). In university studies, dialogue journals have been used, for example, in teacher education to foster reflective practice in students (Bean & Zulich, 1989). New information technology with network systems has made it possible to extend the use of dialogue journal writing to computerised learning logs that enable students to share personal writings with peers and teachers, and read and respond to other people's ideas in a collective network environment (e.g. Audet et al., 1996).

To conclude, journal writing may be used for various purposes and in various ways. It may serve as an important aid in students' knowledge construction and in developing their self-regulative knowledge and skills or it may equally well provide a tool for enhancing social interaction in the classroom.

4.6 Collaborative Writing

Using collaborative writing as a learning tool has been argued for on at least two different theoretical bases: on the basis of the Neo-Piagetian research tradition on the one hand and on the basis of the Vygotskian view of learning as a basically social activity. Piaget's (1963) idea of cognitive conflict or Neo-Piagetians' concept of socio-cognitive conflict (Doise & Mugny, 1984) refer to the mechanism through which an individual realises that her thoughts or ideas are inconsistent with other people's views or new information. This internal conflict leads the individual to reflect on her thinking and may serve to initiate conceptual change. Thus, collaborative writing situations can be seen as generators of discussions leading to higher levels of thinking.

The Vygotskian argument for collaborative learning and writing is based on Vygotsky's (1986, 1978) view of the social nature of learning. According to Vygotsky, learning takes place primarily on the social, interpsychological plane and only secondarily on the intrapsychological plane, that is, when a learner internalises what has first been experienced in social interaction. However, knowledge is not internalised directly but by means of mediating psychological tools, especially language. Through this internalisation communicative language is transformed into an individual's 'inner speech' and verbal thinking. The ideal state for learning is what Vygotsky called the zone of proximal development. This concept refers to the distance between the learner's actual state of development determined by independent problem-solving and the potential level of development that he can reach through the guidance of adults or collaboration with more capable peers. Thus, Vygotsky argued that through social interaction students might reach higher state of development than they would achieve by working and studying on their own.

The degree of collaboration in writing may vary from collaborative planning and using conversation as a writing resource to joint authorship where the partners actually compose a common text. In collaborative planning the participants discuss their ideas about what to write and share their plans and drafts with other collaborators, but finally each of them completes a text of her own. In joint authorship the co-operation between partners may vary between horizontal and vertical collaboration. Horizontal collaboration entails dividing subtopics among the authors while in vertical collaboration they divide the tasks of gathering information, drafting, revising and editing (Flower, Wallace, Norris, & Burnett, 1994; Rubin, 1988).

Modern information technology provides useful tools for writing in collaboration. Bonk, Medury and Reynolds (1994) have categorised collaborative writing tools on five different levels: 1) e-mail messaging tools, 2) delayed/asynchronous collaboration systems, 3) brainstorming and dialoguing devices, 4) direct/real-time text collaboration tools and 5) collaborative hypermedia. While the tools in the two first categories involve only asynchronous communication, the tools on levels 3 to 5 allow also real-time synchronous communication where several users can simultaneously communicate with each other. Various kinds of collaboration tools are nowadays widely used in expert work in most fields of business, economy, administration and services. Therefore, while writing in collaboration and using these tools students also learn other important skills needed in working life.

Although there is a wealth of literature on collaborative writing, most published papers pay more attention to the development of the writing process and writing skills than to domain-content learning (see, for example, Dale, 1996; Dunn, 1996; Flower et al., 1994; Gubern, 1996). Rigorous studies of the learning-related effects of this form of writing are still rare. Some studies of collaborative writing among school-age children suggest that collaborative writing assignments are successful in developing writing and reasoning skills and promoting understanding of the topics to be learned (Dale, 1994; Keys, 1994), but there are also studies indicating that collaboration does not automatically lead children to higher-order argumentation or explorative talk (Kumpulainen, 1996). For higher education students, encouraging examples of using collaborative writing have been reported (Bryan, 1996; Dunn, 1996; Hay & Delaney, 1994), but these studies similarly fail to provide any intensive analyses of the learning processes and outcomes.

4.7 Combining Reading, Writing Tasks and Group Discussions

Traditionally, different forms of class activities as well as different subjects have been separated from each other in education. For example, writing classes have been isolated from domain-content classes and classroom discussions are usually carried out in isolation from and independently of writing tasks. Separate reading and writing classes are of course needed to some extent in order to teach and practise basic skills, but once students have acquired them, integrating different classes and combining different activities may open new avenues for learning. This idea has been applied, for example, in the writing-across-curriculum movement (e.g. Young, 1986).

Studies carried out on different school levels have shown that combining reading and writing tasks or reading, writing and group discussions is a promising approach and may enhance the positive effects of these activities and produce more desirable learning outcomes than when they are used as separate methods (see, for example, Dysthe, 1996; Gaskins et al., 1994; Lonka & Ahola, 1995; Mason, 1998; Tierney, O'Flahavan, & McGinley, 1989; Tynjälä, 1998a; b; Tynjälä, 1999).

The theoretical basis for combining different forms of discourse is still incoherent: cognitive, socio-cognitive and interactionist views seem to compete with each other. From the cognitive point of view, using reading, writing and discussions in combination can be seen as a way of giving students opportunities for constructing multiple representations which, in turn, lead to stronger and more diverse associations between different cognitive elements. Socio-cognitive theories rely on the neo-Piagetian concept of socio-cognitive conflict that refers to a cognitive state brought about by meeting different views and conceptions of phenomena. Interactionist views explain the power of the discourse combination, for example, in Bakhtinian terms of dialogism or multivoicedness (see Dysthe, 1996) and describe how each discourse participant's conceptual systems come to interact with one another and enter into dialogical relationships. In sum, what is needed here is theoretical clarification, including an integration and synthesis of the different positions as well as more empirical studies of the issue.

One experiment combining reading, writing and group discussions was carried out on a university course on educational psychology (Tynjälä 1998a, 1998b, 1999). The contents of the course were three textbooks on learning and human development. The participating students read each textbook while carrying out several writing tasks that compelled them to actively engage with the knowledge they studied. The tasks were planned so that the students could not just reproduce knowledge but they had to transform it in different ways, apply it, criticise it, and so on. These tasks were then discussed in groups once a week during the course. The tasks required the students, for example, to activate their previous knowledge, to compare it with the knowledge presented in the textbooks, to compare different theories or approaches, to examine the theories in the light of their own experiences, to criticise the theories, to apply theoretical concepts to real-life situations, to prepare summaries and to write a fictional or true story using theoretical concepts. In addition to these learning tasks, the students also wrote an extended essay (about 10 pages) during the course. The writing process was supported by collaborative planning (see Flower *et al.*, 1994) that gave the students an opportunity to talk out their essay plans and drafts before completing the essays. Altogether, the course integrated ideas based on cognitive studies of writing and the constructivist view of learning. Accordingly, the group attending the course was called the constructivist group.

The constructivist group students' learning outcomes group were compared with those of a control group which studied the same textbooks by reading them on their own for the examination and attended lectures. The learning outcomes of these two groups were investigated from three viewpoints: 1) as the students' subjective learning experiences, 2) as changes in the students' conceptions of learning (the course dealt with learning), and 3) as measured by traditional examination questions.

An analysis of the students' subjective learning experiences showed that in addition to knowledge acquisition, most constructivist group students emphasised the acquisition of an ability to apply knowledge, the development of their critical thinking skills, changes in their conceptions of the topics studied, and a shift from epistemological dualism towards a more relativistic view of knowledge. These types of description of learning experiences were rare among the control group students. The constructivist group students also wrote higher-level examination answers (as assessed by the SOLO Taxonomy and an epistemic categorisation) than the control group students. In sum, combining reading, writing and group discussions seemed to produce the kind of learning outcomes that correspond with the general aims of higher education, thus fostering the prerequisites of professional expertise (Tynjälä, 1999).

4.8   Writing as a Component of Project-Based Learning

Project-based learning is a form of studying which enables the integration of the learning goals of different school subjects or academic disciplines and the application of theory into practical purposes (Blumenfeld *et al.*, 1991; Poell, Van der Krogt, & Warmerdam, 1998). It also makes it possible to develop in students all the elements of expert knowledge, that is, declarative, procedural and self-regulative knowledge. A project may be the assignment of a single student but usually it is carried out in a group with two to six members. A project has a certain length with the deadline fixed in the initial phase. The aim of a project is usually to design and complete some product, but naturally the main goal of project-based learning is to learn something through the process of project work. The goals of project-based learning include both an understanding of the given subject matter and the acquisition of different skills, such as domain-specific technical skills and co-operation and communication skills, as well as self-regulative skills such as reflective thinking and metacognitive skills.

Projects may proceed, for example, through the following phases: 1) formulation of problems and aims through brainstorming and planning; 2) division of subtasks and labour; 3) collection of materials; 4) implementing the plans; 5) report-writing and evaluation. This type of phase model helps students to organise the work but there is one serious problem. Experiences from project-based courses have shown that the report writing and evaluation phase may come to occupy so much students' thoughts that they begin to equate the report with the project as a whole (Askeland, 1997). The focus has shifted from the learning process to the final report or product. As a result, those students who have developed strategies for writing high-level reports may have gained better grades than those students who have learned a great deal but have focused less on report writing than on the learning process itself.

This problem may be solved by concentrating, both in writing and in evaluation, on the process of project work as such rather than on the product made, and by integrating writing and assessment. In other words, *report writing* is replaced by *process writing* where students reflect on their own work and assessment their progress throughout the project. Instead of 'reports' process writing produces 'records' of the work process (Askeland, 1997, 168). These records may be used as documents for evaluation along with the final product. In addition to written documents, process-based evaluation may also involve oral discussions between the students and the tutor or teacher.

Project-based learning is one way to simulate authentic working life projects and usually one of the aims is that students learn teamwork, cooperation, collaboration and communication, all of which are important skills in today's professional work. Thus, project-based learning can be seen as an authentic learning environment for real-life situations. The writing activities involved in such projects can be similarly organised as authentic tasks. Depending on the subject and the phase of the project, students may be assigned tasks requiring them to write like a project manager, a secretary, an analyst, a consultant, a developer, a researcher, a co-ordinator, an advisor, an engineer, an artist, a journalist and so on. Thus, a project may produce different kinds of records and documents. A final report or some other product is an authentic ending in real-life jobs, and therefore finishing a product should similarly complete student projects. However, as pointed out above, the assessment of a project should not focus only on the final product but also, and very strongly, on the process of learning involved in its making.

An example of project-based learning where writing is used as an important and integral part of project work is a working-life-orientated project-based course, the Development Project Course, being carried out at the Department of Computer Science and Information Systems at the University of Jyväskylä, Finland (see also Eteläpelto & Tourunen, 1994; Tourunen, 1996). The aims of the course are to integrate theory and practice in the domain of information systems design, to provide students with personal experiences in project work and to develop personal transferable skills, such as cooperation and oral and written communication skills. At the beginning of the course the students are divided into project groups, each of which has 4 to 5 members. During the course the groups produce a developmental plan or design some other product for an authentic client company. At the same time they take parallel courses on teamwork and oral and written communication.

Writing plays an important role in coursework, being used as an authentic activity and as a tool for reflection and self-assessment. It is put to the following uses: 1) documenting and reporting different phases of project work (process writing; 'records'), 2) reflecting on the learning processes, and 3) self-assessment and group-level assessment of learning. Thus, during the project the students produce a diverse collection of written materials: project plans, co-operation messages, minutes of meetings, reports on client interviews, plans for and reports of content for the client, computer software designed by the group, self-reflective essays and narratives, journal entries, and so on.

At the beginning of the course all students write a short essay on their conceptions of project work, their expectations and personal learning goals. Through collaborative writing, each group also produces an essay on their starting situation and shared aims. During the course and at the end of the course the students assess their progress and reflect on their work both on the personal and the group level. The students, tutors and representatives of the client company are asked to write assessment documents twice during the project process, halfway through and at the end of the project. Each project group has a journal or diary in which the head of the project writes personal comments and notes on the most significant and important events during the process. (Each member of the group serves as a head of the project on their turn.)

When the participating students' self-assessment reports were analysed in a study of the Development Project Course, it was found that their subjectively experienced learning outcomes could be grouped into five different categories (using the phenomenographic procedure developed by Marton (1988):

1) domain-specific skills (*e.g.* programming, specific methods and tools, understanding end-users' viewpoints, professional attitude, application skills);

2) an overall view of project work (*e.g.* as regards different phases of the project, different roles, planning);

3) co-operation and communication skills (*e.g.* negotiation skills, documentation and writing skills, memo writing, acting as a member of a group);

4) resources management skills (*e.g.* resources allocation, personal and group-level time management);

5) social skills (*e.g.* how to meet new people, how to get along with different people, self-confidence, self-expression, ability to teach and guide other people (as in cognitive apprenticeship).

These learning outcomes were very similar to the learning goals that the students had set themselves at the beginning of the course, and most students felt that they had achieved the goals. In addition, the students also brought up certain outcomes that they had not mentioned as their learning goals, such as a professional attitude and application skills, planning skills and memo-writing skills. Thus, the students felt that they had actually learnt even more than they had intended. It is not possible to analyse here in detail to what extent these outcomes are due to writing and to what extend to other components of project work, but it is clear that writing played an important role in the students' activities during the course. Furthermore, writing proved to be an excellent tool for students to use for reflecting on and self-assessing their learning.

A more detailed study of the use of writing in project learning is only at its early phase, but the experiences gained so far suggest that project-based learning involving extensive use of different forms of writing develops many important skills that are needed in today's working life. Organising learning in the form of a project made it possible to integrate domain-content learning, group work skills and the development of written and oral communication skills.

5   CONCLUSIONS

In this chapter I have examined different forms of writing used in higher education, starting from writing in traditional examinations and continuing through thesis, essay and summary writing towards more novel forms of writing such as journal and collaborative writing. Finally, I presented examples of how writing can be integrated with textbook reading and group discussions and used as an essential part of project-based learning. In general, it can be concluded that different forms of writing and writing assignments entail different kinds of activities and thinking processes which, in turn, lead to different kinds of learning. For example, in examination situations students write from memory, whereas in writing essays or theses they use source materials. The requirement of writing from memory leads many students to surface learning, memorising, reproducing of information and the knowledge telling type of writing while essay or thesis writing is more likely to generate learning processes in which students transform knowledge to construct a personal view of the topic.

From the viewpoint of the development of expertise, each form of student writing has different benefits. Essay, thesis and summary writing make students actively assess information and knowledge, pay attention to the most important parts of the source texts, get the gist of them, make selections what to include their own text, integrate knowledge from different sources or from different sections of the source texts, form their own opinion or conception of the topic and so on. All these processes develop critical thinking and judgement as well as the analysing and synthesising skills that are needed in the knowledge-intensive work of today's professionals. Furthermore, essay writing is likely to generate knowledge transforming processes which may lead to a deeper understanding of domain knowledge and at the same time develop writing expertise (Scardamalia & Bereiter, 1991).

The strength of journal writing lies in the fact that it serves to develop students' meta-cognitive skills and self-reflection, otherwise not very often the focus of teaching and studying. In journals students may reflect on their feelings, beliefs and conceptions and examine the contents in a personal way. Highly developed meta-cognitive and reflective skills are characteristic of experts (*e.g.* Eteläpelto, 1993; Järvinen, 1990); therefore, developing these skills should be an essential aspect of higher education.

Meta-cognitive and reflective skills develop also through collaborative activities as participants have to express and share their thoughts with their peers. Collaboration is also a very important element in the symbolic-analytic jobs (Reich, 1992) peculiar to today's working life. Hence, collaborative writing tasks may provide important learning opportunities as regards not only writing skills but also oral communication skills and co-operation and group work skills.

From the viewpoint of domain-content learning, probably the most beneficial use of writing is to combine it with other forms of discourse and studying. When writing is integrated with textbook reading, group discussion and different project-work activities, for example, students are simultaneously exposed to a broad range of cognitive processes, which may make the effect of each component method stronger than when used separately. Furthermore, this way the benefits of both collaborative learning and individual writing processes can be achieved at one and the same time. A study by Lonka and Ahola (1995) indicates that this kind of activating instruction has long-term effects on student learning, leading to better academic success than traditional instruction.

Bereiter and Scardamalia (Bereiter, 1997; Bereiter & Scardamalia, 1993, 1996) have launched the term 'knowledge building' to describe the kind of activity that they recommend as the basis of the work of teachers and students on all level of the educational system. They make a distinction between knowledge building and learning, the former being the activity of constructing theories, hypotheses, and other knowledge objects, while the latter is the activity of improving one's mental structures. The emergence of the information society, expanding knowledge work, growing information flows and developing network systems mean that it is not all that important to memorise factual information. Instead, it is more important to be able to exploit information and knowledge, critically assess and select the most important information, transform knowledge for novel uses and so on. According to Bereiter and Scardamalia, these kinds of skill do not develop by cramming for a test but, rather, by taking part in a collective effort of knowledge building.

Inspired by the idea of knowledge building as an important educational activity, I suggest that the main practice in higher education should be to encourage students, during their education, to construct knowledge products for their own use (see Bruner, 1996: 22-23). Instead of trying to cope with tests and exams, students could focus on building their own personal collection of useful packages of relevant domain knowledge. These knowledge products could be in the form of essays, term papers, project reports, research papers, videos, posters, slides, portfolios, or whatever other products students might create. Writing plays an important role in making of such products. In an ideal situation, students could find these products so valuable that after their graduation they could serve them as useful resources in dealing with complicated real-life problems. Students' knowledge products would thus constitute a kind of personal library or portfolio. Personal libraries could also be stored in a database or on the Internet for collective use. Naturally, the products themselves will eventually go out of date, but the processes involved in making them will probably last as lifelong transferable skills. When constructing knowledge products with the help of source materials students do not need to concentrate on memorising and cramming for examinations. Instead, constructing different knowledge products requires them to engage in processes of knowledge transforming. As we have seen, different forms of writing and various kinds of tasks can be used to encourage these processes.

ACKNOWLEDGEMENTS

I wish to thank Dr Sarah Ransdell and the reviewers for their most valuable comments on the manuscript. Also, I want to thank Mr Hannu Hiilos for the final checking of the text's English language.

ON THE ECOLOGY OF CLASSROOM INSTRUCTION:

The Case of Writing in High School English and Social Studies

MARTIN NYSTRAND, ADAM GAMORAN, & WILLIAM CAR-BONARO

University of Wisconsin-Madison, USA

Abstract. Drawing from research on emergent literacy and activity theory, this chapter explains an eco-logical perspective on classroom instruction and literacy development distinguished by the reciprocal and epistemological roles of teachers, students, and peers as these roles are shaped through their interactions. The resulting activity networks involve both oral and written discourse, providing a research window on the potential interactions of classroom discourse and writing. This chapter explores such interrelation-ships with quantitative data from 54 ninth-grade English classes and 48 ninth-grade Social Studies classes. The main finding is that classroom discourse contributes to student writing performance to the extent that writing and talk each extend the scope of one another. Evidence from observations and ques-tionnaires revealed many superficial similarities between the two subject matters. Students wrote about as frequently in English and Social Studies, and classroom discourse patterns in both subjects tended heavily towards lecture, recitation, and seatwork. Beyond these similarities, the research uncovered striking dif-ferences in the two contexts as they affected student writing. Though frequent writing activities enhanced writing performance in English, they had the opposite effect in Social Studies. Further probing of writing activities and assignments revealed that writing served different purposes in the different subject areas. With an emphasis on rhetoric and form, English classes displayed more attention to writing as writing. In Social Studies, by contrast, writing was used to teach students methods of close reading. Such differences show that the curricular landscapes of English and Social Studies affected writing performance very dif-ferently, producing two different environments for literacy development.

1   INTRODUCTION

Over the last two decades, researchers have learned much about literacy especially by studying children in settings outside school. These studies include (a) the con-texts in which preschoolers explore interests in writing and reading (*e.g.*, Bissex,

M. Nystrand, A. Gamoran, & W. Carbonaro (2001). On the ecology of classroom instruction: The case of writing in High School English and social Studies. In: G. Rijlaarsdam (Series ed.) & P. Tynjälä, L. Mason & K. Lonka (Volume eds.), *Studies in Writing, Volume 7, Writing as a Learning tool: Integrating Theory and Practice, 57–81.© 2001*. Kluwer Academic Publish-ers. Printed in the Netherlands.

1980; Teale & Sulzby, 1986; Scollon & Scollon, 1980), (b) the role of reading in the development of text-segmentation skills (Nystrand, 1986a), (c) the traditions and messages that parents transmit to their children about the uses of print (Heath, 1983), (d) the game interactions of parents and children (Wertsch & Hickmann, 1987), (e) the tendency of children to combine writing, drawing, and gesture (Gundlach, 1982), and (f) the effects of the social fabric of everyday life on literacy in twentieth-century America (Brandt, 1998, 2001). Dyson (1993, 1995, 1997) has insightfully showed the importance of out-of-school contexts on literacy learning in school. All these studies investigate rich contexts featuring intricate interactions between oral and written language.

Compared to such extensive research on emergent literacy, few studies have until recently examined literacy development in school in any detail to consider, for example, the effects of classroom discourse on writing. There is, of course, considerable recent work on classroom discourse (for a recent review, see Sperling, 1996). Several researchers, including Heath (1983) and Britton (1969), who contended that talk is 'the ocean on which all else floats,' have emphasized fluidity between writing and talk as key to learning. McCarthey (1992) investigated a fifth-grade, African-American student from a writing process classroom who adapted oral language patterns from classroom interaction for use in her own texts. Yet most research examining specific links between the oral and written discourse of the classroom has examined very specialized kinds of talk designed specifically for writing instruction, including response groups and other small-group work, whole-class discussions promoting prewriting, and writing conferences. Though many studies have been made of teacher-student interaction in writing conferences, little progress has occurred, Sperling (1996) points out, in explicitly relating such talk to actual writing development.

1.1 Research on Response Groups and Student Writing Development

In studies of 250 students in 13 classes of freshman composition at the University of Wisconsin-Madison, Nystrand (1986b) found substantial benefits for students writing mainly for each other in small groups as compared to students who wrote only for the teacher and spent no time in groups. College freshmen regularly discussing their papers with peers wrote better and improved their writing ability more over the course of a semester than their counterparts who wrote only for the teacher. The peer-group students' progress was due mainly to the development of superior revising skills. One reason for this was that the students simply did more revising: On average they revised each paper about three times. In addition, as they presented their papers orally to their groups, they developed proofreading skills and typically marked up their papers even before starting group discussion. In a separate study, Nystrand and Brandt (1989) demonstrated the clear effect of group discussion on revision strategies. (For review of research on peer response groups, see DiPardo & Freedman, 1988.)

This is not to say we know nothing about the potential of classroom talk for promoting writing development. The fullest set of studies concerns talk specifically linked to writing instruction. In his meta-analysis of such studies, for example, Hillocks (1986) found that the classroom discourse most conducive to enhancing writing skills involved peer-response groups with an 'inquiry' focus: assigned topics involving analysis of readings or other 'data' and attention to rhetorical strategies. The least effective instruction was lecture-based instruction involving abstract presentations focusing on grammar, mechanics, and features of good writing (Hillocks found that this kind of instruction actually had a negative effect on writing performance). Similarly, Sweigart (1991) found that student-led small-group discussions of nonfiction were superior to both lecture and whole-class discussions in preparing students to write analytic opinion essays, which were scored for clear thesis and elaboration of ideas.

1.2 Research on Whole-Class Instruction and Student Writing Development

A recent study of prewriting that shows just how rich investigations linking classroom discourse and writing can be, is Sperling's (1995) study examining a single secondary lesson in great detail, provocatively tracing the clear influence of classroom talk on student writing, even involving the talk of some students who chose to do no writing. Sperling's close analysis carefully demonstrates the power of analyzing the ideas and content of individual student papers as dialogic responses to the comments and ideas of classmates during classroom interaction.

Nystrand and Graff (2000) show how the instructional environment of a middle-school Language Arts-Social Studies class subverts the teacher's efforts to teach argumentation. In a unit requiring students to write an argumentative research paper, they wrote 'hybrid' texts – argumentative theses followed but not always supported by lists of facts. Nystrand and Graff conclude that the classroom epistemology fostered by classroom talk emphasizing recitation (*i.e.*, knowledge as given) was inimical to the complex rhetoric the teacher was trying to develop in encouraging students to write arguments (*i.e.*, knowledge as constructed).

Overall, however, there are few examinations of the role general classroom discourse plays in writing development when the talk is not specifically about writing or primarily aimed at improving writing skills. When teachers lead open-ended discussions of reading assignments; when they have their students read aloud short stories during class; when they devote considerable time to lecturing on the important points; when students vigorously debate ideas; *etc.*, *etc.*, what, if any, effects do these and other practices have on subsequent student writing and eventually on their writing? What are the effects of different kinds of teacher questions? What kinds of discussion enhance writing? What roles do both teachers and students play in class interactions that make a difference? How do these effects vary from classroom to classroom, and how do the most dynamic classrooms operate? Does classroom discourse affect writing in Social Studies differently than it does in English classrooms? General classroom discourse typically occurs without any reference to writing, and if one has impact on the other, too often we know too little about it. Yet if instruction is to be optimal, teachers need to know as much as possible about all the effects of all their instruction.

1.3 Ecology and Literacy Development

Research on issues such as these requires a conceptual framework powerful enough to encompass and interrelate both oral and written discourse, and we believe research on emergent literacy offers many useful leads. For example, this work clearly shows that contexts of language and literacy development are more than mere settings for development. These environments are intricate and dynamic networks of roles and activities, and must be continuously generated and regenerated by the participants in their interactions with each other. They are achieved and co-constructed. For example, research on emergent literacy shows that a print-rich environment is necessary but not sufficient for the development of literacy. In addition, becoming literate requires readerly interactions between the learner and a facilitator, typically a parent or older sibling. The ritual of bedtime reading enhances literacy development because it defines such a context (Heath, 1980). Writing development, too, is clearly linked to particular interactions writers have with peers and teachers. These environments are not just backdrops for learning; more to the point, in their interactions, the participants actively and dynamically shape each other's writing development.

These interactions set up tight interrelationships and mutual dependencies among the participants, and for this reason, we may understand their activities in ecological terms. Indeed, the character of any given literacy is idiosyncratic to some extent with the particular social and cultural environment that 'sponsors' it (Brandt, 1998). This is not to say that there is anything particularly 'natural' about classroom learning. Ecology here stresses the importance of interrelationships between teachers and students and also among peers as a key force in student learning. Ecology concerns the relation of organisms to their ecosystems, which include other organisms with whom the reference species has a 'symbiotic,' or interdependent relationship. Human ecology concerns the relations of people to their environments (Hawley, 1986). Ecology in our research concerns the relationships of instructors and learners in learning environments. We treat 'instructor' and 'learner' quite broadly here since such learning environments often occur out of school, involving parents, older siblings, and peers.

Ecologists study symbiotic interactions to discover insights about the course and parameters of individual organisms' behavior and development. The ecosystems they study vary tremendously in size and scope, some as large as a river basin or watershed, others as small as the side of a desert highway which, because it gets ample moisture in the form of runoff from the pavement, supports plant life that is more lush than other plants just a few feet away in the dry surrounding desert.

Learning ecosystems range from whole-class instruction to bedtime reading rituals and response groups. It is important to note that any given learning environment is more than the physical space it occupies. Many function only at certain times involving particular activities and participants. Hence if bedtime reading occurs in a particular spot, in a favorite chair or in bed, for example, this activity system (Engeström, Miettinen, & Punamški, 1999; cf. Leont'ev, 1978) comes alive as a unique space for literacy learning only when the reader and the one-read-to curl up together with a good story at bedtime. For the rest of the day, the spot plays many other functions, potentially setting up other ecosystems. In other words, ecosystems are defined not simply by physical spaces but by the participants' interactions and the functions activated at the time of their interaction. This is why it is the ritual of a parent reading to a child at bedtime, and not just the place of reading, that constitutes the learning ecosystem: The activity assigns particular roles to the participants, who, through their very interactions, shape and support the parameters of the learning environment. In short, learning ecosystems are activity settings: Bedtime stories are part-and-parcel of going-to-sleep routines, enacted by the nurturing interactions of skilled readers and the ones read to; response groups are effective when they create contexts that enable writers to relate their composing and revising to the likely responses of their readers (Nystrand, 1986b); and whole-class contexts shape learning as teachers enact assumptions about what counts as learning and knowledge, typically realized by the kinds of questions teachers ask their students as well as how they respond to them (Nystrand, 1997). Each of the critical interactions in these settings defines literacy ecosystems.

1.4 Ecological Features of Literacy Learning Environments

Ecologically, learning environments are distinguished by the reciprocal, mutually dependent roles of their particular members: What one does has implications for what the other can do. In environments dedicated to learning, the roles are also epistemological, and it is the discourse between participants that defines the operational epistemology of the group.

Reciprocal Roles. Literacy learning ecosystems are shaped by the interactions of parents and children; teachers and students; experts and novices; *etc.*, and it is the roles of the participants that shape these interactions. These respective roles are reciprocal, which is to say, the role of one (*e.g.*, teacher) entails the role of the other (*e.g.*, student). Reciprocity is an important principle of any social interaction (Schutz, 1967), and the character of any semiotic space is largely defined by the roles of the conversants (hence, textual space is a function of writer-reader interaction (Nystrand, 1982, 1986c); learning space is shaped by the reciprocal roles of teacher and learner (Nystrand, 1997).

The defining nature of reciprocal roles in ecology of learning is evident in Bruner's (1978) concept of scaffolding. Scaffolding occurs when an adult or more able peer initially shows a learner the essential moves in a new activity, making all or most of them himself, but then, in subsequent interactions, gradually handing things over to the learner. In such a coordinating effort, the instructor 'scaffolds' the learning and activity of the learner by striking a balance between what the learner can do herself while providing support for what she is not yet able to do by herself. Continually honoring the expanding role and perspective and emerging skills of the child, the expert gradually allows the learner to assume more responsibility for the task as the learner's potential skills are transformed into actual ones. The context is dynamic, evolving according to the shifting roles of the two. Development is elegantly understood here as the learner's expanding role enabled by the instructor's

Receding Adult Role
EXPANDING CHILD ROLE

Figure 1. Reciprocity in scaffolding: Adult role recedes as child role expands.

receding role in a joint activity; their roles can shift precisely because reciprocity remains constant (see Figure 1).

Epistemological Roles. Because such interactions comprise learning environments, the participant roles are also epistemological affecting whether knowledge is 'precast' and transmitted by the teacher or dynamically co-constructed through classroom interaction. Classroom discourse is the chief medium for the construction of classroom epistemology (Applebee, 1996), for in classroom interaction, student roles are largely shaped if not assigned by the roles teachers assume through questions, tests, and responses to student answers, writing, *etc*. For example, our previous studies have showed that discussion, which is more coherent than question-answer recitation, is also a more effective medium of learning than question-answer recitation (Nystrand, 1997; Nystrand & Gamoran, 1991). Learning is clearly promoted, for example, when teachers effectively build on students' prior knowledge and current understandings by following up on student responses. By doing so, teachers validate particular student ideas by incorporating their responses into subsequent questions, a process Collins (1982) calls 'uptake.' In the give and take of such talk, student responses and not just teacher questions shape the course of talk. The discourse in these classrooms is therefore less predictable because it is 'negotiated' or co-constructed – in character, scope, and direction – by both teachers and students as teachers pick up on, elaborate, and question what students say (Nystrand, 1990b, 1991). Such interactions are also often characterized by 'authentic' questions – asked to obtain valued information and opinions, not simply to see what students know and don't know; authentic questions are questions without 'prespecified' answers (Nystrand & Gamoran, 1991). Unlike recitation, in which the teacher's questions are prescripted according to points of information students must learn, discussion is more fully shaped by open-ended interaction, and is more likely to be thematically organized as the conversants respond to and follow up on – in short, develop what has been said into a coherent network of conversation turns.

By asking authentic questions, teachers elicit students' ideas, opinions, and feelings, and in so doing, they make students' prior knowledge and values available as a context for processing new information. In this way, authentic questions, like writing that follows up discussion, contribute ecologically to the coherence of instruction by enlarging the network of available meanings in the class. By contrast, the coherence of instruction is likely to suffer if, as in recitation, the teachers' questions are exclusively prescripted according to what students are supposed to learn. Skilled teachers are adept at phrasing questions with one eye on the text and the other on the class's current understanding at each and every point of the unfolding discussion. Epistemologically, such dialogically organized instruction treats present-tense, constructive, sometimes tentative knowing – *i.e.*, the class's current understanding – as the foundation of past-tense knowledge (what gets remembered) and therefore learning. In this way, full-blown discussion ecologically elaborates a network of conversation turns, each utterance sequentially contingent upon both the previous and subsequent turns. It is in the context of this network that class understandings emerge.

By conceptualizing the classroom as a dynamic and integrated system of resources for learning, an ecological perspective on classroom instruction assumes that development in one area often impacts and/or possibly inhibits development in another. This approach builds on what is known about the nature of classroom discourse and about effective writing and reading instruction respectively, but goes beyond to investigate how each mode of discourse can complement, optimize, and constrain the others. Amidst education research traditions that too often treat writing, reading, and classroom discourse as discrete domains, an ecological perspective is indispensable for understanding how these different modes of discourse can interact to promote overall literacy development.

This conception of instruction has been recently supported by both the 1996 National Council of Teachers of English and 1994 National Council of Social Studies standards-based reform documents that envision communities of language users and inquiry as the foundation for learning and student achievement.[1]

2 WHEN WRITING AND CLASSROOM DISCOURSE ENHANCE EACH OTHER: AN ECOLOGICAL STUDY

We may expect classroom discourse and writing to enhance each other to the extent that classroom talk extends and integrates writing into the established discourse, *i.e.*, to the extent that teachers treat writing tasks as conversation turns of sorts. This happens when talk motivates writing, and/or vice-versa, so that the one follows up the other. When writing and talk interact in this way, the writing carries on what began as talk, in which case the talk is prewriting, or the talk carries on what began as writing, in which case the writing may be said to focus the talk. The overall effect is to increase the coherence of instruction. Here's an example of talk closely interrelated with writing from a ninth-grade English class. The teacher, Ms. Lindsay, is leading a discussion of plot summaries students have written for a chapter from Mildred Taylor's *Roll of Thunder, Hear My Cry*. In the following excerpt, Ms. Lindsay is writing on the board, trying hard to keep up with John, one of her students in this ninth-grade class, who has just read aloud his plot summary.

---

[1] *www.ncte.org/standards/standards.shtml; www.ncss.org/standards/*

'I had a lot of trouble,' says Ms. Lindsay, 'getting everything down [on the board], and I think I missed the part about trying to boycott.' She reads from the board: ''and tries to organize a boycott.' Did I get everything down, John, that you said?'

'What about the guy who didn't really think these kids were a pest?' replies John.

'Yeah, okay,' says Ms. Lindsay. 'What's his name? Do you remember?' John shakes his head, indicating he can't remember.

Without waiting to be called on, Alicia, another student, volunteers, 'Wasn't it Turner?'

Looking around the class, Ms. Lindsay says, 'Was it Turner?' Several students say, 'Yes.'

'Okay,' continues Ms. Lindsay, 'so Mr. Turner resisted white help. Why? Why would he want to keep shopping at that terrible store?'

John quickly answers, 'There was only one store to buy from because all the other ones were white.'

'Well,' Ms. Lindsay objects, 'the Wall Store was white too.'

Another student, Tom, now addressing John, wonders, 'Is it Mr. Hollings' store? Is that it?'

'No,' John answers. 'Here's the reason. They don't get paid till the cotton comes in. But throughout the year they still have to buy stuff – food, clothes, seed, and stuff like that. So the owner of the plantation will sign for what they buy at the store so that throughout the year they can still buy stuff on credit.'

'So,' Ms. Lindsay says, reading aloud what she puts up on the board: 'he has to have credit in order to buy things, and this store is the only one that will give it to him.'

Another student, Felice, speaks up. 'I was just going to say, it was the closest store.'

Barely looking away from the board now, Ms. Lindsay replies while continuing to flesh out the paragraph building on the board, 'Okay – it's the closest store; it seems to be in the middle of the area; a lot of sharecroppers who don't get paid cash – they get credit at that store – and it's very hard to get credit at other stores. So it's going to be very hard for her to organize that boycott; she needs to exist on credit.

'Yeah?' she says as she then nods to yet another student. Discussion continues.

This excerpt is noteworthy because it starts with John's written summary, which the teacher writes on the board as John dictates it to her, and then uses discussion as a way of further developing John's ideas. More specifically, by scaffolding his responses with particular questions, Ms. Lindsay teaches him how to interpret literature. Here writing focuses talk which, in turn, further develops John's literary thinking. Presumably his written summary will develop if he revises it, for what began as a report now has the orientation and potential of an essay. The discussion has helped him articulate a focused thesis about why there was only one store to shop at. When we also consider that both writing and discussion here develop out as a reading assignment, we can see how instructional time in this class is highly effective and efficient because the writing, reading, and talk all pull together, and so work coherently and epistemologically to develop a network of understandings about the novel.

Our previous research (Gamoran & Nystrand, 1991; Nystrand, 1997; Nystrand & Gamoran, 1996) showed that academic achievement in both literature and Social Studies is enhanced when writing, reading, and classroom discourse are coherent, sustained, and focused on academic subject matter. In English instruction, we expect that literature achievement will be enhanced to the extent that writing, reading, and classroom discourse are integrated in study of a particular drama or novel. We expect that such integrated instruction will be superior to instruction which treats literature independently of writing, as when, for example, students read a novel and work on study questions for a few days, and then turn to unrelated writing tasks on others. Integrated instruction increases its coherence, which in turn promotes learning because students are best able to digest new information when they can easily relate it to what they already know. Similarly, in Social Studies, we expect that writing about Social Studies topics will be enhanced by a coherent focus in classroom reading, writing, and talk around Social Studies concepts and issues.

Yet our experience and expectations lead us to believe that writing is used differently in Social Studies and English. Traditionally English and language arts classes have been more concerned with writing than Social Studies teachers have been. With new emphasis on the importance of writing in all subjects, however, this situation may be changing, so our study sought to examine this issue in our large sample of schools, classes, and students. Put differently, we expected that, though the quality of classroom discourse positively affects writing performance, curriculum potentially mediates these effects by significantly altering the ecology of instruction. By reanalyzing previously collected data (Nystrand, 1997), we sought to unravel these effects by testing the following hypotheses:

Hypothesis 1. In normal instruction, classroom discourse and writing tend to proceed independently of each other, *i.e.*, teachers infrequently relate the two as a result of planning.

Hypothesis 2. Despite the infrequency of planned interactions between classroom discourse and writing in most classes, we expected that classroom discourse enhances writing to the extent that writing promotes coherence by enlarging the network of conversation turns, and we expect that writing will develop more fully to the extent that writing and classroom discourse regularly interact, *i.e.*, classroom discourse leads to writing and writing leads to talk.

Hypothesis 3. Finally, we expect writing to develop differently in English and Social Studies classes to the extent that these two curricula alter the ecology of instruction in the two kinds of classes.

3   DATA AND MEASURES

Most research on the dynamics of classroom discourse has involved close analysis of instruction especially of the sort conducted by Dyson (1993, 1997), Heath (1978), Langer (1995), McCarthey (1992), and Mehan, H. (1979). Case studies are more nuanced and attuned to the dynamics of classroom interaction than are large-scale quantitative studies. What the latter lack in nuance, however, they potentially make up in power, for they can focus across numerous classes to reveal relationships and significant patterns and effects not always found in individual case studies. Hence, in order to test a number of hypotheses about the general effects of classroom discourse on learning and to examine the mediating role of curriculum in writing performance in English and Social Studies, we undertook a quantitative analysis of data from our previous studies of instruction.

Our data were collected over an entire school year from 9 Midwestern high schools, including 3 in small-town/rural locales, 1 large suburban school, 3 large urban schools (1 in an upper-middle-class area and 2 in a working-class locale), and 2 urban Catholic schools whose students were mainly middle-class. In English, we gathered data from over 1,100 students in 54 ninth-grade classes. In Social Studies, the two smallest rural schools did not have year-long ninth-grade classes, but we were able to gather data on over 1,000 students in 48 classes in the other 7 schools. About 90% of students who began the school year in the selected classes participated in the study, which included fall and spring testing and questionnaires for students; spring questionnaires for teachers; and four observations of each classroom. In each of the observations, the class sessions were tape recorded, and, using a specially designed computer program, CLASS 2.0 (Nystrand, 1990a), observers systematically recorded and coded all teacher and student questions, and also noted the nature and topic of activities in which teachers and students were engaged.

Our database also includes qualitative information on the handouts teachers distributed in class and the long-term writing assignments they required of students. At the beginning of the year, teachers received a folder in which they were asked to collect copies of each handout they distributed. In addition, teachers used logbooks to record the content they covered in class and note each week's reading selections. At the bottom of the coverage logs, teachers were asked to describe any long-term writing assignments they gave to students. For this chapter, we use the handout materials and writing assignments to examine the content of students' writing task.

3.1 Background Measures

One aspect of a classroom ecosystem is the composition of its student population. Moreover, to study the effects of instruction, it is important to take account of pre-existing differences among students. Consequently, we obtained information about student background through student questionnaires. These data were coded as dummy variables for student race (1=Black), ethnicity (1=Hispanic), and sex (1=female). We also constructed a scale for socioeconomic status (SES), an un-weighted additive composite of student reports of mother's education, father's education, the higher of mother's or father's occupation on an updated Duncan SEI scale (Stevens & Cho, 1985), and possession of home resources.

The ranking or status of a class may also constitute an important ecological element, and our analyses indicate whether students were enrolled in honors, regular, or remedial classes. We used an 'other class' category for a small number of school-within-school and heterogeneous classes.

3.2 Achievement Tests

We obtained data on student achievement in the fall and spring. In the fall, we administered a writing task in both English and Social Studies classes, and separate literature and Social Studies achievement tests in the two different subjects. In the spring, we administered a test of literature achievement in the English classes and a test of Social Studies achievement in the Social Studies classes. The spring tests included open-ended essay questions, which we are using in this chapter to measure students' writing performance in the two subject areas. The two readers' scores were averaged, and wherever there was a difference of more than one point on either measure, samples were reread by a new pair of readers. Each student's initial writing score was computed as the sum of the two measures.[2]

English and Social Studies: Test of Initial Writing Achievement. Following the work of Nystrand, Cohen, and Dowling (1993), we defined expository writing as sustained reflection in which the writer records and processes information to various degrees. Basing our work on this construct, we assessed writing samples in terms of both (a) degree of reflection and (b) extent of text elaboration. We asked students to write brief personal essays, describing some experience that taught them something they valued, and explaining why it was important. This sample was scored by two readers on each of two dimensions: (a) level of abstraction, based on Britton *et al.*'s (1975) categories of transactional-informative prose; and (b) coherence and elaborateness of argumentation, based on the 1979/1984 NAEP criteria for informative writing (in Applebee, Langer, & Mullis, 1985).

English: Test of Initial Literature Achievement. Measurement of students' start-of-the-year capabilities with literature used a power test taken from the National Assessment of Educational Progress (NAEP), a standard, nationally administered test of literature in America and involved a series of multiple-choice questions concerning a set of poems and narrative passages. In addition, students were asked to explain their response to one of the short stories, and this writing sample was scored using the National Assessment of Educational Progress 1979 criteria for the identification and substantiation of personal emotions and feelings elicited by a short story (Applebee, Langer, & Mullis, 1985). These samples were read by two readers and

---

2 On the 5-point Britton scale, readers agreed within 1 point for 96.3% of the papers; on the 4-point NAEP scale, readers agreed within 1 point for 95.5% of the papers.

reread by a new pair of readers whenever there was a discrepancy of more than one point.[3]

Social Studies: Test of Initial Social Studies Achievement. In Social Studies, students filled out a multiple-choice test of general Social Studies knowledge in civics, history, and geography. Items for the test were drawn from public-release items from the National Assessment of Educational Progress (NAEP).

English: Test of Achievement in Writing about Literature. In the spring, we administered another literature test, asking questions about various aspects of works they had studied during the year. As part of this test, students wrote a brief essay requiring them to select a character they admired from one of the novels, short stories, or dramas they had read, and to both describe this character and explain their admiration for him/her. This writing sample, like the one collected in the fall, was assessed using the same rubrics for (a) degree of reflection and (b) extent of text elaboration. To facilitate comparisons across subjects, we have standardized the achievement tests to have a mean of 0 and a standard deviation of 1. Although the samples for the two tests are not identical, they are similar enough, with overlapping memberships, to make such comparisons reasonable. However, we have not standardized the independent variables, so the regression coefficients can be interpreted as indicating the impact of a one-unit change in the independent variable on a standard deviation in test score results. For example, the coefficient for 'Gender' indicates the difference between females and males on the tests; the coefficient for 'Uptake' indicates the change expected on the basis of a one percent increase in uptake (since uptake is coded in percentages); and so on.

Social Studies: Test of Writing Achievement in Social Studies. In Social Studies classes, we administered a test that posed a series of questions from recall to short essays about a specific topic students had studied during the year. The topics varied, depending on what had been covered in class. As part of the test, we also asked students two open-ended questions about any other topic they had studied in Social Studies during the year. Responses to these questions are used in this study as indicators of student writing performance in Social Studies. The responses were scored by two readers on three dimensions: level of abstraction, amount of information, and accuracy of information. The scores for each dimension were summed across dimensions and averaged across readers (interrater-correlation of scores was .87.) Then the three dimensions were compiled into a single score using a formula derived from a pilot study in which three high school Social Studies teachers had marked a set of similar tests. The formula gave most weight to amount of information, second to level of abstraction, and third to accuracy.[4]

---

[3] *There was perfect agreement among readers for 92.6% of the samples. Each student's initial literature score was computed as the average of the two readers' scores, plus the multiple-choice scores.*

4 *Additional technical information about all tests and measures, including information about validity and reliability, will be found in Nystrand (1997).*

Measures of Instruction. Classroom observations, teacher questionnaires, and student questionnaires generated data on writing activities and classroom instruction which we use for the analyses in this chapter.

Writing Activities. During each class observation, we recorded all instructional activities in sequence. These data allowed us to track how often class activities involved writing, as well as what types of writing occurred, and the extent to which writing and talk were related.

In addition, our teacher survey elicited three indicators of how much writing was assigned to each student: (a) frequency of writing at least a paragraph, (b) frequency of writing more than 2 paragraphs, and (c) frequency of writing 1 page or more. All frequencies were coded in times per month. For regression analyses, we used the average of these three measures to compute the frequency of extensive writing (this scale has an alpha-reliability of .86). We also included a measure of how often students choose their own writing topic, coded in times per month, from a single question on the teacher survey.

Student questionnaires indicated how often students reworked their written texts. In addition to noting the frequency of rewriting, we created separate indicators for editing, which we restricted to work on spelling, punctuation, grammar, and/or usage; and for revising, by which we meant reworkings of ideas and information, as well as issues of organization and development.

On the questionnaires, students indicated how often they rewrote their work, and what they worked on when rewriting. We created the indicator of editing by multiplying the response for the frequency of rewriting by the sum of students' responses to whether, if and when they revised, they worked on spelling, punctuation, grammar, and/or usage. Thus, for example, a student who reported revising once a month, and who worked on both spelling and punctuation, would have a value of 2 on the editing scale (1 time/month x 2 editing activities = 2). The scale has a minimum of 0 (for students who never worked on editing in revision) and a maximum of 80 (for students who revised daily but worked on all four areas of editing). We also created an indicator of revising by multiplying responses to the same question about frequency of revision by whether, if and when they revise, students worked on ideas and information, and on organization and development of the paper. This variable has a minimum of 0 (for students who never revised) and a maximum of 40 (for students who revised daily and worked on both types of revision). Finally, we also asked students how often they completed their written work, and coded this variable as a percentage.

Classroom Discourse. Observations and teacher questionnaires both contributed to our measures of classroom discourse. From the observations, we computed the average amount of time spent in lecture, question-answer recitation, and discussion. In our study, discussion was narrowly defined as free exchange of information among students and/or between at least 3 students and the teacher that transcended the usual initiation-response-evaluation (IRE) sequence of classroom discourse (Mehan, 1979) and lasted longer than 30 seconds.

Observers also coded the questions posed by teachers on a variety of dimensions, including authenticity (whether the question avoided a pre-specified answer) and uptake (whether the question incorporated a previous student response). These variables are coded as a proportion of total teacher questions, averaged across observations. Observers also noted what proportions of students were visibly off task during instruction, and these data too were averaged across the four observations. Finally, teacher questionnaires yielded an indicator of coherence that reflected how often students wrote about and discussed their readings, related their readings to other readings, and related discussions to previous discussions.

The scale for coherence is coded in times per week based on responses to the following questions:

'About how often do students in your class write about (or in response to) things they have read?'

'About how often do you discuss writing topics with your students before asking them to write?'

'About how often do you and your class discuss the readings you assign?'

'When you ask students about their reading assignments in class, how frequently do you attempt to do each of the following: 'Ask them to relate what they have read to their other readings'

'About how often does your class relate its discussion to previous discussions you have had?'

'About how often do you and your class discuss things students have written about?'

This scale has an alpha-reliability of .68.

4   RESULTS

First we present descriptive findings on the amount of writing, editing, revising, and classroom discourse, and the relations between writing and discourse. Then we present analytic results on the impact of classroom discourse on writing. Finally we provide a content analysis of the handouts and long-term writing assignments, to help us understand some of the subject-matter differences that emerged from the statistical analyses.

4.1 Writing and Classroom Discourse

How much writing do students do? Are there differences between English and Social Studies? How does writing relate to classroom discourse? Conventional wisdom suggests that students write in English classes more than in Social Studies, yet little is known about the relation between classroom discourse and writing in either subject. To address these issues, we present data from surveys and observations that describe the character of writing and discourse in ninth-grade English and Social Studies classes. Results are reported in Table 1.

Table 1. Characteristics of writing activities and the discourse environment.

English (N=54 classes)	Mean	Standard Deviation
Writing Activities		
Frequency (times per month)[a]		
At least a paragraph	4.52	3.04
More than 2 paragraphs	2.03	2.54
1 page or more	2.00	2.08
Choice (times per month)[a]	2.61	3.38
Completion (percentage)[b]	85.91	6.88
Rewrite (times per month)[b]	2.37	1.46
Discourse Variable		
Lecture time (minutes)[c]	8.42	5.84
Question-answer time (minutes)[c]	17.58	6.55
Discussion time (minutes)[c]	.24	.50
Authentic questions (percentage)[c]	26.57	19.19
Uptake (percentage)[c]	25.69	11.83
Coherence (times per week)[a]	12.84	6.76
Off-task (percentage)[c]	3.77	4.06

Social Studies (N=48 classes)		
Writing Activities		
Frequency (times per month)[a]		
At least a paragraph	5.06	3.47
More than 2 paragraphs	1.99	1.89
1 page or more	1.83	2.08
Choice (times per month)[a]	.81	.93
Completion (percentage)[b]	83.52	9.91
Rewrite (times per month)[b]	1.34	.85
Discourse Variables		
Lecture time (minutes)[c]	6.21	6.12
Question-answer time (minutes)[c]	23.82	8.74
Discussion time (minutes)[c]	.52	1.31
Authentic questions (percentage)[c]	30.48	20.05
Uptake (percentage)[c]	26.95	14.01
Coherence (times per week)[a]	10.82	6.63
Off-task (percentage)[c]	3.28	3.68

[a] *Teacher reported.*
[b] *Aggregated from student reports.*
[c] *Observed.*

Amount of Writing, Choice, and Revision. We were surprised to find that the frequency of writing was similar in English and Social Studies. We expected to find more writing in English, but instead teachers in both subjects reported that students were required to write at least a paragraph a little more than once a week, and they were asked to write more than 2 paragraphs, as well as 1 page or more, about once every two weeks. In English, students could choose writing topics about every other week, but in Social Studies, such choice was limited to less than once a month, on average. Also, editing and revising were more common in English than in Social Studies. On average, students reported they revised or rewrote their papers about every other week in English, but little more than once a month in Social Studies. Completion of writing assignments averaged 86% in English and 83% in Social Studies, according to student reports. Overall, the relatively large standard deviations compared to the means indicate substantial variability from classroom to classroom in both subjects.

Classroom Discourse. Generally, classroom discourse was very similar in English and Social Studies. In both subjects, the vast majority of class time was devoted to a combination of lecture, question-and-answer recitation, and seatwork. English teachers lectured and directed seatwork a bit more, and recitation was more prominent in Social Studies, but the overall character of class time was very similar. Discussion was rare in both subjects. On average, discussion took less than 15 seconds a day in English, and about 30 seconds in Social Studies classes. In English classes, 61.1% of all classes had no discussion at all, and only 5.6% had more than a minute daily; only 1 class of the 54 averaged more than 2 minutes. Similarly in Social Studies, 62.5% of the classes had no discussion at all, 10.4% had more than one minute daily, and only 4.2%, or 3 classes, averaged more than 2 minutes per day.

In English classrooms, authentic questions were asked in all the ninth-grade classes we observed; half the classes routinely had 25% or more. In Social Studies, one class exhibited no authentic teacher questions and, as in English, half the classes averaged 25% or more. The average for authentic questions was about 27% in English and 30% in Social Studies. We also observed that 26% of teacher questions in English and 27% in Social Studies exhibited uptake. Coherence, characterized by writing about reading selections, talking about writing, talking about readings, and so on, occurred about 13 times per week in English and 11 times per week in Social Studies, according to teacher reports. Again, the standard deviations are large compared to the means, indicating that classes differ substantially from one another in both subjects.

Classroom Writing. Writing was a rare event in the classrooms we studied with none occuring in over half the lessons we observed; Social Studies used writing slightly more than English (57.6% of observed lessons vs. 53.7% in Social Studies). When writing did occur independently from talk, it most commonly involved seatwork (10.2%). Short writing tasks were discussed in only 7% of the lessons we observed, and in none of the lessons was discussion interwoven with longer writing tasks (*e.g.*, essays). These results are summarized in Table 2.

For the most part, these general descriptions of writing and discourse conform to expectations. The only unexpected finding, that the amount of writing is similar in English and Social Studies, simply indicates that, on average, students do not write very much in either subject. Classroom discourse is dominated by teachers; most questions have prespecified answers and do not build on students' ideas; and question-answer sessions rarely become the kind of free-flowing exchanges of information that we have called discussion. Is there a pattern here? The next question is to ask whether writing activities and classroom discourse are related to one another.

Table 2. Classroom uses of writing in 431 grade 9 English and Social Studies lessons. Percentages.

	Social Studies Lessons		English Lessons		Total Classes	
	All	Writing	All	Writing	All	Writing
LESSONS WITH NO PLANNED WRITING TASKS	57.6	---	53.7	----	55.5	----
TALK ABOUT WRITING						
Grammar lessons	0.0	0.0	2.5	5.6	1.4	3.1
Writing lesson	0.0	0.0	0.9	1.9	0.5	1.0
WRITING WITHOUT TALK						
Extended writing in class, but not discussed	1.5	3.6	6.4	13.8	4.2	9.3
Clerical work (copying down assignments & taking notes)	4.0	9.5	3.4	7.4	3.7	8.4
Tests or quizzes* undiscussed in class	8.0	19.4	8.6	18.5	8.4	18.8
Seatwork with no discussion	9.0	21.4	11.2	24.1	10.2	22.9
TALK AND WRITING AS EXTENSIONS OF EACH OTHER						
Recitation as extension of short writing task (homework, Seatwork, tests, & quizzes)	19.2	45.2	16.7	36.1	10.9	24.5
Recitation as extension of longer writing task (*e.g.*, essays)	2.5	5.9	3.4	7.4	3.0	6.8
Discussion interwoven with short writing task	0.0	0.0	1.3	2.8	0.7	1.6
Discussion interwoven with longer writing task	0.0	0.0	0.0	0.0	0.0	0.0
Individual seatwork	12.1	28.6	15.5	33.3	13.9	31.3
Collaborative seatwork	6.1	14.3	5.6	12.0	5.8	13.0
Small group work	9.1	21.4	9.0	19.4	9.0	20.3
N	198	84	233	80	431	192

Tests and quizzes were undercounted in our study because we sought to avoid observing classes when they were scheduled.

Relations between Classroom Discourse and Writing. As noted above, classroom discourse and writing typically seem to proceed independently of each other in most high school instruction. Table 3 presents correlations between five indicators of writing activities (frequency, choice, completion, editing, and revision) and seven aspects of classroom discourse (lecture, question-answer, discussion, authenticity, uptake, coherence, and off-task behavior). The correlations indicate that the two aspects of classroom life have little to do with each other. Of seventy correlations reported in Table 3, only six are statistically significant at the .05 level – more than expected by chance, but few enough to refute any clear relationship between classroom discourse and writing activities. The only possible pattern that appears in the correlations is that Social Studies classes devoting more time to discussion also require more writing, allow more student choice, and foster more substantive revision of student work. This pattern may be evidence of a more open, interactive, and inquiry oriented type of classroom, but the rarity of discussion should caution us not to over interpret the finding. The pattern does not appear in English, where there is no discernable pattern at all. The Social Studies data also hint at the possibility that rates of completing student work are higher in more coherent classes, *i.e.*, where reading, writing, and talk are more frequently integrated, and where teacher questions build on student responses. However, only the correlation with uptake is statistically significant. Overall, the picture is one of disconnection between writing and discourse.

Table 3. Correlations between writing activities and the discourse environment.

Discourse Variable	Frequency[a]	Choice[a]	Completion[b]	Editing[b]	Revision[b]
English (n=54 classes)					
Lecture time[c]	-.07	-.01	.16	-.13	-.11
Question-answer time[c]	-.27*	-.22	.17	-.09	-.06
Discussion time[c]	.14	.17	.09	-.06	-.14
Authentic questions[c]	-.06	.11	-.33*	.02	.02
Uptake[c]	.16	.01	-.05	.14	.03
Coherence[a]	-.03	-.04	-.13	-.01	-.04
Off-task[c]	-.06	.26	-.27	.07	-.04
Social Studies (n=48 classes)					
Lecture time[c]	-.03	.03	.00	-.11	-.19
Question-answer time[c]	-.18	-.09	-.03	-.04	.02
Discussion time[c]	.41*	.67*	.08	.26	.47*
Authentic questions[c]	.00	-.02	-.09	-.18	-.07
Uptake[c]	.19	.15	.36*	-.13	-.03
Coherence[a]	.30	-.25	.24	.03	.16
Off-task[c]	-.07	-.35*	-.21	-.02	-.15

[a] *Teacher reported.*
[b] *Aggregated from student reports.*
[c] *Observed.*
*p < .05.

Effects of Classroom Discourse on Writing. The core of our analysis examines the relationship between features of classroom discourse and writing achievement. Does coherent, engaging classroom discourse enhance students' writing? Table 4 presents the results of regression analyses in which we examine the extent to which variation in student background, the amount and character of assigned writing and reading tasks, and features of classroom discourse influence student performance on the spring writing sample for English and Social Studies (our dependent variables). The regressions were carried out at the student level, with class-level variables assigned to the appropriate students.

Table 4. Effects of classroom discourse on writing.

	English		Social Studies	
Background				
Gender (Female =1)	.232**	.057	.120*	.054
Race (Black=1)	-.091	.110	-.098	.091
Ethnicity (Hispanic=1)	.002	.102	-.155	.100
SES	.085*	.040	.021	.037
Fall writing	.046	.024	.105**	.021
Fall subject test[a]	.020**	.006	.023**	.003
Honors class	-.094	.168	.154	.160
Remedial class	.110	.179	-.241	.232
Other class[b]	.123	.193	.746**	.222
Writing Activities				
Frequency	.094**	.021	-.091**	.022
Choice	-.079**	.016	.064	.047
Completion	.006**	.001	.004**	.001
Editing	-.013**	.004	.002	.007
Revising	.021*	.009	.002	.013
Classroom Discourse				
Lecture	.010	.005	.026**	.007
Question-answer	.017**	.005	.021**	.004
Discussion	-.052	.064	.022	.050
Authentic Questions				
Honors classes	.009	.005	.004	.004
Regular classes	-.003	.002	-.001	.002
Remedial classes	-.017**	.005	-.011	.008
Other classes	-.021**	.004	-.006	.007
Uptake	.011**	.003	.006*	.003
Coherence	.022**	.005	.039**	.008
Off task	-.023*	.009	-.029**	.010
Adjusted R^2	.298		.416	

Dependent variable is subject-specific writing. N=979 students in English and 894 students in Social Studies.
[a] *English: Reading power test. Social Studies: Social studies general knowledge test.*
[b] *'Other Class' includes school-within-school and heterogeneous classes.*
* $p < .05$ ** $p < .01$.

Because our model takes into account conditions at the beginning of the school year, such as social background and prior writing skills, and examines the relations between instruction that occurs during the year and writing at the end of the year, we view our analysis as describing a causal process. Of course, one can never completely rule out the possibility that unmeasured conditions, rather than the instruction we assessed, contributed to the results. Consequently, conclusions about causality must be treated with caution.

Instructional Effects. The second columns listed for each subject include the background variables and add indicators of classroom instruction, including writing activities and classroom discourse. How do discourse and writing activities affect students' writing skill? Although classroom discourse and writing activities proceed independently, classroom discourse clearly influences students' writing performance. Table 4 shows that in both subjects, writing performance was higher in classes in which more time was spent in oral activities; in which fewer students were off task; and in which teacher questions involved more uptake. Coherence – the extent to which writing related to reading, reading to talk, and talk to writing – significantly affected writing performance in both Social Studies and English. Discussion time had no significant effects, probably because it was so rare. Following our earlier analyses of literature achievement, our model allows the effects of authentic questions to differ across honors, regular, remedial, and other classes. In English, we find, as in our previous work, a positive coefficient for honors classes (the coefficient falls just short of significance at the .05 level) and significant negative effects in remedial and other classes (Gamoran & Nystrand, 1992). This pattern seemed to reflect different uses of authentic questions: in honors classes, authentic questions typically focused on the literature students were reading, which was the subject of our spring writing assessment. In remedial classes, teachers rarely asked authentic questions about literature: They mainly asked test questions about literature focused on plot summaries, and the authentic questions they did ask seemed mainly used to engage students' attention, not to focus thinking about literature. Not surprisingly, then, authentic questions in remedial classes actually detracted from writing about literature (see further Gamoran & Nystrand, 1992). In Social Studies classes the coefficients for authentic questions also differ in sign across class types, but the coefficients are close to zero and nonsignificant.

Results for 'other' classes are due to the idiosyncratic nature of our 'other' category and should not be interpreted as a finding about heterogeneous versus homogeneous grouping. In English, the 'other' category included a school-within-a-school in an urban environment, plus a small rural school. In Social Studies, the 'other' category included the same school-within-a-school, and also a Catholic school. The contrast between the Catholic school and the rural school very likely accounts for the differing results for the 'other' category across subjects. How large are the observed differences? They range from modest to substantial. Evaluated in a causal framework, an increase of 10% in the percent of questions with uptake would result in a rise in writing performance of just over a tenth of a standard deviation in English (10 x .011 = .11) and about half that impact in Social Studies. A teacher who increased coherence from 13 to 20 times per week (an increase of about one standard deviation) would expect to see better writing by about .14 standard deviations in English (7 x .022 = .144) and twice that much in Social Studies. In a chaotic classroom – for example one in which off-task behavior rose by 10% – one would expect to see a drop in writing performance by approximately a quarter of a standard deviation in both subjects. In light of the limited time span covered by the analysis (one school year), differences of 10% of a standard deviation or more should be regarded as meaningful.

Effects of discourse are generally similar across subjects, but effects of writing activities differ: Statistical tests indicate that none of the coefficients for discourse variables differ significantly across subjects, but the coefficients for frequency of writing and choice of writing are significantly different in English and Social Studies. Perhaps the most striking contrast across the subject areas is that the frequency of writing exerts a positive impact on writing in English, but a negative effect in Social Studies. At the same time, student choice of writing topics exhibits a significant negative coefficient in English, but not in Social Studies. These contrasts warrant further exploration, which we carry out below with a content analysis of writing assignments. In both subjects, students who reported that they complete more of their writing tended to score higher on the spring writing task. In English, substantive revision tends to enhance writing development while editing for grammar, spelling, punctuation, and usage retards it; these effects do not appear in Social Studies, where both editing and revision were perhaps too infrequent to matter for students' writing development.

4.2 Content Analysis of Social Studies and English Writing Assignments

One of the our more puzzling findings was that some variables had positive effects in English and negative effects in Social Studies while others had negative effects in English and no impact in Social Studies. In order to understand some of these inconsistencies, we contrasted the respective instructional landscapes of the two subjects by closely examining the content of the course materials and long-term writing assignments in the classrooms we observed. We discovered that writing serves quite different purposes in English and Social Studies, even though in some superficial ways, *e.g.*, frequency, it was similar in both subjects.

4.2.1 Writing in Social Studies: A Way of Teaching Reading

A content analysis of the course materials of the classrooms studied revealed that the nature of the writing tasks in Social Studies and English fundamentally differed. In Social Studies, writing was used mainly to teach reading for information. The overwhelming majority of Social Studies writing assignments (short answer questions and short essays) required recapitulating and reporting to the teacher facts learned in class or found in a textbook. When Social Studies teachers were asked about the extent to which they emphasized facts relative to the implications of facts, most teachers said they tried to split their time evenly between the two tasks. However, this pattern was not evident in the vast majority of writing assignments that students had to complete.

We did encounter a handful of Social Studies teachers whose writing assignments were based on authentic questions requiring students to use analytical skills and argue for or against a position, and justify their position with evidence, *e.g.*, 'Consider the consequences of Congress having the final authority to impeach the president, and argue whether or not Congress should have that power'; 'Consider whether third parties are a constructive mechanism for engendering political change, and support your position with evidence'; and 'If you were a current-day muckraker, what would you write about?' These questions all went beyond simple recall, and challenged students to take and defend positions in writing.

Nonetheless, these teachers were the exception, and very few Social Studies teachers encouraged students to use critical thinking skills to build persuasive arguments in essay form. Rather, their questions typically required no critical thinking skills whatsoever. Some teachers required students to write short answers in response to a reading passage which they provided. Again, these assignments emphasized recall rather than critical thinking.

As the descriptive statistics in Table 3 indicate, revision was relatively rare in Social Studies classes. The content analysis revealed that when students were asked to rework their writing, the work mainly involved editing for spelling, punctuation, and grammar; it rarely involved revising the substantive content of their essays. Not surprisingly, these same teachers devoted little attention to students' writing processes, though on rare occasions some instructors did stipulate certain text elements for adequate response – 'Your answer must be at least three paragraphs,' 'Your answer must include an introduction and a conclusion,' *etc.* It not surprising that students who did more of this type of writing – reporting their reading – actually did worse than students who wrote less: The more time students spent doing this type of writing, the less time was left over to do activities that actually improved writing achievement.

Writing assignments in Social Studies that gave students some choice were among the most demanding, and had positive effects on writing. When students were given a choice about what to write about in Social Studies, their choices were relatively limited, and they were forced to write on substantive topics. The topics tended to be serious issues that forced students to go beyond personal experience and required use of evidence to support claims. These writing assignments almost always posed authentic rather than test questions. Here is an example:

Social Studies Essay Exam

The following topics are statements regarding some aspect of the Middle East. For your essay you must agree or disagree with the topic statement. An essay in good form will state your position on the topic, support this position in the body of the essay and conclude with a summary paragraph. All work should be presented neatly, be written in ink or typed, be spelled correctly and written in complete sentences. You will be graded on how well you support your opinion, not on the opinion you hold. Good support would show that you have read the class readings or other supplementary material and must be expressed in you own words. Each essay should be 2-3 pages long.

Choose one of the following:
- The relationship between the Bedouin and the villagers established a successful Middle East economy.
- The Palestinian question could be resolved with a plan of coexistence within the state of Israel.
- Presence of the superpowers has stabilized the situation in the Middle East.
- What American policy in the Mid East should be (consider the need for oil Soviet involvement, need for development of nationalization in the Mid-East)?
- What it will take for Israel to become a safe home for the Jewish people?

Writing assignments like this clearly challenge students to think, and they pose substantive writing tasks. Our end-of-the-year measure of writing in Social Studies offered similar choices. Students wrote two separate essays. In the first, they wrote about an important person (their choice). They then explained as specifically as they could (a) who this person was, (b) what they knew about this person's life, and (c) why the things this person did and/or said were important. In the second essay, students wrote about an important election, discovery, invention, war, or labor strike (their choice). They were asked to explain as specifically as they could (a) what the event was, (b) whom it affected, and (c) how it affected them. This is the most plausible explanation for why 'choice' had a positive effect on writing in Social Studies classes.

4.2.2   *Writing in English: More Attention to Writing as Writing*

As in Social Studies, most writing assignments in English entailed cursory attention to the surface features of writing, with no real insight into the writing process. For example, students were often asked to write an essay that included certain elements such as an introductory paragraph with a thesis statement, three paragraphs which included supporting evidence for the thesis, and finally a concluding paragraph. Nonetheless, for the most part, English teachers paid attention to writing as writing, not just as a source of information as in Social Studies classes. English teachers typically provided a template that students were required to follow when writing. In the interviews with teachers, teachers commonly referred to this type of writing as 'decent' or indicative of a 'well-constructed essay.' As for the substance of these essays, they typically involved analysis some of the basic elements of a novel or short story. This was a reflection of the general goals that teachers reported holding for their English classes: to teach students to 'understand' and 'appreciate' literature.

A few teachers went deeper than merely providing a template for students to follow when writing. These teachers actually gave students insights into the structure of exposition, including attention to the form and organization of exposition. As for the substance of the writing, these teachers also expected students to analyze the texts they were reading more closely. Students were often asked to pay attention to how texts worked, as well as the style and organization of the writing when analyzing texts. Overall, the attention to the writing process in English classrooms addresses the issue of why students who did more writing were better writers.

Most English teachers required students to revise their writing, but as in Social Studies, the majority of these revisions entailed spelling, punctuation, and grammar. While teachers reported in interviews that they were not overly concerned with these aspects of writing, they were the most common types of revisions. There were only a few teachers who required more substantive revisions that focused on the organizational and aesthetic qualities of the essay. Finally, one teacher required students to read each others' work and make comments on their classmates' papers. Students in this class were urged to make substantive comments regarding the form and organizational aspects of writing. Since this type of revision was much more common in

English classes than in Social Studies, it is not surprising that it has positive effect in English but no effect in Social Studies.

A number of classes used writing assignments in ways that were similar to the typical Social Studies writing assignment: the main focus was on recalling information (about literature rather than historical events), and little attention was paid to the stylistic or rhetorical (*e.g.*, how to organize an essay) aspects of writing. Overall, creative writing (*i.e.*, fiction writing or wiring about personal experiences) was rare. Nonetheless, in English, there was substantial variety in the nature of the writing assignments in the observed classrooms, and when students could exercise choice in topics in English, their choices were often more open than in Social Studies. One type of task offering students choice of topic posed an authentic question and was substantive in nature, for example, 'How is *Great Expectations* a series of lessons learned the hard way?' Our end-of-the-year measure of writing in English was similar to this: Students wrote a brief essay requiring them to select a character they admired from one of the novels, short stories, or dramas they had read, and to both describe this character and explain their admiration for him/her (see above). In other assignments, students were asked to pick a social problem (*e.g.*, an ecological problem), do research on it, and write a short story about it. Some choice assignments posed miscellaneous creative prompts, such as 'Create a story of explanation for a plant, an invention' or 'Create a diary of 'A week in a life of ...,'' *etc*. The third type of choice assignment centered on some type of personal introspection. For example, students wrote an essay on three of their own personal characteristics. Other topics included 'How I changed and what I learned' and an experience from the previous day. In short, there was more variety in the 'choice' assignments in English, and the assignments tended to be less rigorous and substantive than the more issues based topics in Social Studies. This may explain why, on our assessments of writing, choice of topics worked against students in English but helped students in Social Studies.

5   CONCLUSION

To sum up, our study found a clear, though hardly simple relationship between classroom discourse and writing. Overall, even though writing activities and discourse practices are not closely linked, certain aspects of classroom discourse tend to enhance writing. For example, class talk, particularly when characterized by uptake, promoted students' writing development. Coherence among writing, reading, and talk also improved writing. Another key here was the student's own contribution: Controlling for writing skills and other background conditions at the beginning of the year, our analyses found that students who complete their written work, as well as classes where fewer students are off task, exhibit better writing at the end of the year.

Nonetheless, we found some surprising and initially puzzling differences in the effects of classroom discourse on writing in the two subjects. Though students wrote as often in English as in Social Studies, as reported above, frequency of writing enhanced writing in English, but had the opposite effect in Social Studies. Similarly, though students chose writing topics twice as frequently in English as in Social Studies, such choice was a liability in English but an asset in Social Studies. We came to understand these differences only when we looked closely at writing practices in the two subjects. Then we discovered fundamental differences in that the purposes of and emphases on writing. In its emphasis on rhetoric and form, English classes displayed more attention to writing as writing. In Social Studies, by contrast, writing was used almost exclusively to teach students methods of close reading, with little more than cursory emphasis on writing, limited almost entirely to copy-editing. Though choice of topics was more open in English, editing and revising were more than twice as common in English than in Social Studies. Such differences clearly show that, even though students write about as frequently in both English and Social Studies, the curricular landscapes of the two subjects are very different insofar as writing is involved. This study raises cautions for writing across the curriculum reforms. Though such efforts have usefully heightened the collective consciousness of teachers in all corners of the school about the importance of writing in as many subjects as possible, proponents often assume writing is categorically valuable. Yet, as the findings of this study show, clearly, writing is not writing is not writing. As far as writing development goes, the two curriculum areas we examined defined quite different niches of literacy development.

Niches, not just contexts. Indeed, context is far too lame a term to explain our results. Insofar as writing plays out differently depending on the interaction of teacher and students in different classroom settings, it is important to understand that these contexts are variable and dynamic – constantly changing and changed by the interactions of the conversants. In the classrooms we studied, we were dealing not simply with the effects of more or less classroom discourse on writing, more or less authentic questions, *etc.*, but more accurately different ecologies of learning constituted by classroom interactions and activities especially as these enacted classroom epistemologies. Further studies will need to clarify these important and complicated relationships. Such work should help teachers create a rich language environment and conduct classroom discourse that is conducive to learning.

ACKNOWLEDGEMENTS

This chapter was prepared at the National Research Center on English Learning and Achievement (CELA), Wisconsin Center for Education Research (WCER), School of Education, University of Wisconsin-Madison. The Center is supported by the U. S. Department of Education's Office of Educational Research and Improvement (Award # R305A60005). However, the views expressed herein are those of the authors and do not necessarily represent the views of the supporting agencies.

WRITING TO LEARN, WRITING TO TRANSFER

PIETRO BOSCOLO* & LUCIA MASON**

*University of Padova, Italy, **University of Lecce, Italy

Abstract. This chapter is focused on writing to develop thinking and reasoning about complex phenomena in the elementary school. It introduces a study aimed at investigating whether writing as a learning tool could be used by students first for understanding in history and then for understanding in science by transferring a disposition toward writing as a meaningful activity in knowledge construction. Making writing a meaningful activity for students implies leading them to experience the different functions it can have in the learning process: not only to record information, but also to expose, reflect, discuss, argue, and communicate. Thirty-two fifth graders divided in two groups, experimental (writing) and control (non-writing), were involved in the implementation of a history curriculum unit on the discovery of America and of a science curriculum unit on the human circulatory system. The findings provide evidence that writing can be effectively introduced across the curriculum to support higher-order thinking processes in order to produce understanding. The experimental group students were able to transfer the attitude, which characterized their writing activity in history to the domain of science, reaching a deeper conceptual understanding in both disciplines, as well as more advanced metaconceptual awareness of their learning. It may be concluded that if knowledge construction and reconstruction in the classroom is sustained by activities requiring the deep engagement of students as intentional learners who solve knowledge problems, then such an engagement can be activated by writing as a tool for thinking and reasoning to transform knowledge.

1 INTRODUCTION

This chapter deals with writing as a possible means to sustain students' learning and understanding in different curriculum content areas. Our study was aimed at investigating how fifth graders could use writing to develop thinking and reasoning about complex phenomena in history and science.

The general theoretical framework is based on a constructivist epistemology, which gives great emphasis to students' active construction of knowledge. Knowledge is actively constructed as the knower interprets new information and data through his/her prior conceptions and beliefs. Thus, meaningful learning is a continuous process of knowledge construction and re-construction. In this perspective, writing could have a complex role as a tool for learning. In recent years, several studies (*e.g.* Connolly, 1989; Fellows, 1994; Holliday, Yore, & Alvermann, 1994; Keys, 1994; Newell & Winograd, 1989; Prain & Hand, 1996; Rivard, 1994; Roth &

P. Boscolo, & L. Mason (2001). Writing to learn, writing to transfer. In: G. Rijlaarsdam (Series Ed.) & P. Tynjälä, L. Mason & K. Lonka (Volume Eds), *Studies in Writing, Volume 7, Writing as a Learning tool: Integrating Theory and Practice, 83* – 104.© 2001 Kluwer Academic Publishers. Printed in the Netherlands.

Rosaen, 1991; Zinsser, 1988) on writing to learn have shown that writing can be a useful aid to learning in various content areas – particularly science – in that it may help both comprehension and retention of information and concepts as well as reflections on ideas and conceptions. This study was aimed at investigating writing as a meaningful activity that pervades different curriculum domains. Making writing a meaningful activity for students implies leading them to experience the different functions it can have in the learning process: not only to record information, but also to expose, reflect, discuss, argue, and communicate. We assumed that through this experience students might acquire new ideas about writing and its functions, which they could then apply to different curriculum domains.

In the following sections, central issues concerning writing to learn, as well as learning in the domain of history are introduced. The rest of the chapter describes an experimental study. Two groups of elementary school students, writing and non-writing, are compared to see whether, and to what extent, writing as a learning tool can improve students' understanding in history and how its potential power can be transferred to learning better in science also.

2   WRITING AS A LEARNING TOOL ACROSS THE DISCIPLINES

Since the seventies, writing has been considered as a learning tool. Research on the relationship between writing and learning has been developed in many countries. In particular in the US, the so-called 'Writing Across the Curriculum' (WAC) movement has led to the implementation of a comprehensive educational program at every school level (*e.g.* Young & Fulwiler, 1986). What is the power of writing in the content areas?

Writing does not automatically mean improvement in learning. The primary purpose of writing to learn is to involve students in a cognitive activity that activates and fosters higher order thinking skills for learning. This in turn leads to developing, and not, or not only, displaying knowledge (Rosaen, 1989). As noted by Schumacher and Gradwohl Nash (1991) in their review, some outstanding scholars in composition have pointed out that writing by its very nature has characteristics that make it a powerful tool in the learning process. We only mention here the classic scholars who have produced seminal works. Emig (1977) underlined that writing facilitates the integration of ideas, requires establishing relationships, provides tangible feedback and activates personal involvement in the material. Applebee (1984) clarified the nature of the relationship between writing and reasoning. Langer and Applebee (1987), by investigating how writing shapes thinking, highlighted the various aspects of the role of writing in learning and argued that different types of writing activities, entailing different thinking processes, have different effects on learning.

Since these seminal works, a considerable theoretical and empirical research has been carried out to study the role of writing in relationship with learning and understanding in content areas. On a theoretical level, for example, Rosaen (1989) has synthesised three main aspects that make writing a means of learning. First, writing makes it possible to express one's thoughts in a way, which can always be re-examined, for further clarification or exploration. Second, writing entails a cognitive activity that can stimulate learning. Writing down thoughts is a way for writers to represent a knowledge object to themselves, thus making sense of new knowledge in the light of prior knowledge and beliefs. In other words, writing requires making systematic connections and relationships that are particularly suitable for producing a meaningful understanding of subject matter. Third, writing has the potential to help students monitor their own learning process, fostering their metacognitive awareness of the process of developing understanding in the domain because they are stimulated to pay attention to their cognitive activity while they write.

Recently, Tynjälä (1998) has underlined that empirical research about the effect of writing on learning has produced contrasting results and proposes some reasons to account for them. These reasons mainly refer to the research methodology used in assessing learning outcomes, the nature of the writing tasks used, and the ways in which students perceive and approach the tasks. Writing seems to be suitable for tasks which require students' deep understanding through a change of prior conceptions and development of their thinking skills rather than a mere accumulation of new factual information. It has also been found that different writing tasks may produce different kinds of learning as they imply different thinking processes and can be perceived and approached superficially or at a deeper level by students.

To sum up, it can be said that writing can improve students' learning by promoting active knowledge construction that requires them to be involved in transforming rather than a process of reproducing. Through writing they have the opportunity to manipulate, integrate, and re-structure knowledge by using, and reflecting on, their existing conceptions and beliefs in a continuous process of developing meaningful understanding.

3 WRITING IN HISTORY

In educational research various aspects related to history learning have been investigated only quite recently (Carretero, Jacott, Lopez-Manjon, & Limon, 1994). Developmental psychologists have studied children's understanding of concepts in the domains of politics and economics (*e.g.* Berti, 1994; Berti & Bombi, 1988; Furnham, 1994), adolescents thinking about political and historical issues (*e.g.* Torney-Puta, 1994), and the epistemological underpinning of historical reasoning in adults. What has been investigated in particular, although not very extensively, are students' conceptions of history (Halldén, 1993) and the types of explanations produced in giving accounts of historical phenomena (Dickinson & Lee, 1986; Halldén, 1994, 1998), the different types of instructional explanations given in history classes (Leinhardt, 1994), what students learn from historical texts (Britt, Rouet, Georgi, & Perfetti, 1994; Rouet, Favart, Gaonac'h, & Lacroix, 1996; Wineburg, 1991b), also dealing with uncertainty (Perfetti, Britt, Rouet, Georgi, & Mason, 1994), and the process of evaluating documentary and pictorial evidence (Wineburg, 1991a). Moreover, with respect to elementary school children's learning in the classroom, it has been documented how they are able to partake in small group discussions to collaboratively reason on and understand historical topics when considering a different culture (Fasulo, Girardet, & Pontecorvo, 1999), or key issues of historical methodology (Fasulo, Girardet, & Pontecorvo, 1998).

Regarding conceptual understanding in history, Voss and Wiley (1997) have clearly pointed out three ways students may undergo cognitive restructuring in this domain. These have been taken into account in the study introduced below: (1) restructuring conceptions and beliefs about events; (2) restructuring the concept of historical explanation, for example shifting from a personified explanation to one that emphasises institutions; (3) restructuring epistemological beliefs about the role of the historian and the nature of history itself. In this respect, many students at various educational levels do not realise the interpretative role played by historians, therefore restructuring may require realising that history is constructive, subjective, and argumentative in nature.

Of particular interest here is the use of writing in history teaching and learning. To our knowledge, writing as a tool for understanding historical topics has not received much attention and needs to be explored. In the very scanty literature available, there is a study by Greene (1994) investigating college students' writing. He examined how two different writing tasks, a report and a problem-based essay, affect the production of students' texts by using prior knowledge and information from six different source texts about the subject of their course, 'European Lifestyle and Culture'. He found that all students writing reports understood that the task required them to rely extensively or exclusively on the sources, whereas most of those who wrote problem-based essays understood that they should integrate prior knowledge with source information. In contrast, historians, who were asked to accomplish the same tasks, perceived writing reports and problem-solving on the basis of their understanding of the field readers' expectations. Rouet *et al.* (1996) examined the process of writing from multiple documents about a historical controversy in the history of the Panama Canal. The documents were two historian's essays presenting two opposing interpretations, two different accounts by individuals who took part in the events directly, two official documents that played a role in the controversy, one textbook-like excerpt that was mostly factual and did not refer to the controversy. Writing was produced by novice and expert history students who were asked to write a short essay to express their opinion on the historical controversy. An analysis of the claims, arguments and evidence expressed in their texts revealed that novices were more likely to take a position on the controversy and argue for it, driven by their personal beliefs and opinions, rather than by an overall view of the argument structure of the controversy. The experts were more likely to evaluate and discuss problems and evidence as they could be understood from the documents read. The evidence the experts referred to was more often of a factual nature, whereas novices appealed more to arguments introduced in second-hand accounts.

Much closer to our research interest is Rosaen's (1989) work. After reviewing writing in the content areas, she described the use of writing to learn in an elementary classroom during implementation of an America history unit by examining both teachers' and students' interpretations of the learning activities. In particular she compared writing and drawing. While in their writing children focused on questions which they interpreted as the content about which they should write, in the drawing activity, which was optional and not judged for quality, they perceived room to explore and manipulate ideas. Only the drawing activity acted as a tool for generating ideas and helped students construct new knowledge. The writing activity did not help them go beyond mere knowledge telling, but writing and drawing combined gave students the opportunity to move toward knowledge transformation.

In the study introduced below writing in history has been explored with young students, fifth graders, as a way of constructing meaning and understanding in history at different moments during implementation of a history curriculum unit. The use of content area writing was intended to help children construct new knowledge during the writing process. Writing provides occasions for them to think about the topic, see new relationships and explanations about the events examined, and to monitor their developing understanding.

4   WRITING AND TRANSFER

While several studies have been conducted on writing as a tool for learning, few, if any, have investigated if, and to what degree, the use of writing in a specific content domain can be generalised to another domain or discipline, or, in other words, to what degree writing to learn can be transferred from one domain to another.

There are two opposing views of writing instruction regarding transfer. The first, and older view maintains that writing is a set of general skills that can be mastered through formal instruction and applied to different tasks and situations, in school and out. Although unsupported by empirical research, this view is still deeply rooted in many teachers and learners. In the United States the 'General Writing Skill Instruction' (GWSI) has been strongly criticised by the social constructivist approach to literacy (*e.g.* Nystrand, Greene, & Wielmert, 1993; Petraglia, 1995; Russell, 1997). The second perspective views writing as a situated, highly contextualised activity. According to this perspective, writing is not a general ability, but a literacy practice that may assume different roles and functions in specific contexts and activity systems. Thus, it is not to be considered as related to a specific curriculum area only – language skills – because it should pervade all curriculum domains (Writing Across the Curriculum). As an activity theorist has recently argued (Russell, 1995), WAC has a clear objective: the study and improvement of the role of writing in teaching and learning in specific disciplines and professions.

These two perspectives represent two opposing conceptions of teaching writing for transfer. The first optimistically assumes that by learning to write in a limited number of academic genres, students should become flexible writers, that is, able to write quite different text types when needed. The second approach, which stresses the multiplicity of genres related to specific contexts/activities, rejects, or even ignores, this general view of transfer.

In this study we adopted a constructivist perspective of writing, as mentioned in the introduction, that is, the ways children use writing are mediated by their views on this activity. Therefore, we assumed that having children use writing in different ways (unusual but functional to specific activities) may contribute to fostering not only writing skills, but also a representation of writing as a multifunctional activity.

Writing usually has a rigid place in the elementary school curriculum, closely related to language skills. Children learn to write in a few and often stereotyped genres, mainly regarding the communicative functions of writing: to narrate personal or invented events, recount the results of classroom activities and demonstrate what they have studied. What is unusual in most elementary schools, at least in Italy, is the use of writing as a conceptualisation tool, that is, as an effective support for school activities such as history and science, which are traditionally based on oral communication and/or discussion. Effective support means that writing can have a variety of functions closely related to specific classroom activities: recording results, ideas and information, reasoning, expressing, communicating and discussing ideas and doubts, *etc.*.

Bereiter (1995: 22) introduced a nice distinction between transfer of principles and transfer of dispositions. The first depends on a learner's depth of understanding and occurs when he/she recognises new cases of a general principle. The second type of transfer does not regard knowledge, but a learner's attitude towards knowledge. It occurs when a student, through a learning experience, develops the disposition to engage in the activity or assume the attitude that characterises that experience: for instance, to argue, discuss, think scientifically or question beliefs. The main difference between these two types is that the transfer of a concept or principle is achieved when the concept is incorporated into the learner's cognitive system, whereas the transfer of dispositions occurs when an attitude is created within him/her.

In the study introduced below transfer of writing was intended according to this second meaning, that is as the transfer of a disposition. We chose two domains of the elementary school curriculum quite different from both the epistemic and instructional points of view: history and science. Of course, history and science are disciplines with different rules and procedures of knowledge construction, and this difference emerges also in elementary school, where children learn some crucial aspects of the two domains through different activities. For instance, they are involved in observations and hands-on activities regarding scientific phenomena, whereas they learn the importance of various types of documents in history. In spite of these differences, writing could be used as a means of learning in both disciplines, *e.g.* to expose, reason, reflect, argue, communicate about ideas and beliefs, inform, explain. Thus, we assumed that if students developed the disposition to engage in a meaningful writing activity within the curriculum domain of history, they could transfer this disposition to another domain, science, if the same instructional conditions are fulfilled.

Writing as a tool to learn in science has been investigated much more than writing for historical understanding (see Mason, 1998, in press; Mason & Boscolo, 2000). Researchers have demonstrated that it can facilitate organisation, integration and synthesis of ideas, establishment of relationships, clarification of thoughts, monitoring and regulation of the learning processes.

5   AIMS OF THE STUDY

The purposes of the present study were to see:
1)   whether students could learn to use writing for the first time as a means to express, reflect and reason on ideas, descriptions and explanations, monitor and communicate in the process of understanding in history;
2)   whether writing in the service of learning facilitated the understanding of a new history topic through restructuring contents, types of explanation, beliefs about the nature of history and the historian's role, as well as students' awareness of the concepts they had learned;
3)   whether the use of writing to learn in history could be transferred to learning in another domain, that of science. In other words, to see whether students, when asked to write in science, could use writing to understand scientific concepts. This would show they could write for different purposes as they had done in the history domain by transferring their disposition toward writing as a meaningful activity for knowledge-building;
4)   whether writing in the service of learning also facilitated an understanding of the new scientific topic which required conceptual change as well as students' metaconceptual awareness of the changes occurring in their cognitive structures.

6   THE STUDY

6.1 Participants

Thirty-two fifth graders (18 boys and 14 girls) attending a public elementary school in the Padova area (Northern Italy) were involved in the study. They shared a homogeneous middle class social background. The experimental group was made up of 20 students for whom the writing activity in the service of learning took place in history and science classes. A group of 12 students comprised the control group who did not undertake the writing activity but did all other activities. The two groups were randomly assigned to the two conditions.

6.2 Subject Matter

A curriculum unit on geographical discoveries, in particular the discovery of America was implemented in the history class and lasted about two and half months (ten weekly sessions of one hour and fifteen minutes each). The unit aimed to promote students' cognitive restructuring in the three ways pointed out by Voss and Wiley (1997), that is: (a) change of conceptions about events; (b) change of the concept of historical explanation; (c) changes of conceptions about the historian's role and the nature of history itself (at fifth grade level).

In the science class a curriculum unit on the human circulatory system was implemented and lasted about one month (two weekly and two twice-weekly sessions for a total of six sessions). The science unit was implemented after the history one had been completed. It was aimed at promoting restructuring of alternative conceptions about the role of the heart, blood and the circulatory system.

6.3 Classroom Context

The teachers were experienced and motivated and taught both history and science to the same group of students. They are used to collaboratively plan their classroom activities and analysing the results at weekly meetings. These activities include establishing purposes, contents, methods, tools, and materials for each discipline. The teachers were aware of the importance of the classroom-learning environment in motivating and supporting students' construction of their own knowledge. They were very concerned with promoting a true dialogue in the classroom between the students themselves and between teachers and students. They have been used to engaging students in group discussions in order to facilitate and sustain meaningful learning. The same kind of interpersonal relations between students, and between teachers and students characterised classroom life. The second author was in both the experimental and control group classroom as participating observer during several sessions on the history and science curriculum units. She could check that these were implemented in the same way, the only exception being the writing activity.

In the history class the main activity for both groups was based on the use of written historical documents to help students learn not only the new contents, but also the historian's job as a scientist, that is to also learn how historical accounts are produced. In some cases, the documents provided different interpretations of the same historical event to give students the opportunity to reflect on the non-existence of 'pure' facts but rather on biased interpretations of the facts. In most cases, the documents were adapted from original sources by the researchers in collaboration with the teachers to make them understandable to fifth graders. Both the experimental and the control group students were involved in reading and examining the same historical documents and in lively discussions about the same knowledge problems in the history class.

In the science class too, both groups of children were involved in the same observations, in reading the same materials, and discussing the same knowledge problems. In both conditions, writing and non-writing, class discussions took place in almost every session devoted to implementing first the historical and then the scientific curriculum unit. In addition, the same worksheets were given to the students. Thus, we can say that the teachers' classroom behaviour regarding the instructional intervention was the same except for the use of writing. They applied a controlled method and the differences observed between the two groups were not due to a particularly positive teaching performance by the teacher of the experimental group. Obviously, it is not possible to maintain that two teachers were the same as one, rather that their classroom behaviour was very similar and was the same when considering the implementation of the instructional intervention, with the exception of the use of writing.

Both groups carried out the usual writing tasks in history and science classes, that is, summaries and reports on a schema given by the teacher at certain points in the curriculum units. Only in the experimental condition was writing for learning systematically carried out individually, while in the same time the control group was engaged in drawing or writing syntheses about the topics as dictated by the teacher. In very few sessions the writing tasks were the same for both groups (see Appendix). It is worth noting that although the experimental group teacher had never used writing to promote learning in any discipline, she had been trained to do it. She introduced the different functions of writing in the history class by both giving instructions on how to use writing and 'modelling', *i.e.* showing the children its various aims. From the beginning of the history activity she made the children aware that note-taking, commenting on, reasoning and reflecting upon ideas, expressing doubts, synthesising what has been learned, could all be writing activities. The children were invited not to worry about the errors they made in writing. If they felt unable to express a thought or comment, the teacher would help them clarify their ideas. At the beginning of each session the teacher and children used what they had written as a link with the previous session. The students' written production was considered as a personal way of reasoning and reflecting on a knowledge problem, and a useful way of recording and communicating their own understanding.

At the beginning of the science curriculum unit the students were told by the teacher that writing could also be used in science to think, reason, reflect, and communicate about their ideas, beliefs, explanations, *etc.* as they had already done in history.

6.4 Tasks and Scoring

In both groups the conceptual understanding of the history target topic, the discovery of America, was assessed by five tasks whose scores represented the dependent variables.

1) Four open-ended pre- (to identify students' *prior knowledge*) and post-instruction written questions on geographical discoveries at the end of the 15th century. The answers to each question were scored on the basis on their correctness by giving 1 point to each item of correct information (maximum 10 points).

2) A post-instruction written text on *topic knowledge* about what they knew of the discovery of America. It was scored according to the expression of the following contents: causal statements; Columbus's navigation equipment and crew, his beliefs and scientific knowledge, native Americans' beliefs and customs, Columbus and slaves, the activities of the 'conquistadores', extermination of native Americans, the Pope's position, Venice's economic decline, the development of colonies. To correct information on each content element 1 point was assigned (maximum 12 points).

3) A short post-instruction written text concerning *awareness* of what had been learned. It should be pointed out that in this study, both for history and science learning, only one aspect of the *metacognitive competence* was addressed, that is, awareness of own conceptions, beliefs, explanations, *etc.* that underlies and may constrain learning. A successful process of knowledge revision implies that students become aware of their ideas and presuppositions brought to the classroom in order to recognise their limitations and fallacies and to manage to change them, at least to some extent. Very often, learning a new topic involves not only a change in specific ideas but also the development or refining of metaconceptual awareness. The students were asked to write whether they had

changed their explanations of the historical facts examined and write their comments on what they had studied and understood. For each reflective aspect (mention of prior and current explanation, why the change occurred, comments on what had happened in the past and on what they learned) 1 point was given (maximum 5 points).

4) Five pre- and post-instruction open-ended written questions on *epistemological beliefs* about the historian' s work and knowledge construction in the domain. For clarity, it is worth mentioning these questions. They included 'What is history?', 'How do the people who write history books know of the past they write about?', 'What problems may historians have when they try to understand the past?', 'Is it possible to explain the same fact which happened in the past in different ways? Why?', 'If there are two different explanations of the same fact in the past, how is it possible to understand which is the most correct?'. For this task a qualitative analysis was performed by assigning the answers to different categories: low, middle or high level.

5) A pre- and post-instruction task taken from Kuhn, Weinstock and Flaton (1994: 384), *the Livia task*, which involved two historians' conflicting accounts of the fictitious 'Fifth Livian War'. It was given to see whether the students could perceive differences in the accounts. They were asked to 'Describe what the war was about and what happened'. Only if they perceived the differences in the accounts that made impossible to describe what had happened 1 point was assigned to this task.

In both the experimental and control group the conceptual understanding of the science target topic on the human circulatory system was assessed by the six following tasks which were scored by giving 1 point to each item of correct information.

1) A pre- and post-instruction *drawing of the blood' s journey* through the body (maximum 5 points).

2) Short pre- and post-instruction written texts on what the students knew *about the heart and blood* (maximum 13 points).

3) A short post-instruction *topic knowledge* written text on the human circulatory system (maximum 4 points).

4) A post-instruction open-ended written question about the crucial *relationship between the heart and lungs* (maximum 4 points).

5) A post-instruction open-ended *transfer* written question on what happens if a baby is born with a septal defect, that is a gap in the septal wall between the two sides of the heart (maximum 2 points).

6) Five post-instruction written questions were asked to ascertain students' *meta-conceptual awareness* (see above). For clarity it is worth mentioning these questions, which included: 'Do you think your ideas about blood circulation have changed?' If so, 'What were your initial ideas?', 'Why did you have those ideas?', 'What are your current ideas?', 'Has changing your previous ideas been easy or difficult and what made it easy or difficult for you?'. The 'yes' answers scored 0 points when a student was not able to express any metaconceptual awareness while 1 point was given for mentioning each of the following as-

pects: initial ideas, why they had changed, current ideas, double circulation as the main idea, how they managed to change previous ideas (maximum 5 points).

All scores were attributed separately by two independent judges. Overall agreement was very high (95%) and disagreements were resolved by discussion in the presence of the authors. Correlation analyses between the scores in the different tasks used to assess learning in history and science revealed that they only moderately correlated as any significant correlation was larger than .35. This indicated that the measures used were not repetitions of the same construct but rather they tapped different aspects of the students' learning in the two domains.

Moreover, it should be said that there were no differences between the two groups for any measure, in history or in science, at the beginning of the curriculum unit implementations in both curriculum domains.

The teachers were informed of the results presented and discussed in a meeting.

7   RESULTS

7.1 Writing in History

The only aspect that differentiated the experimental from the control group was the use of writing to assist learning. The written production showed that the students in the experimental group learned to use writing for different aims which required an active elaboration of knowledge. More specifically, writing was carried out by the students for three main functions:
1)   to give explanations and to elaborate knowledge to develop new understanding of the topic;
2)   to make comments on what they had read and discussed to construct their own interpretations of specific events;
3)   to express their own doubts about what had puzzled or still puzzles them and any change of beliefs and explanations.

The means by which these functions were carried out are presented below with examples taken from the students' written productions. These examples are not intended to be exemplary instances but rather they have been selected to illustrate more effectively the ways writing contributes to a deeper understanding in history.

1) a. *Writing to express one's initial explanations* to start a discussion. To lead the students to an understanding of the commercial reasons for the long voyages at the end of the 15th century, the teacher asked why spices and precious metals were so important at that time. A student wrote:[1]

> I think that spices were so important because they were very useful for healing people as a type of medicine. They could also be made into perfumes to be worn or as a type of sauce to put on food to make it more tasty. I also think that precious metals were very

---

[1] *The children's written production has been translated trying to keep the same 'style' as in the original Italian version.*

important because many things could be made from them, things which were necessary for the very rich people, the very rich merchants, for example gold coins. They were very difficult to find so their price was very high. It was very hard to cast metals. As times became more modern, they were more expensive but it was less hard to find them. (*Anna*)

1) b. *Writing to express explanations as a result of what has been newly understood.* Here is an example of a text produced after reading two documents about the economic situation at the time of the geographical discoveries.

I have understood European expansionism in this way. Spices and metals were very important to Europeans. Spices were fundamental because at that time it was very difficult to preserve meat as there were no refrigerators. Spices were rare so not easy to find. Europeans had to go overland to the East, to India, passing across territories occupied by the Turks who asked them to pay taxes. Venetian merchants had more spices so they used to sell them to other European countries and the trade made them rich. Metals were also very important and it was not easy to cast them to make coins. Princes and kings of that time were obviously rich and had many soldiers in their services. But they had to pay them with coins made from metals that they did not have. Europeans had to pay higher and higher costs to Venice to get spices and also metals so it became necessary for them to find spices and metals by themselves using a different route to the East, a route over the sea. The only routes they had were: (1) toward the South but they had to circumnavigate Africa and nobody had done it before so they did not know if it was really possible; (2) toward the West to reach the East with the idea that the Earth was a sphere and not flat. (*Mirko*)

1) c. *Writing to infer knowledge from pictorial documents.* While 'reading' a reproduction of Columbus's meeting with the natives of Guanahani Island in 1492, which can be found in the public library of New York, a student wrote:

Looking at this reproduction I know that the land was fertile because I can see many trees and plants. The natives gave presents to Columbus and the other people so they were kind and generous. They do not have weapons so they are peaceful, they do not like wars or are afraid. Their did not wear clothes, they wore only very simple and short things. Columbus went ashore in a very straightforward way. You can see this by looking at the expression of his face, his body position, and his attitude toward the natives who offered gifts. (*Michele*)

1) d. *Writing to make hypotheses.* After reading the papal bull in which Alexander VI promulgated that he would give land forever to those who arrived there, a question arose: why was the Pope so interested in 'the new lands'? In trying to formulate hypotheses, a student wrote to make her conjectures of a personalised nature explicit:

In my opinion there are two ways to answer the question we are dealing with. (1) The first is that the Pope was cruel and greedy as he wanted to have a lot of money so he promised people that they would get money as a reward if they conquered new lands. In this case he gave permission to live in the American lands, but the proceeds of what the new habitants made also passed to the Pope as a 'ransom'. (2) The second is that the Pope was a good person and liked to assign these lands to the people who arrived there to give people the opportunity of new conditions and a new style of life. (*Elena*)

2) a. *Writing to make comments on contrasting documents.* The students read two documents, one written by Juan Ginés de Sepúlveda, a Spanish humanist, and another by Bartolomé de las Casas, a Dominican preacher. These documents depicted American natives in totally conflicting ways. The students were then asked to com-

ment on how it was possible to give such opposing accounts of the same people. A very lively discussion on this question took place in both groups. Two students' written comments after the discussion in the experimental group follow. The idea that a document supported the actions of the 'conquistadores' appears briefly in the first while it is elaborated more in the second.

> One document is more balanced and objective, the other justifies that they wanted to kill the natives. Sepúlveda judged people according to two scales. On the highest there were the Spanish people, on the lowest the natives as their servants. (*Alessandro*)

> The document by Sepúlveda wants to explain why natives are inferior to Europeans. According to him, natives are slaves by nature. As they had never come in contact with the life and culture of Europe, they are considered stupid and wild. Although it is known that these people are able to do things that Europeans cannot, they are judged stupid and inferior all the same so Europeans could do anything they wanted to them. In my opinion, the second document written by Bartolomeo de las Casas is totally different as we read that natives were not so stupid and primitive. The documents are so different because the two authors had totally different points of view about what was happening between Europeans and natives and each of them wrote what he believed. (*Jacopo*)

2) b. *Writing to interpret what appears as an amazing event.* The students read a document which impressed them a lot about the first ship-load of slaves taken by Columbus on one of his next voyages. They discussed how he was able to take people away as slaves. Collaborative reasoning and argument on this knowledge problem led to a first contextualisation of the event. Let's look at what two students wrote. The first is a more personalised account; the second refers to the context in which the events happened.

> I believe that Columbus made natives slaves so that the king and queen would give him more gold coins, as there would be servants in the royal palace. (*Giulia*)

> In my opinion it happened because Columbus saw that they were peaceful, so he tricked them. The Spanish were much more powerful and if the natives had refused, they could have killed them. At that time the Spanish thought that the natives were inferior to them, they did not have any value, so they could possess them. At that time the law allowed people to take weaker people as slaves whereas nowadays the law is more just and careful, although in some parts of the world it is still possible to treat people as slaves. (*Federica*)

3) a. *Writing to communicate what has not been understood.* The learners were told that writing could also be used to communicate what puzzled them so that they could then be helped in finding an answer to their knowledge problems in a collaborative way. Some examples of questions of a different nature:

> It is not yet clear to me if Columbus was immediately aware of being in a new land or if only Vespucci recognised that. I have also not figured out why European colonisers took native Americans prisoners and even though they could see that the prisoners were not strong and could die, they still continued to make them slaves. (*Matteo*)

> I see that I have not understood the Pope's behaviour toward the colonisers because he was more powerful than the king and queen, and the decline of Italy as a consequence of geographical discoveries. (*Andrea*)

3) b. *Writing to express changes of beliefs or explanations.* At several points students wrote to reflect on the changes occurring in their cognitive structures. Here is an example of a text with metacognitive reflections:

> Before reading the historical documents I believed that the people who lived in America before Columbus's arrival were much wilder and primitive than they really were. I have changed my beliefs as I have read about their culture and now I know different things. Moreover, I thought that when Columbus arrived in America the natives attacked him and his people wanting to kill them. By reading historical documents I saw that my ideas were not correct anymore. Now I know that populations before Columbus welcomed him as if he was a God descended from heaven. They were peaceful and fearful people. (*Camilla*)

> I have understood that people, especially poor people, at that time were the crews on the ships and they travelled for money, not for their adventurous spirit, for curiosity, or to get to know different things. It took months and months to arrive anywhere, it was not easy at all to reach new places, they ran into many problems and difficulties. Before my idea was that to travel overseas was easy and exciting, like a holiday. (*Emanuele*)

To conclude, it should be noted that the students (although not all of them in all situations) could use writing not only for knowledge telling but also for knowledge transforming (Bereiter & Scardamalia, 1987) while they were engaged in meaning making.

It should also be pointed out that our underlining of the students' high level engagement in knowledge problems does not mean that they always produce high levels of description and explanation from a historical point of view. Nevertheless, they were involved in connecting, integrating, and synthesising information to understand and build knowledge. Personalization in historical descriptions and explanations, as pointed out by Halldén (1998), was also found in these students.

7.2   Writing and Historical Understanding

Open-ended questions. As an effect of the instructional intervention aimed at stimulating and supporting understanding, the students constructed new knowledge by enriching and changing their prior explanations. An ANOVA for repeated measures indicated that both experimental and control groups improved their conceptual understanding as measured by the open-ended questions, $F (1, 30) = 54.11, p <. 001$. The ANOVA also showed a significant group x time interaction. Indeed the experimental group reached a higher level at the end of the instructional intervention than the control group, $F (1, 30) = 14.10, p = .001$.

Interestingly, the type of explanation given as an answer to the question about why America was discovered changed more among the students who had the opportunity to use writing to learn. The explanations were categorised as *intentional* ('America was discovered because Columbus wanted to become famous and be remembered by everybody'), *scientific-technological* ('America was discovered because at the time there were new navigational instruments and types of ships to make long journeys overseas'), and *economic* ('America was discovered because it was necessary to find a new route to get to India for the spice trade and not to go overland and pass through the territories occupied by Turks'). A McNemar test was performed for each group to see whether the explanations changed from the beginning to the end of the instructional intervention. It revealed ($p < .001$) that the experimental group students in particular shifted much more from an intentional to an economic cause.

Topic knowledge text. A one-way ANOVA revealed a significant difference between the experimental and control group on the text about all the students knew on the discovery of America: the former outperformed the latter, $F (1, 30) = 4.63, p < .05$.

Metaconceptual awareness written text. A one-way ANOVA showed significant differences between the two groups, $F (1, 30) = 10.87, p < .01$, regarding their awareness of what they had learned and the changes that occurred in their explanations, and their comments. Two examples of short reflective texts produced by two experimental group students follow. The first shows the student's awareness of her newly developed explanation about the causes of the discovery of America. The second shows the students' awareness that knowing new things can lead to changing one's own views and that it is needed to contextualise a historical fact.

> I have changed my explanation of C. Columbus's journey. I thought that he left with the three galleons because he wanted to discover a new world which he knew was called America to became famous. Moreover, I thought that the native inhabitants of America fought against him as soon as he arrived there. Now my explanation is that he discovered a new continent by chance as he was looking for a new commercial route and he did not know that he was the first to go there. I also see that the natives were very peaceful and generous people. (*Milena*)

> History is very interesting for me as I like to know what happened in the past and knowing this makes you change your ideas and explanations. For example, I did not know that after the discovery of America such cruel things happened because the Spanish made war against the native inhabitants. I never suspected the existence of 'conquistadores' and their great cruelty. But at that time the law allowed people to be made slaves and for them to be transferred to another land by a very long and difficult journey in which they could die because of the cold weather and new illnesses. (*Michele*)

Open-ended questions on epistemological beliefs. The intervention in the history class was based mainly on reading and analysing written documents which could provide conflicting accounts of the same questions. It was not only aimed at helping students master key historical concepts but also to stimulate more advanced beliefs about the nature of history, the historian's job as a scientist, and knowledge construction in the domain. A McNemar test was performed for each group to see whether the answers given at the end of the history education experience were more sophisticated. The test showed ($p < .01$) significant differences for the experimental group concerning only two of the five questions, that is: 'Is it possible to explain the same fact which happened in the past in different ways? Why?', and 'If there are two different explanations of the same fact in the past, how is it possible to understand which is the most correct?'. At the end of the history activities, more students in the experimental than in the control group also showed more advanced epistemological beliefs in answering the two last questions than at the beginning. The justifications given by the 13 students who explained why more explanations can be given for the same historical fact appealed to the different theories that historians may have when they interpret the past. At the beginning, they mainly referred to the fact that there are many different ways to make an explanation. Moreover, the experimental group students progressed more than the control group in saying what has to be done to decide which of the two explanations of the same historical fact is more correct. At the end of the activities in history they maintained more frequently than the control group students that it is necessary to investigate more to collect evidence for or against the given explanations, while at the beginning they mainly said that it is necessary to ask an expert, or see which explanation is richer, longer or more meaningful ($p < .05$).

No differences were found between the groups in their answers to the first three questions before and after the intervention. All students but one maintained that history is about studying and knowing what happened in the past, in answer to the first question. The only student who gave a different answer at both the beginning and end maintained that 'history is a reconstruction of the past which is made through ruins and documents'. Most students in both groups, at the beginning and end, said that historians study what has already been written in books or use ruins or documents, which appear to be considered by students as self-evident in answer to the second question. Concerning the third question, most students in both groups maintained, at both the beginning and end, that the problems encountered by historians may include not finding remains, not being able to decode very old documents, and not finding enough evidence.

'*The Livia task*'. This task was about two historians' conflicting accounts of the fictitious 'Fifth Livian War' (Kuhn, Weinstock, & Flaton, 1994: 384) and aimed at seeing whether the students noticed differences between the accounts. A McNemar test revealed ($p < .01$) that only the experimental group improved their performance significantly.

7.3   Writing in Science

The science curriculum unit did not last as long as the history unit; therefore students had less opportunity to practice writing. However, their written production showed that they could use writing as a learning tool by transferring their disposition to engage in writing as a meaningful activity in science classes. They wrote short texts revealing their attitude toward knowledge building and learning which had been developed in the history classes. In particular, their written productions showed that they were able to use writing for the same aims as in history classes, in particular for two of the three functions described above, that is:

1)   to give explanations and to elaborate knowledge to develop a new understanding of the topic;
2)   to express their own doubts about what has puzzled or still puzzles them and any changes in beliefs and explanations.

The students accomplished the first function by making their own initial ideas explicit (conceptions, explanations), by reasoning upon these ideas and the ideas of others, communicating what they had newly understood, and giving final explanations of the phenomena examined. They accomplished the second function by expressing what they found difficult to understand and explaining any change of conceptions.

The following are two examples of short texts that illustrate, respectively, the two functions of writing in the science class.

> Today we have talked about the heartbeat. We have been to the gymnasium to compare our heartbeats with our teacher Egle's chronometer at different times: at rest, after walking, after running slowly and very fast. We discussed a lot our experience and came to these conclusions:
>
> - We can hear the heartbeat in different points of our body (chest, neck, wrist);
> - when we make an effort the heartbeat increases and we need to breath faster and have more oxygen available;
> - not all people have the same number of heartbeat. It may happen only by chance.
>
> Now we have a problem. Some of us think that in elderly people the heart beats slowly for some reason, others think exactly the opposite for different reasons. We have not been able to find a solution because our ideas are still contrasting. We have to think further about it. Next week we will go into it in greater depth. (*Anna*)

> I thought that the lungs had nothing to do with the blood circulation. I did not know that they give oxygen to the blood. I knew that they are important but I believed that they were useful only for holding the air for breathing. I did not have the idea that the blood is related to the lungs. I was convinced that the blood circulated by means of the heart which exploited a mysterious force to make the blood travel through our veins. (*Edoardo*)

7.4 Writing and Scientific Understanding

Blood journey in our body. An ANOVA for repeated measures indicated that both experimental and control groups showed graphically a more advanced representation of the blood circulation in the human body, F (1, 30) = 67.51, $p < .001$. The ANOVA also showed a significant time x group interaction as the experimental group reached a higher level at the end of the curriculum unit implementation, F (1, 30) = 5.14, $p = .05$.

Short texts on the heart and blood. An ANOVA for repeated measures did not show any significant difference between the two groups: both progressed in enriching their conceptual structures of new information.

Topic knowledge text on the blood circulation. As an effect of the instructional intervention aimed at stimulating and supporting conceptual understanding, the students were required to construct new knowledge by changing their prior conceptions. The experimental group outperformed the control group in learning through conceptual change. A one-way ANOVA revealed that the former learned better, F (1, 30) = 6.26, $p < .05$.

Open-ended questions on the relationship between the heart and lungs. Confirming a better understanding of the blood circulation in the human body, the experimental group students gave a more correct and complete explanation of this relationship, as emerged from a one-way ANOVA, F (1, 30) = 5.77, $p < .05$.

The transfer question. A one-way ANOVA also showed a significant difference between the experimental and control group on the questions requiring application of the newly learned concepts of the structure and function of the heart: the former outperformed the latter, F (1, 30) = 4.27, $p < .05$.

Metaconceptual awareness questions. A one-way ANOVA showed significant differences between the two groups, F (1, 30) = 33.50, $p < .001$, concerning the students' awareness of the changes which occurred in their conceptual structures. The students who had the opportunity to use writing to reflect on their conceptions and monitor their developing understanding reached higher levels of metaconceptual awareness. Two significant metaconceptual reflections written by two experimental group students are reported here to illustrate their awareness of what has changed and how. Metacognitive reflection allowed them to be aware of the process that led them to integrate the new ideas into their conceptual structures.

> Before I thought that the blood did not reach the head because I often heard people say something like this: 'Do not do this, blood will go to your head, be careful', so I thought it was not a good thing to have blood in your head. Now I know that the blood reaches every cell, also in the head where the brain is. I know this because we have studied the blood's journey through our body and because I have seen a baby's head and could see the veins in the head very well. I am convinced about this. It has not been very difficult to change what I used to think because I followed the discussions and explanations in the classroom (*Giulia*).

> The ideas I had before were not very good because I did not know, for example, what a lung was and its function with respect to the blood. Through this work I have been able to understand that the lungs are essential for purifying the dirty blood. Moreover, I did not know that oxygen was in the blood, transported by red cells, and that the heart is fundamental to being alive as it makes the two circulations possible. To understand the new concepts has not been particularly difficult because when you like a topic you study it with pleasure, the reasoning comes very easily and you remember the reasoning you have done (*Luca*).

8   DISCUSSION AND CONCLUSIONS

The first purpose of the study was to see whether fifth graders could use writing as a tool to express, reflect and reason on ideas, descriptions and explanations in the process of understanding historical events. The findings indicate that the experimental group students were able to write for different aims which required an active manipulation of information. They showed they could be involved in knowledge transforming processes while writing for learning.

The second purpose of the study was to find out whether writing in the service of learning facilitated understanding of the new history topic. The data show that it contributed significantly to a better understanding in history at the three levels pointed out by Voss & Wiley (1997): the restructuring of contents, change of explanations, and change of some beliefs about the nature of history and the historian's role. The experimental group students reached a higher conceptual understanding of the discovery of America and changed more the type of explanation they gave for this event by having learnt better that there was an economic cause behind it. They also changed more some of their epistemological beliefs by recognising the interpretative nature of historical facts and the need for further investigation of different accounts of the same fact to collect evidence to support or deny them. Moreover, the experimental group students improved significantly in their recognition of the differences between the two historical accounts of the fictitious 'Fifth Livian War'.

There were significant differences between the two groups for only two questions about this kind of belief. It can therefore be noted that written questions, although open-ended, are not the most adequate means for assessing matters such as epistemological beliefs in young students. They may be very limited in eliciting all they believe. It may be speculated that interviews would allow deeper investigation into their beliefs and a more accurate picture of what they think about the nature of a discipline and knowledge construction in the domain.

It would appear that writing has also contributed significantly to creating or refining students' awareness of what they have learned, especially their initial and current beliefs and explanations, as the experimental group expressed a higher level of metacognitive reflections.

The third purpose of the study was to see whether the use of writing as a learning tool in history could be transferred to learning in science. Although the science curriculum unit was not as long as the history one, giving the students less opportunities to practice writing, they showed a capacity to transfer the disposition to be engaged in writing as a meaningful activity. In science they also expressed the attitude which characterised the writing experience in history, that is the use of writing for different functions in the learning process.

The fourth purpose of the study was to see whether writing also facilitated understanding the new science topic that required conceptual change. The findings indicate that the students who transferred the uses of writing from history to science actually reached a deeper conceptual understanding of the new topic by producing changes of conceptions in their cognitive structures and transferring the newly constructed concept of double circulation, and a higher metaconceptual awareness of those changes. Interestingly, the experimental group did not outperform the control group in the task, which implied only accretion of factual knowledge, that is, a lower level of cognitive performance.

Following the line of research initiated with previous works (Mason, 1998, in press; Mason & Boscolo, 2000), the study provides further evidence that writing can be effective in building new knowledge in complex domains. It indicates that the use of writing in the service of learning in a curriculum domain can be successfully applied to another domain by transferring a disposition which represents an attitude toward knowledge and learning.

From an educational point of view the study points out that writing can be effectively introduced across the curriculum to support higher-order thinking processes in order to produce understanding. Knowledge construction and reconstruction in the classroom is promoted and sustained by activities requiring the deep engagement of students as intentional learners who solve knowledge problems. Writing as a tool for thinking and reasoning to transform knowledge can activate such an engagement.

We would like to conclude with a text, written by a learner considering all the work done in history on geographical discoveries. It clearly shows how much teachers and researchers may learn from students' comments about a constructivist learning environment which has given them the opportunity not only of learning through different and meaningful activities but also of evaluating what has been done in the classroom.

> I would like to write my judgement on the work we did in history on geographical discoveries. I liked the topic we did but I disliked the fact that sometimes when one of us said something about an experience or asked something, the teacher said 'we do not have enough time to talk about that'. Historical documents have been of a great help as they make me think and reason on the ways of life in the past. In my group we discussed quite a lot the topics which were more difficult to think and write about. Discussing is a way to talk together and ask questions that you would normally never ask. For me writing was very useful as it makes you revise your ideas and what you have done in each class. All discourse has been deepened further because a discourse about only the main problems does not make you understand well. I do not think that cards are important, we can make them in our notebooks. For me the time we have devoted to this work is about right, right for carrying out a topic of this size. Our teacher sometimes allowed us to be quite relaxed but she also made us do a lot of work, reading, drawing and writing a lot. I tried to play my role in the group, by intervening very often and asking questions. The only thing I wish to propose for the next work is that the teachers leave us to talk, discuss, raise questions and ask other things much more. In conclusion I liked this work as I see I have learned, although not in the best way.
> (*Edoardo*)

These words lead us to reflect on the students' very strong need to be deeply personally involved in meaningful learning. Although the teachers and researchers who created a learning environment may believe that it gives the students the best opportunities for meaningful learning, these opportunities might not be enough. Thus, to reflect on learners' reflections about what they experience at school, and the limitations of their experience, should be a frequent activity to be carried out by those who are interested in creating increasingly better contexts to build knowledge in the classroom.

ACKNOWLEDGEMENTS

We wish to thank the class teachers, Egle Boffo, Fides Curzolo and Tiziana Zanetto for their great interest and precious co-operation in this study. Also, of course, a special thanks to all the students.

APPENDIX

List of sessions for the historical and science classes with the writing tasks carried out by the experimental and control groups.

History classes

Session 1   Write everything you know and think about the importance of spices and metals in the 15° century (both groups).

Session 2   After reading new information on the importance of spices and metals in the 15° century, write your explanations about the reasons for the first very long sea voyages (experimental group only).

Session 3   Write what ideas and beliefs were held by Columbus according to what you have understood (experimental group only).

Session 4   Write what you have understood about Columbus' travel diary (experimental group only).

Session 5   Write all the information you can by carefully observing the reproduction of Columbus's landing in the Guanahani islands in 1492 (both groups).

Session 6   Write your comments on the documents you have read about native Americans (experimental group only).

Session 7   Write your hypotheses about the papal bull you have just read (experimental group only).

Session 8   Write your interpretation of what we have read in the document about Columbus's shipload of slaves (experimental group only).

Session 9   Write if there is anything that is still puzzling you or you feel you have not yet understood well (experimental group only).

Session 10   Write your comments on the work done in history. You can say if you have liked it and why, if you have found it interesting and why, if you have found it different from the previous work done in the classroom and why; your proposals for the next work (both groups).

Science classes

Session 1   After discussing the heartbeat, write your ideas on the heart and blood (experimental group only).

Session 2   Write what you can discover from this picture of the blood in our body (both groups).

Session 3   Write what you think about the two opposing ideas that have emerged from today's discussion on the blood circulation (experimental group only).

Session 4   Write your explanation about what the lungs have to do with the blood. Have you changed your initial ideas on this? (Experimental group only.)

| Session 5 | Write if there is anything that is still puzzling you or you feel you have not yet understood well (experimental group only). |
| Session 6 | Write your final explanation about why there are two types of circulation in our body (experimental group only). |

NB Session 7, was implemented in language skills class only: Write an invented story – for both groups, but only for the experimental group were the 'characters' given: *i.e.* the heart, lungs, red and white blood cells. For the control group the characters were not related to the science unit).

SEQUENTIAL WRITING TASKS' INFLUENCE ON SCIENCE LEARNING

BRIAN M HAND*, VAUGHAN PRAIN** & LARRY YORE***

*Iowa State University, USA, ** La Trobe University, Bendigo, Australia, ***University of Victoria, Canada

Abstract. Recent enlarged accounts of science literacy emphasize that student learning should move beyond a narrow focus on technical knowledge to an understanding of the nature, rationale and procedures of science as well as a commitment and capacity to communicate scientific understandings to diverse readerships. This chapter explores the implications of this redefined view of science literacy for effective task design in writing for learning in science. We report on two case studies that sought to identify the effects on student learning of science and science literacy when they engaged with different single and sequential writing tasks. The results of the study indicated that students who wrote to explain their ideas performed better on subsequent tests than students who undertook only the usual writing tasks. Students who undertook a sequence of two connected writing tasks also performed better on higher order questions than students who did not undertake such tasks.

1   INTRODUCTION

Contemporary science literacy has refocused its historical emphasis on technical conceptions and scientific terminology to emphasize a set of abilities, plausible reasoning, habits of mind, unifying concepts, and communications. Furthermore, the target of science literacy has been expanded from future scientists and engineers to include all students and adults. Science literacy involves the cognitive abilities and emotional dispositions to construct science understandings, the big ideas of science, and communicative skills to inform and persuade others to take informed actions on these ideas. This interpretation of science literacy encompasses the nature of science, scientific inquiry, and scientific epistemology; the understanding of the major unifying concepts of science; and the oral and written communication abilities to engage in the academic or public discourse about science, technology, society, and the environment. Clearly, talking science, reading science, and writing science are

Hand, B., Prain, V. & Yore, L. (2001). Sequential writings tasks' influence on science learning. In: G. Rijlaarsdam (Series Ed.) & P. Tynjälä, L. Mason & K. Lonka (Volume Eds), *Studies in Writing, Volume 7, Writing as a Learning tool: Integrating Theory and Practice*, 105–129.© 2001 Kluwer Academic Publishers. Printed in the Netherlands.

not only desired outcomes of science literacy but are potential means to achieving science literacy.

The writing-to-learn science movement attempts to capitalize on this renewed emphasis and to utilize writing tasks as discourse opportunities that enable students to construct science understanding and science communication proficiency. Ideally, the authentic science writing tasks of professional scientists and engineers can be infused into science instruction to promote consolidation of and reflection on science learning and to promote technical writing abilities for all students (Yore, Hand, & Prain, 1999). Non-traditional science writing tasks (poems, prose, science fiction, *etc.*) can be utilized to enhance students' motivation and to encourage their personal identification with science ideas. This chapter attempts to anchor a recent study of junior secondary students' writing-to-learn science in the current international science education reforms and implementation literature, in the nature of science, science inquiry and scientific epistemology, and in the educational research on models of writing, genre and writing-to-learn science.

2   BACKGROUND

The international science education reforms in Australia, Canada, New Zealand, the United Kingdom, and the United States of America (AAAS, 1990, 1993, 1998; CMEC, 1997; Curriculum Corporation, 1994; Department of Education, 1995; Ministry of Education, 1993; NRC, 1996) identified science literacy for all students as their central focus. Each reform specified a set of abilities, concepts, emotional dispositions, and epistemological understandings. The nature of science and the subsumed habits of mind (psychological propensities) address the public concerns about how science, technology, society, and the environment are related, the differences between science and pseudo-science, science as inquiry and technology as design, patterns of argumentation, canons of evidence, and the sceptical stance of scientists. Effective science writing (process) and science writings (product) clearly reflect the nature of science in that unique terminology, a mixture of written language and mathematical symbols and genre are used to capture the scientific inquiry, illustrate the plausible reasoning, and transmit the claims, evidence and warrants of the argument. Writing-to-learn science advocates believe that both the process and the product can be utilized to increase scientific knowledge, enhance a scientific epistemology, and assess science literacy.

2.1 Nature of Science

Contemporary science literacy includes the nature of science, but there is a lack of consensus about the essential character of science (Driver, Leach, Millar, & Scott, 1996; McComas, 1998; Norris, 1997; Nussbaum, 1989). Post-modern cultural relativists refute the traditional absolutists' view of documenting reality and the modern evaluativists' claims to durable standards of truth, objectivity, and reputable method (Figure 1).

How does scientific knowledge develop?

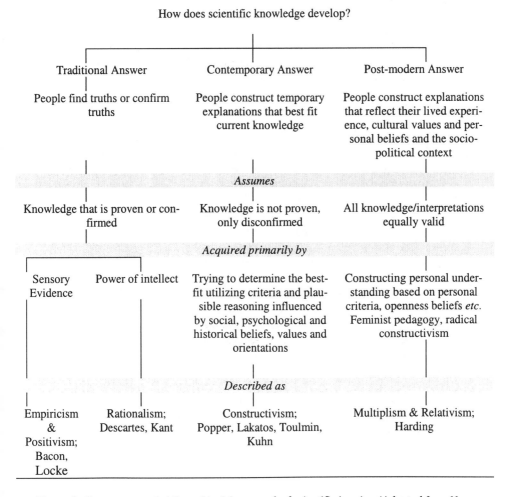

Figure 1: Concept map of philosophical framework of scientific inquiry. (Adapted from Nussbaum, 1989.)

The National Science Education Standards (NRC, 1996: 6) emphasize the provisional nature of knowledge claims in science but also argue that there is a general consensus about how knowledge is claimed, tested, and refined. The science education reform documents in Australia, Canada, New Zealand, the United Kingdom, and the United States of America acknowledge that scientists differ routinely about research questions and interpretation of evidence, and publish conflicting experimental results or draw different conclusions from the same data (McComas & Olson, 1998). However, ideally, scientists recognize this conflict and work towards finding evidence to resolve disputes. This evaluativist view of science entails assessing the results of scientific investigations, alternative interpretations, theoretical

models, and the explanations proposed by scientists against evidence from nature
(Yore & Shymansky, 1997). Although scientists may disagree about explanations of
the phenomena, about interpretations of the data, or about the value of rival theories,
they agree that questioning, response to criticism, and open communications are
integral parts of the scientific enterprise. Scientific knowledge evolves, and major
disagreements are eventually resolved through such interactions between scientists.
In this sense, the nature of science is conceptualized as a form of inquiry that shapes
a worldview, ways of knowing, and plausible reasoning, and generates an accepted
body of explanations.Science distinguishes itself from other ways of knowing and
from other bodies of knowledge through the use of inquiry, empirical standards,
logical arguments, and scepticism to generate the best temporal explanations about
the natural world (NRC, 1996). Scientific explanations must meet certain criteria.
They must be consistent with experimental and observational evidence about nature;
and they must make accurate predictions, when appropriate, about the systems studied. Evaluations should be logical, respect the rules of evidence, be open to criticism, report methods and procedures, and make knowledge public. Explanations
about the natural world based on myths, personal beliefs, religious values, mystical
inspiration, superstition, or authority may be personally useful and socially relevant
but they are not science. Science literacy should incorporate a conception of science
as a human construction of knowledge from which the human or fallible element has
been limited but not fully excised (Cleminson, 1990).

Students need to understand that science is an intellectual activity requiring more
than technical competence. They must engage their own epistemological beliefs
about knowing, justification, and logic central to scientific reasoning. Addressing
the lack of congruence between the students' beliefs and the modern epistemological
commitments of science is central to promoting science literacy. Activities in the
classroom should take on the authentic characteristics of scientific inquiry as students develop their epistemological commitments and understandings about the nature and rationale of science. Critical discussions of these inquiries can help students
begin to understand science as a way of knowing related to, as opposed to distinct
from, other ways of knowing.

2.2 Epistemology and Plausible Reasoning

Hofer and Pintrich (1997) emphasized that epistemology needs to focus on 'individuals' beliefs about knowledge as well as reasoning and justification processes
regarding knowledge' (p. 116). Driver et al. (1996) continued:

> An understanding of the scientific approach to inquiry ... involves an epistemological
> dimension: all empirical inquiry is planned and carried out within a framework imposed
> by its conceptual and theoretical structures which the inquirer brings to bear on it. ...
> Similarly, epistemological considerations underpin an understanding of the limits of ap-
> plication of the scientific approach and of the demarcation between science and non-
> science. (p. 14)

Plausible reasoning is critical to the learners' epistemological understandings in that
it anchors the learners' understanding of the processes and the basis of knowing science. Students' epistemological beliefs about science are based on their understand-

ings of the nature of science and the nature of knowing science (Carey & Smith, 1993). Songer and Linn (1991) found that students who view science as tentative and dynamic were less likely to perceive science learning as rote memorization of isolated infobits.

Students' understandings of the nature of knowledge are perceived as a progression from viewing knowledge as absolute to a more relativistic view to an evaluativist view (Kuhn, 1991, 1993). Students move from conceiving of knowledge as fixed, where absolute truth exists with certainty, to knowledge as tentative, where temporary truth exists within limits. Knowledge moves from accumulation of facts to highly interrelated concepts. The continuum of knowing, viewed as the source of knowledge and justification for knowing, moves from knowledge originating outside the self and residing in external authority that transmits the knowledge, to self as knower where knowledge construction occurs in interactions with others, prior knowledge, and concurrent experience with the environment. Thus, learners are viewed as shifting from spectators to active constructors of knowledge who evaluate knowledge claims using evidence, expertise, and creditability of source.

As students navigate the pathways of various inquiries trying to construct knowledge (Figure 2), they are required to apply different forms of plausible reasoning to address problems, questions, evidence, warrants and claims (Yore, 1992).

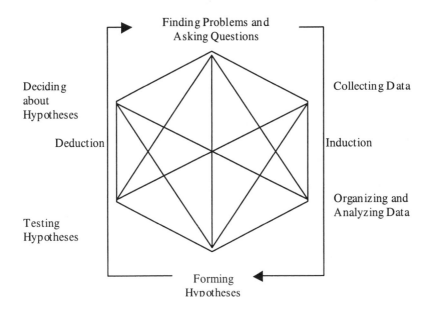

Figure 2. Scientific inquiry.

The historical science of Francis Bacon and the embryonic explorations of young children emphasize inductions where specific experiences and individual events are synthesized into generalized patterns (Driver *et al*, 1996). Holland, *et al* (1986) stated induction involves 'inferential processes that expand knowledge in the face of uncertainty' (p. 1). The uncertainty is indirectly related to the students' prior knowledge and associated experiences with the phenomenon, but absolute certainty cannot be achieved by induction (Mc Comas, 1998). The rationalism of Immanuel Kant and the post-lecture experiments of traditional science classes emphasize deductions where established generalizations are verified by documenting the occurrence of specific events (Yore, 1992). Johnson-Laird (1988) suggested that deductive reasoning requires students to search for unknown events based on the logical extension of a concept or model that does not increase the information contained in the fundamental premises taken collectively. The contemporary science of Thomas Kuhn and the constructivist learning implied by the National Science Education Standards (NRC, 1996) emphasize hypothetico-deductive reasoning where a hypothesis serves as a blueprint for inquiry in which a tentative causal relationship guides a falsification test (Yore, 1993). Hypothetico-deductive inquiry requires students to find a problem, ask a researchable question, form a hypothesis about the cause and the effect, make predictions assuming the hypothesis to true and to be untrue, design an experiment, collect and analyze data, and interpret the data in light of the earlier predictions in order to construct an argument that makes a claim based on the evidence and the embedded logic. The spontaneous discoveries of scientists and the creative insights of children emphasize abductions where students extract patterns from observations, measurements and events in a holistic manner (Hanson, 1958; Holland *et al*, 1986). Abductions appear to involve perception of the whole in the form of a gestalt – a unified whole, a configuration, a pattern or an organized field having specific properties that cannot be derived from the summation of the component parts – or a metaphor – an application of an idea that does not literally denote the second idea in order to suggest comparisons and potential relationships. Abductions occur when the input data interact with the student's perspectives to stimulate a spontaneous, imagined, conceptual 'abstraction that drops idiosyncratic details differing from one exemplar to another and leaves only what holds in common' (Johnson-Laird, 1988: 242). Clearly, science instruction that promotes effective learning and constructivist epistemologies involves far more types of inquiry and plausible reasoning than typically illustrated by the mythical scientific method.

2.3 *Writing-to-Learn Research*

Writing across the curriculum has been earmarked with a series of grassroots efforts in which numerous effective programs went undocumented. More recently writing-to-learn studies have been reported in the research journals, but limited results are available for science (Rivard, 1994). Furthermore, little research has considered epistemological and cognitive aspects of the interactions of the nature of writing, the nature of science, and the nature of science literacy (Rowell, 1997). Several science educators have identified the potential time-efficiencies and dual goals of writing to help students construct knowledge about science and insights into science writing (Holliday, Yore, & Alvermann, 1994; Keys, 1999; Prain & Hand, 1996a, 1996b).

2.3.1   Models of Writing

The dominant knowledge telling model of writing in science in schools has various limitations. This model fails to engage with the transformational and recursive possibilities of science writing, does not consider the unique characteristics of scientific discourse, reduces the pedagogical purposes for writing in science, underestimates the potential variety of writing tasks in learning science, and ignores the understandings of participants – teachers and students. Holliday *et al.* (1994) identified a potential basis for change:

> Writing, like interactive-constructive reading, depends upon the writer's prior domain and strategic knowledge, purpose, and interest. Bereiter and Scardamalia (1987) described the interactive and constructive processes involved in the knowledge-transforming model of writing that parallels the generative model of science learning in that it involves long-term memory, working memory, and sensory-motor activity. The knowledge-transforming model appears to be far more interactive and recursive than linear. The tasks of goal-setting and text production do not fully reveal the complex cognitive, metacognitive, and memory factors involved in the retrieval of conceptual and discourse knowledge from long-term memory and the executive control, strategic planning, and construction taking place in short-term memory. (pp. 885-886)

Students utilizing the knowledge telling model systematically select a topic, recall understanding, draft a product, proofread the draft, and produce a final copy. Frequently, the writing process was linear, void of any classroom interaction or engagement with the norms of different kinds of science writing, and emphasized the mechanical correctness of language. Scardamalia and Bereiter (1986) encouraged teachers to help their students move from this predominant knowledge telling writing, which involves converting knowledge from long-term memory into written words essentially unaltered, to a knowledge transforming approach in which knowledge is actively reworked to improve understanding – 'reflected upon, revised, organized, and more richly interconnected' (p.16). While such a model poses far greater cognitive challenges for student writers, such an approach offers far greater gains in terms of learning through writing. Certainly students should be encouraged to develop a far more conscious and reflective attitude towards the possible purposes for writing about science.

The knowledge transforming model can be used to clarify the role of content knowledge about the nature of science and the target topic, the discourse knowledge about and management of written science discourse, patterns of argumentation and genre, and science writing strategies' influence on the science writing process. Keys (1999) believed that writers increase their content knowledge during the interactions of the content and discourse spaces. She stated:

> In the content space, the problems and beliefs are considered, while in the discourse space, the problems of how to express the content are considered. The output from each space serves as input for the other, so that questions concerning language and syntax choice reshape the meaning of the content, while efforts to express the content direct the ongoing composition. (p. 120)

Utilizing the knowledge transforming model as an operational framework would encourage science teachers to get students spending more time setting purposes, accessing and building content knowledge, specifying audience, thinking, negotiating, strategic planning, reacting, reflecting, and revising. Explicit instruction embedded in the authentic context of scientific inquiry can clarify the following: the nature of writing is as a symbol system: the function-form relationships of scientific genre: the author's responsibilities to the audience; the interactive, constructive, generative nature of science language; the relationship between evidence, warrants, and claims; and what, how, when, and why to use specific writing strategies. While such a focus represents an ambitious agenda, these elements need to be considered as an integral part of science courses in which student writing promotes science learning (Ferrari, Bouffard & Rainville, 1998; Yore, Hand & Prain, 1999). Embedded instruction needs to convert the metacognitive awareness into action to improve self-regulation (planning and generating ideas, translating ideas into text, checking and revising text) and actual writing performance (Hayes & Flower, 1986; Sawyer, Graham & Harris, 1992).

2.3.2   Genre

One major strand within recent writing for learning science has been the focus on genres, both in terms of the micro and macro structures of text types (Halliday & Martin, 1993; Keys, 1999) and the sociocultural factors that have shaped these text types, the idea of science writing as an evolved set of cultural practices (Bazerman, 1988; Kelly & Chen, 1999). From this perspective students need to know how knowledge is claimed and argued for in science in different contexts, as well as understanding the purposes of particular linguistic features in different text types as part of these claims. As Kelly and Chen (1999: 910) have argued, there is the need for 'the unpacking of scientific norms...if classroom activities aimed at reproducing authentic scientific contexts are to be successful at affording opportunities for students engaging in scientific discourses'. However, surveys of teachers and analyses of school writing tasks reveal that teachers are unfamiliar with many genres and narrative and factual recounting activities predominate (Wray & Lewis, 1997). Effective writing-to-learn science programs, then, need to provide explicit instruction, and writing tasks need to engage in a full range of genre – the specific function-form relationships of science writing (Table 1). Narrative involves the temporal, sequenced discourse found in diaries, journals, learning logs, and conversations. Narratives (document recollections, interpretations, and emotions) are far more personal and informal than most scientific writings, but they provide opportunities for the writer to connect personal experiences with science ideas. Description involves personal, commonsense and technical descriptions, informational and scientific reports, and definitions. Frequently, descriptions will be structured by time-series of events, scientific classification systems or taxonomies, or accepted reporting pattern of information (who, what, where, when, why). Explanation involves sequencing events in cause-effect relationships. Explanations attempt to link established ideas or models with observed effects by using logical connectives of 'if this, then this'. Instruction involves ordering a sequence of procedures to specify directions, such as a manual, experiment, or recipe. Instructions can effectively utilize a series of steps in which the sequence is established by tested science and safety. Argumentation involves logical ordering of propositions to persuade someone in an essay, discussion, debate, report, or review. Arguments attempt to establish the boundaries and conditions of the issue, logical sequence of the claims, evidence and warrants, and then to systematically discredit, reject, or reinforce components of the issue, to clearly disconfirm or support the basic premises.

Each genre is flexible, and the writer must control the form to address the function or purpose. No lengthy piece of text uses a single genre (Anthony, Johnson, & Yore, 1996). Analysis of effective writing illustrates microstructures embedded within the macro-structure. In argumentation, a writer might start with a descriptive passage to engage the reader, later use an explanation passage to illustrate a critical cause-effect relationship, and in closing may use an instruction passage much the way a judge clarifies the issues, claims, critical evidence, and the charge to a jury. Prain and Hand (1996a) utilized writing type (booklet, travel brochure, letter to editor, article, *etc.*) to capture the essential aspects of genre, to recognize the variation of microstructures in text, and to represent the variety of writing tasks literate adults, engineers, and scientists use.

Table 1. Genre, purpose, outcome and audience of writing-to-learn science (Adapted from Gallagher, Knapp & Noble, 1993).

Genre	Purpose	Outcome	Audience
Narrative	Recording emotions and ideas	Attitudes	Self and others
Description	Documentation of events	Basic knowledge	Others
Explanation	Causality	Cause-effect relationships	Others
Instruction	Directions	Procedural knowledge	Others
Argumentation	Persuasion	Patterns of argument	Others

2.4 Writing-to-Learn Science

Connolly (1989) suggested that this new writing-to-learn rhetoric was compatible with constructivist perspectives of science learning and illustrated that the symbol systems used to communicate play a critical role in constructing meaning. He emphasized:

> Writing-to-learn is not, most importantly, about 'grammar across the curriculum' nor about 'making spelling count' in the biology paper. It is not a program to reinforce standard English usage in all classes. Nor is it about … mastering the formal conventions of scientific, social scientific, or business writing. It is about the value of writing 'to enable the discovery of knowledge'. (p. 5)

However, writing-to-learn science tasks also provide authentic opportunities to develop scientific vocabulary, grammar, spelling, punctuation, patterns of argumentation, and technical writing utilized in the science and technology professions. Writing to learn and technical writing have much in common; effective instruction should utilize authentic technical writing tasks where possible to promote science learning, reflection, and practical technical writing for science and technology professionals and adult lay people alike (Yore, Hand. & Prain, 1999).

Howard and Barton (1986) stated that the 'idea is to learn to think in writing primarily for your own edification and then the eyes of others. This approach will enable you to use writing to become more intelligent to yourself – to find your meaning – as well as to communicate effectively with others' (p. 14). The following principles should guide the development of writing-to-learn tasks in science (Tchudi & Huerta, 1983):

- Keep science content central in the writing process.
- Help students structure and synthesize their knowledge.
- Provide a real audience for student writers that will value, question, and provide supportive criticism.
- Spend time prewriting, collecting information from various sources (concrete experiences, print materials, experts, electronic data banks, visuals, *etc*.), sharpening focus, and strategic planning.
- Provide on-going teacher support, guidance, and explicit instruction.
- Encourage revisions and redrafts based on supportive criticism to address conceptual questions and clarify understandings.
- Clarify the differences between revising and editing (format, spelling, mechanics, grammar).

3   ASSUMPTIONS OF THE STUDY

The research project was guided by various assumptions about how writing serves science learning, as well as the need for a sequence of tasks to promote writing for learning as knowledge transformation (Bereiter & Scardamalia, 1987; Tucknott, 1998). This writing should aim to develop students' knowledge of the nature of science, its epistemological commitments and reasoning processes, including what counts as effective evidential claims and persuasive explanation in science (Hand, Prain, Lawrence, & Yore, 1999). The knowledge transformation model of writing suggests that the design of effective writing tasks should be sufficiently complex to require higher-order thinking through reformulation of ideas and, hence, promote meaningful learning. This complexity will entail generating and integrating content, signalling authorial purposes, anticipating and meeting reader needs, organizing content in an appropriate genre, and using appropriate language and terminology in an interconnected recursive process. Therefore, effective task design or task sequence should encourage students to move beyond simple retelling of information to a far more complex conscious engagement with the dialectical process of addressing these interconnected rhetorical and content issues.

Flower (1994) and Grabe and Kaplan (1996) identified the need to recognize the importance of context in student writing performance, here defined as the particular features and demands of specific writing tasks. Therefore, this study addressed the significant challenges junior secondary students face when engaging the processes of scientific reasoning through writing by designing tasks and instructions that provide sufficient scaffolding and explicit teaching to support this learning. Collectively, the instruction and tasks acknowledge that there are dangers in compartmentalizing elements in the knowledge transformation model, when in fact all the components of 'knowledge, skills, goals and feelings' are interrelated, and 'over time these separate components come to form a more organic whole' (Bereiter, 1990: 613).

The writing tasks required students to reword their understandings of a topic to meet the needs and interests of an unknown non-expert audience, thus increasing the cognitive demands of the task beyond simply retelling their ideas to the teacher. The instruction explicitly addressed students' understanding of audience and strategies to address the expectations and knowledge needs of their readers by considering the order, focus, kind, and amount of explanation presented in their writing. Students need to understand how to clarify concepts for non-expert readers by making links between these concepts and the readers' current knowledge. The sequential tasks focused on reworking texts to provide opportunities for students to identify the audience's influence on content and focus.

Students' genre knowledge, including understanding of the function-form relationship between the purposes of different kinds of writing and their structural features, is also important in effective writing for science learning. This issue was addressed through the provision of additional guidance in constructing scientific explanations; the study used a series of science writing heuristics (SWH) as one of the writing tasks. This modified version of the traditional laboratory report uses a series of questions and templates (frames) to provide scaffolding and prompts to develop students' reasoning when they generate meaningful inferences from evidence to support claims about a topic. The SWH seeks to develop students' understanding of the nature of science as a form of inquiry and argument by providing opportunities for students to reflect on how persuasive explanations are developed in science, and to understand their own epistemological and metacognitive strategies in learning science. The other writing task used in the study was the personal letter. This task was chosen because students already have knowledge of the purposes, structure, and language of letter writing. The students' familiarity with these features meant that they could tackle successfully the demand of explanation, compare-contrast, and rewording understandings of science concepts without having the additional burden of an unfamiliar genre. Other student writing undertaken in the study included concept maps, notes, summaries, diagrams, review sheets and tests, including short-response and extended-response items.

4   AIMS OF THE STUDY

In seeking to identify the effects of sequential writing tasks on students' learning in junior secondary science, the study had the following aims:

1)   Identify differences in the performance of control and experimental groups of students in answering lower-level and higher-level test questions.

7)   Identify the experimental students' perceptions about the values and effects of the sequential writing tasks on their science learning.

8)   Document the conditions necessary to maximize the impact of writing-to-learn strategies in science.

9)   Identify the implications for designing, implementing, and evaluating writing tasks for learning in junior secondary science.

5   METHOD

This study was conducted in a junior secondary school in a regional city of Victoria (Australia) and was completed over a two-semester period, involving two similar classes in each semester with the same experienced, well-informed teacher teaching all classes. The study was in essence two separate but related comparative case studies to examine the outcomes for students using a single writing-to-learn task and sequential writing-to-learn tasks in answering lower-level and higher-level cognitive questions on typical science tests. Writing tasks were designed to focus on learning science knowledge, on the enhancement of understanding the nature of science, and on the development of students' metacognitive abilities to construct understandings and to monitor their own learning strategies. In the first semester, two Year 10 classes (15-16 year olds) used either no unusual writing tasks or a single writing task, while in the second semester, two Year 9 classes (14-15 year olds) used no unusual writing tasks or a series of writing tasks. Both qualitative and quantitative methods were used to examine the predicted differential effects of no unusual writing tasks, a single writing task, and sequential writing tasks.

5.1 Case Study 1

The first case study compared the performance of two similar, but non-randomly assigned, Year 10 science classes studying genetics. The experimental (N=23) and control (N=23) classes were determined by a toss of a coin. The instruction was the same length and covered the same topics and writing activities (note taking, review sheet, and unit test) for both classes, except the experimental class completed a letter-writing task designed to require causal explanation for a non-expert peer audience. Both classes were allowed to generate study summaries as review for the unit examination. The unit of study explored sexual reproduction and the transfer of genetic traits from parents to offspring. Dominant and recessive traits were considered as the result of paired chromosomes with matched or unmatched genes.

A contemporary focus was provided by exploring 'Dolly' and genetic cloning issues. Students read and summarized newspaper reports of cloning of 'Dolly' and also referred to additional library resources to clarify their understanding of the cloning process. The implications for human cloning were also explored, with students identifying ethical and other issues arising from this topic. The teacher did not provide an 'authorized' (canonical) definition of terms to the experimental class but expected individual students to develop their own definitions through class discussion and reference to the textbook and other sources. After this work, students were expected to explain what they understood about the nature of cloning in a letter to a friend their own age who was not familiar with the topic. The students were told that they had to use scientific terminology in their letter but they also had to explain these terms without resorting to 'authorized' definitions from their textbook or other sources. They were given no specific instructions about the structure of the letter but were told that the letter should make the subject interesting to the intended reader.

The 30-item unit examination measured lower-level recall and comprehension of ideas related to each topic with 17 true-false, 8 multiple-choice, and 5 short-answer questions developed over several years. The test items were examined by experienced science educators for construct validity and judged to be reasonable measures of the lower-level content outcomes for the unit. The total possible score for the test was 34 points. An innovative analogy question was developed to access higher-level understanding: it required students to compare and contrast genetic cloning and photocopying. This extended-response question placed greater writing demands on students than was expected by the other test questions. The total possible score for the analogy question was 6 points. Scoring for the analogy was based on the scale of complexity used to answer the question. Low-level responses, such as cloning involves transfer of genetic material or photocopying is a mechanical process that does not involve cells, scored few marks. Answers that addressed the complex issues of cloning compared to photocopying scored higher marks. T-test analyses of the final examination results were conducted. Five students from both the control and experimental groups were interviewed upon completion of the unit. The interviewees were selected by the teacher as representative of the performance range in the class of able, average, and less able students. A semi-structured interview protocol focused on the students' engagement with the letter-writing task (experimental group), the production of the review sheet, and their engagement with the additional test question.

5.2 Case Study 2

The second case study compared two similar, but non-randomly assigned, Year 9 classes studying reflection and refraction of light. A coin toss was used to determine the experimental class (N=25) and the control class (N=27). The instruction was the same length and covered the same topics and usual writing tasks (note taking, concept maps, summaries, review sheet) for both classes, except that the experimental class completed a series of additional writing tasks – SWH forms and letter. The SWH is a framework to facilitate scientific explanations in conjunction with the completion of laboratory work and consists of two components (Hand & Keys, 1999). The first component is a series of pre-investigation activities to promote students' thinking about laboratory concepts and might include the development and discussion of concept maps, initial observations, writing questions, and brainstorming ideas. Students can negotiate their understandings in different contexts, including on their own, with peers, with textbooks or other sources, and with the teacher. Students were asked to identify their current understandings about the nature of light, specific terms associated with this topic, and to make predictions about the properties of light under different conditions. The second component incorporated a template designed to facilitate students' reasoning in constructing explanations from their observations (see Figure 3). Through a series of questions, the students were required to make careful substantiated links between observations, claims, and evidence. The framework differs from the traditional laboratory report in that students were expected to provide precise, coherent reasons for their knowledge claims based on evidence. If their explanations differed from those found in textbooks, after these were consulted, then the students were expected to review their claims and evidence. The SWH is also intended to strengthen students' understanding of the nature and rationale of scientific inquiry and to promote reflection on their own learning processes, as well as strengthening their concept knowledge about the topic.

1. Beginning ideas	What are my questions?
2. Tests	What did I do?
3. Observations	What did I see?
4. Claims	What can I claim?
5. Evidence	How do I know? Why am I making these claims?
6. Reading	How do my ideas compare with other ideas?
7. Reflection	How have my ideas changed?

Figure 3. Science Writing Heuristic provided to students to use when completed laboratory activities.

The light unit involved the usual inquiries into how light travels, what happens when light encounters opaque objects, what happens when light encounters transparent objects, and how the principles of refraction are used to explain concave and convex lenses. Initially, students constructed concept maps to explore their understandings of light and discussed their own meanings for terms such as 'bouncing' or 'bending' to account for the properties of light hitting a mirror. Students shone a light through a rectangular prism and developed their own descriptions of the path of the light in this experiment. They also examined the path of light through additional objects over several lessons, including triangular prisms and lenses. The SWH template (see Figure 3) was introduced to the experimental students and explained as a way to organize and justify their explanations of these experiments. The students were encouraged to ask questions about the order of prompts in the template and to consider how it differed from the usual science report. The teacher stressed that the students needed to explain very precisely the basis for their claims about the properties of light in each experiment. The learning cycle enabled students to investigate freely a series of problems using the SWH template.

During the course of the topic, the students completed five templates as they negotiated their ideas in groups and with the teacher. Because the structure and demands of the template were new to the students, it was necessary to undertake this number of attempts, with some students finding the cognitive demands of this task very challenging.

The researchers also recognize that this task does not match all the conditions proposed in the knowledge transformation model of writing for learning in that students do not have to signal authorial purpose, anticipate and meet reader needs, or organize content in an appropriate form or genre. However, this task still requires students to generate and integrate content, and use appropriate language and terminology and, therefore, represents significant worthwhile challenges for students in promoting higher-order thinking. After the completion of the templates, the teacher tried to clarify key concepts in relation to light, reflection, and refraction. The experimental students then wrote a letter to a high school student at the same grade level who was about to study a unit on light in an American school. The teacher advised them that their letter should include a description of the laboratory processes, their recently acquired knowledge of the nature of light, and their views about the purpose and value of the SWH for learning about the topic. The letter provided an opportunity for the students to connect SWH scientific reasoning and the rationale and basis for scientific inquiry. As with the other personal letter task, students were not given prescriptions about the structure of the letter but were told that they had to use appropriate scientific terminology and to explain terms clearly but without resorting to 'authorized' definitions. Students were asked to consider what their American peers might be expected to know about the topic and to consider what might be the best order in which to present explanations and clarifications. The students were also asked to consider which concepts were most important, which descriptions were necessary, and whether examples might be needed to help with explanations. These focus prompts were intended to provide a basis for clarifying audience needs, planning organization, reviewing composition, and to enable students to monitor their own success in achieving their writing purpose.

The control class completed the light unit using the learning cycles approach, but teacher-directed discussion and lectures were used to formulate the conceptions during the invention phase. Students used textbooks to elaborate their understanding of the target concept. Opportunities to explore understanding through social negotiation with each other were not provided to these students, and they did not complete any unusual writing types as part of the learning process. After the science concepts of light, reflection, and refraction were established, both classes applied their understanding to analyzing and understanding optical lens systems.

Science achievement was measured with a 78-item true-false, multiple-choice, and short-response item examination developed earlier by the classroom teacher. Total possible score for the examination was 82 points, comprising 77 points for the recall (true-false and multiple-choice) items and 5 points for the short-response comprehension item. The test was examined by experienced science educators for construct validity and judged to be a reasonable measure of the lower-level learning outcomes for the science unit. An analogy question was added to assess higher-level understanding; it required students to describe and explain what would happen to the laser beam and the bullet as a laser-targeted bullet entered a body of water. The total possible score for the extended-response analogy item was 8 points. Students were given low scores if they only extended and labelled the diagram provided. High scores were given to illustrated diagrams with accompanying explanations relating to refraction, mediums, and energy.

T-test analyses of the final examination results on lower-level questions and the higher-level question were used to examine differences between the experimental and control groups. Students from the experimental class (N=12) were identified to be interviewed at the end of the teaching unit using the same selection procedure as in the first case study. The interviews centered on students' engagement with the SWH, the letter writing task, and the perceived learning value of the writing tasks.

6   RESULTS

As outlined in the previous section, this study consisted of two parallel comparative case studies designed to examine collectively the differential effects of no unusual writing tasks, a single writing task, and sequential writing tasks on lower-level and higher-level science achievement. Thus, the results are presented as two separate case studies, but the discussion will draw comparisons across the two case studies. It should be noted that in each case the only difference between the experimental and the control group was the type of writing that they were required to undertake and the embedded discourse required by the task. The experimental groups were asked to undertake non-traditional writing tasks as part of their science instruction whereas the control groups followed traditional science writing activities.

6.1 Case Study 1

The descriptive results of the common test items that both experimental and control classes completed at the end of the topic are outlined in Table 2. T-test results indicated no significant differences ($p < .05$) on either the lower-level items ($t = 0.49$) or the higher-level item ($t = 0.62$). Initial analysis indicated that the experimental students did not perform any better on the test questions than the control students and that a single writing task may not have influenced science achievement.

Table 2. Case 1 Descriptive statistics (mean, standard deviation) for the lower-level and higher-level test questions.

Classes	Lower-level Items (max=34)	Higher-level Item (max=6)
Control (n=23)	22.6 (6.5)	3.1 (1.8)
Experimental (n=23)	23.7 (8.0)	2.9 (1.1)

It must be pointed out that the teacher was not given specific instruction or guidance as to the construction of the test apart from the request to incorporate the higher-level cloning analogy question. Thus, the lower-level items represent what an experienced, well-prepared science teacher believes is important and were not oriented towards higher-level understanding. Therefore, the inclusion of the writing task did not disadvantage the experimental students. A post hoc analysis of the analogy question indicated some useful information in terms of conceptual clusters addressed within this question. The higher-order conceptual cluster included such concepts as recognition of different types of cloning, differences between nuclear transfer technology and true cloning, cloning gives a three-dimensional copy while only surface structure is copied in photocopying, photocopying is in common usage while cloning involves specialized usage, cloning does not mean the copy will be exact, and that the environment may influence outcomes. Fifteen students in the experimental classes used higher-level concepts to address the cloning-photocopying question, while only five of the students in the control class used concepts identified as being in the higher-order cluster. Chi-square analysis of the difference between the two groups in terms of using higher-order concepts was significant, $\chi^2(2) = 7.17, p < .05$. The language used by the students in answering this question was also noted as important. Students in the experimental class tended to use more scientific terminology and tended not to use the teacher's language to answer the question. By contrast, students in the control class had more responses that were shorter in length, less reflective, and used the teacher's definitions of relevant content to answer the questions. These results may be reflective of the difference in emphasis for students in the experimental class, who were not given teacher-authorized definitions of concept terms but were expected to have generated these through their discussion, research, and letter-writing task. As such, they were willing to use their own language and developed more diverse concepts in their answers on the test.

When experimental students were interviewed about their initial reaction upon reading the cloning question, two of the five students thought the question was *stupid*. However, both these students indicated that they were able to answer the question. One student said *I was surprised that I knew so much*. The other student indicated that she was initially confused about the comparison but found it interesting. She further added that she *would like to have taken the question home to do because [I] could have included a lot more if I had more time to formulate ideas*. Another student stated that the cloning question was *easier than anything else on the test*. The five control students were interviewed about the analogy question. Two said the question was *all right*, with one of them indicating that she wrote *a fair bit because [I] knew a lot about cloning from [my] Psychology [course]*. One other student indicated that she had also previously completed an assignment on cloning and found the question easy. However, of the other two students, one *didn't really understand the question* and the other gave only a brief answer.

In undertaking the construction of a one-page review sheet, the students in each class appeared to adopt different strategies. The control students interviewed indicated that they focused on glancing through the textbook or their class notes and tried to use their own words. For example, one student indicated that he *kind of [used] my own words; different from the textbook; wrote the way I thought, the way I interpreted it.* Experimental students interviewed were more prepared to use color coding to identify important points and attempted to link important words with lines. Of the five students interviewed from the experimental class, two indicated that they were prepared to *select things that I thought would be on the test*, although both indicated that they had not guessed exactly what would be on the test.

6.2 Case Study 2

Descriptive results for the lower-level items and higher-level items are provided in Table 3. T-test analyses of the differences indicated a marginal difference in scores on the lower-level items ($t = 2.87$, $p < .01$) and a significant difference on the higher-level items ($t = 4.98$, $p < .001$) between the experimental group and the control group.

Table 3. Case 2 descriptive statistics (mean, standard deviation) for the lower-level and high-level test questions.

Class	Lower-level Items (max=82)	Higher-level Item (max=8)
Experimental (n=25)	55.7 (9.9)	6.4 (1.5)
Control (n=27)	44.6 (16.6)	3.3 (2.8)

These results indicate that using sequential writing tasks as a learning tool appears to be of significant value in the learning process for this science topic. Students who experienced SWH and letter writing appeared able to answer both the lower-level and higher-level questions better than students who did not experience any unusual writing tasks. Unfortunately, the experimental and control group differed in performance in other content units in the class. Thus, an analysis of covariance (AN-COVA) was conducted to more conservatively assess the effect of writing to learn independent of pre-existing difference. Group (experimental vs. control) was the independent variable while scores on a common geology examination given earlier in the school year served as the covariant. After removing the effects of the previous science performance on the current test results, the writing-to-learn group performed significantly better on the higher-level analogy question than the control group, F (1, 41) = 15.85, $p < .001$, but the difference between the two groups on the lower-level items was not significant, F (1, 41) = 4.85, $p = .032$. This pattern of results adds confidence to the conclusion that use of sequential writing-to-learn tasks facilitates students' learning of higher-level light concepts without impeding the learning of lower-level concepts.

On completion of the unit, twelfe experimental students were interviewed to examine their understanding of the various writing tasks. The students interviewed had completed all the writing tasks, the five SWH templates, the letter, and the test. Analysis of the interviews centered on examining students' understandings of the writing tasks, including any perceived difference in the tasks and the value of using writing as a learning tool, that is, whether students began to understand metacognitive advantages of using writing-to-learn strategies. Assertions from the interview are expressed in **bold type**, supportive quotes are expressed in *script type*, and the authors' elaboration is expressed in normal type.

Girls were better able than boys to articulate the value of using the SWH templates in constructing their own understandings. Girls tended to be more focused on their own knowledge construction and valued what they constructed for themselves, whereas the boys were more focused on ensuring that they just reported what happened. This was particularly evident when addressing the claims and evidence section of the SWH template. For example:

> *J (high-achieving girl):* When you got to the evidence you might think this isn't a claim at all and if you had to write down why it was then maybe your claim changed because you were reflecting on what you had done and then you realized that this is not the claim that we're saying. We've got evidence for one thing and claiming for another thing, so you might change it.

> *A (low-achieving girl):* Good ... pretty good idea with the claims because then you go and see what you thought about what you'd just done. I think *[when]* doing the claims it was easier to put an end result with what happened.

> *B (high-achieving boy):* The evidence was a bit harder because it was really the same thing by prac or by your own knowledge. It wasn't hard because once you did something and you knew what happened you just wrote it down.

When asked if there was any need to change their answers on their templates when they were given the opportunity to use textbooks to reflect on what they had written, all the students treated the textbook as the authority. In particular, the boys did not see the need to reflect on what they had written because it was the *same as the textbook*.

Students discovered that they had to change the style and focus of writing when they moved from the SWH to the letter. Students talked about having to change their writing from the normal complex writing for the teacher to make it simpler for peers in America, illustrating the importance of considering the audience, for example:

> *J (high-achieving girl):* Yes, to try to tell someone else what you had been doing, what you have learnt and about the new process in which you had done it, it really got you thinking about what you had actually learnt and it made you think about it more, whereas if you had just done it from a textbook as normal, you sort of say, Oh well I've done that now it's out of the way. This way you had to think about it and you had to tell someone else who knew nothing about what you've been doing, you had to justify what you've been saying in your letter and you had to make sure that they would understand it also changing it to make it simpler so anyone can understand it. That way you can translate it sort of, you can make sure that you've really learnt it, because you can change it to suit you.

> *C (high-achieving girl):* Yes I thought you had to use simple language so that they'd know what you were talking about, so they could understand as well. It just made it easier for them to understand, you just have to use simple language.

J (low-achieving boy): It is harder to write for another person than a teacher because it's another person your age and you have to speak their way, whereas the teacher will accept any sort of words.

M (average-achieving boy): It's hard because teachers know exactly what you're talking about whereas the students will not know what you're talking about on the topic.

Students discovered that they needed to take into account the audience's needs in writing about science and they perceived this to be a valuable task. The need to explain science ideas in language appropriate to the target audience was recognized as being necessary but difficult.

D (averaging-achieving girl): Yes, because otherwise they wouldn't be able to understand it sort of. Like when I first started the topic I didn't know what all the words were. Like I didn't know non-transparent. It was hard to change the harder science words into normal words. Like it's hard to describe transparent objects and that. It's easier just to say non-transparent.

However, not everyone believed that the letter writing activity was a more difficult task than normal writing for the teacher.

T (average-achieving girl): I write things down, like you might do a summary of an experiment, first you have to think about your ideas simply and then you have to make it sound better, you have to make it sound more mature. *When asked about whether the letter was more difficult, she responded:* No I don't think so because you only really had to do one step, you didn't have to make it more complicated.

Students' metacognitive awareness begins with their ability to reflect on the value of writing and its learning advantages. Some of the students began to describe the value for them in completing the writing tasks in comparison to traditional copying and rote memorization tasks.

J (average-achieving girl): You're the person whose thinking about what should be eliminated and what should stay. When you're copying off the blackboard you tend to just write it, you don't even tend to read it. It was interactive, everyone was together and everyone had their own opinions and you had to work with a team as well as the science and writing down, you didn't have to worry if the words were right, as long as you and your group knew what you meant. Then later on when you got to the claims you could word it correctly. ... It was difficult but again as we went on we were getting the hang of it because you had to adjust from something so different from the textbook, the writing it down and being told what's right and what's wrong, to your own ideas and having to justify your own ideas.

A (low-achieving girl): I think it goes through your brain more because with the book it has sort of the answers in the book and you've just got to pick out the bits that apply to the question. Whereas with this you are actually thinking on your own account what you've done and you have to think a bit harder, but after you've thought it out and stuff it comes together. ... Probably the test was a lot easier to understand too because I think if we'd just done the answers out of the book we'd be trying to think back to what we'd actually read. A lot of people write down the answers and they don't really think about what they've just written because it's just in the book there for them.

The collective comments from all the interviewed students in the experimental group support the view that the sequential writing tasks were beginning to promote students' understanding of the value of these tasks to learning in science.

7   DISCUSSION

In discussing the results, the authors would point out that the practical nature of the situation constrained the implementation of an ideal research design. These constraints required that we assign whole classes to the treatment and control conditions. The data were analysed however as if students were randomly assigned to the treatment. For this reason some degree of caution should be exercised in interpreting the results. While this analysis may not be sufficiently conservative several of the results attained a level of significance of $p < .001$, indicating that the results may be robust given a more conservative test. The results of the two case studies indicate that there are various benefits from using writing-to-learn strategies within science classrooms. These benefits not only address the actual results on science achievement but also focus on the metacognitive understandings that students develop when completing the writing tasks.

When examining the relative student performance on the higher-order test question in each of the case studies, it can be seen that there is clearly better performance achieved by students who participated in the writing-to-learn treatment. Even though in Case Study 1 there were no significant differences between the groups on the lower-level test results and the results on the higher-level test question, there was a significant difference in the type of conceptual clusters used to answer the analogy question. Similarly, in Case Study 2, there was no significant difference ($p < .05$) for the lower-level items; but there was a significant difference between the treatment and control group when answering the higher-level test question.

Clearly there were differences between the two case studies in terms of the number of different writing experiences with which the students were engaged. In Case Study 1, the students only engaged in one writing task, while in Case Study 2 the students engaged in sequential writing tasks designed to (a) focus their attention on claims, evidence, and warrants and (b) require them to transform observations into inferences, claims, and explanations. While results from Case Study 1 indicate no significant difference in performance on the analogy test question, in Case Study 2 there was a significant difference for the higher-level question as predicted. This raises the issue of whether there is a necessary cumulative beneficial effect when using writing-to-learn strategies within or across topics and the further issue of which sequence of writing tasks within and across topics may be most beneficial in developing students' scientific concept knowledge. As already indicated in this chapter, the broad issue of effective writing task design is further complicated by the requirement that such tasks should also promote enhanced students' scientific literacy, entailing knowledge of scientific inquiry, epistemology, reasoning, and habits of mind as well as technical communication abilities. Clearly this represents an ambitious and exacting set of requirements for task design or sequence, and the learning effects reported in this study have been influenced by the modest scale and nature of the tasks undertaken. While it is not be possible to claim that this study demonstrates that all the experimental group students have developed knowledge transforming capacities when they write, the reported comments indicate that some students have become more reflective about their writing practices, and more aware of how their writing can serve their learning. For students to achieve all the dimensions of science literacy proposed at the start of this chapter will require a far more extended program of writing experiences and reflection.

However, this study suggests that a sequence of writing tasks can enable students to review and revise their understandings without loss of interest in the topic through perceived repetition, and that the sequential tasks can promote new links between concepts to be constructed thus enhancing meaningful understanding and promoting knowledge transformation. These links represent opportunities for students to negotiate and strengthen understandings of concepts across the discourses of science and the broader society – not as a one-way process but rather as necessary border crossings implied in contemporary understanding of science literacy (Rowell, 1997). The requirement that students inform a non-expert reader about the nature of light through writing a letter is a practical example of the way that writing to learn in science can engage with communicative issues entailed in new understandings of science literacy. This study also indicates that an effective sequence of writing tasks in science will need to serve a diversity of functions and give explicit recognition and strategies to engage each dimension of science literacy. As already suggested, these tasks will need to go beyond the usual focus on student concept acquisition to a greater emphasis on understanding and communicating through various kinds of texts what counts as persuasive scientific reasoning and its justification to diverse audiences. In this way writing for learning in science can genuinely engage with expanding students' understandings of the nature of science and the nature of science literacy.

This study also indicates that attempts to use writing activities in school science to enhance students' understanding of science literacy face considerable challenges. These include students' current understandings of the nature and reasoning demands of science, implementation and teaching issues, and the question of effective design of tasks. Although the writing tasks in the study led to significant results for Case Study 2, the quality of reasoning in written products often failed to meet the researchers' expectations. For example, the SWH was intended to support students' construction and understanding of what counts as adequate explanation in laboratory work; and most students were able to state a claim from a practical activity. However, many students had difficulty constructing a written explanation in terms of evidence for the claim. They were clearly unfamiliar with the inductive, deductive, and hypothetico-deductive requirements in science and needed considerable teacher scaffolding to understand the purpose and demands of the SWH. The development of students' understanding of the nature of plausible reasoning in science will require extended opportunities to construct carefully framed explanations. In the letter-writing task, only two students were able to incorporate all four light concepts addressed in the laboratory work. Various factors may have contributed to this outcome, including student unfamiliarity with this kind of task in science, confusion about the task requirements, problems in negotiating the topic focus or concept ex-

plication, or limited concept knowledge. Thus, while all students completed the letter-writing task, not all were able to produce the quality in terms of explicit elaboration of the science concepts involved. Students need very explicit teacher guidance
in negotiating task demands, even if as indicated by some student comments, they
appreciate the value of reformulating their knowledge for different readerships in
this way. However, given these outcomes, the results on the analogy test question
demonstrated a significant difference. While the sample sizes were small, the results
suggest that even though students are unable to complete all elements of the writing
tasks to the desired level, there are benefits in undertaking the tasks. While initial
learning gains may be smaller than expected and the demands on students in writing
to develop science literacy should not be underestimated, there are some positive
outcomes in terms of student performance on higher-level test items.

The study also confirms many of the researchers' assumptions about, and raises
other related issues concerning, effective writing task design and task sequence for
learning about science concepts and about the nature of science and science discourse. An effective task sequence requires students to transform their knowledge
through addressing content and rhetorical issues as they reword texts to meet altered
writing purposes, address generic and discursive demands, and consider audience
needs. No single sequence of tasks on a topic is likely to meet all these criteria, but
particular tasks and task instruction can focus explicitly on one or more of these issues as part of the process of promoting students' science literacy (Tucknott & Yore,
1999). Science literacy ultimately implies that students should see themselves as
writers in and of science, who understand the premises and bases of both scientific
discourse and popular discourse about science. This perspective suggests that students will need to write in a diverse range of genres for varied readerships and purposes if science literacy is to be achieved. While there has been recurrent argument
about which genres and genre knowledge should take precedence in routine science
lessons (Halliday & Martin, 1993; Hildebrand, 1998; Keys, 1999; Yore, Hand &
Prain, 1999), there is clearly a case for students to practice a diverse range of genres
as the basis of science literacy.

One of the most powerful positive points to arise from the case studies was the
evidence of student metacognitive understanding of their own learning processes in
science arising from engagement with these writing tasks. While previous studies
(Prain & Hand, 1999) indicated that students were able to develop some metacognitive understandings of how and why to tackle these tasks, this was the first time that
students were able to clearly articulate the value of different writing tasks in relation
to their own learning. The students recognized that the need to switch from the 'authorized' science vocabulary of their teacher and textbooks to the everyday language
and metaphors for their peers improved their understanding of the science concepts.
The students also articulated the strategies needed to make this topic meaningful to
their audience of peers. While students were able to explain the benefits gained in
having to switch between different writing tasks, they varied in their conception of
the degree of difficulty involved in switching between tasks. Students who were
more responsive to the audience in terms of the letter-writing activity tended to recognize that, while the task appeared to be simple, there was much thinking required
to translate science words and concepts into language appropriate to the target audi-

ence. The change in audience from the teacher to peers was crucial in encouraging the students to think more carefully about the language and concepts they were using and their responsibilities to the readers. They all indicated that writing for the teacher enabled them to leave some points implicit or unelaborated because of their teacher's expertise. However, in writing for peers, ideas and assumptions had to be made explicit and justified. Their choice of words needed to be more precise or elaborated, and this meant a deeper understanding of the concepts was required. This knowledge transformation activity promotes a much greater awareness of the links between individual concepts and a conceptual network for the students and among the technical vocabulary of science, everyday language, and metaphors to explain concepts. Student comments indicated that they recognized that the tasks made increased demands on their conceptual understandings and communication abilities, but these are exactly the goals and benefits of using writing-to-learn strategies in science classrooms.

There are also several implications arising from this study in terms of designing, implementing, and evaluating writing tasks for science learning. First, the study indicates that students will need very explicit support in understanding what functions writing can serve in science and which precise strategies are needed to achieve these purposes. The enlarged conception of science literacy advocated makes new ambitious demands on what teachers are expected to know and students are expected to learn about the nature of science and scientific reasoning through writing in science. While this study has highlighted some of the considerable challenges in devising and implementing effective writing tasks, it is equally clear that these issues need to be addressed if learning science through writing is going to lead to the gains claimed by its many advocates.

8   CONCLUSION

The results from this study indicate there are benefits in using writing-to-learn strategies in the science classroom. These benefits not only apply to performance on higher-order test questions but also to students' metacognitive awareness of the writing process and the value of writing for enhancing learning. While this study did not seek to test the extent to which the writing tasks altered the students' self-conception as writers in and of science, this aspect also represents a possible gain from writing tasks that encourage students to cross discursive boundaries in representing their scientific knowledge. The results of this study provide evidence that writing-to-learn strategies can have beneficial effects in promoting knowledge transformation for students and hence deeper learning.

ACKNOWLEDGEMENTS

The authors wish express their general thanks to colleagues and graduate students who have contributed creative insights, corrective criticism, and supportive efforts. A special and specific recognition is given Carolyn W. Keys, University of Georgia, for her contributions to the conception of the case studies and the science writing heuristic.

NOTE TAKING AND ESSAY WRITING

VIRPI SLOTTE & KIRSTI LONKA

University of Helsinki, Finland

Abstract. This chapter concentrates on the relationship between the quality of note taking during writing and subsequent outcomes – as measured by the content and quality of essay-type answers. During their research project the authors studied the notes of more than 1200 students in order to answer the questions: What kinds of note taking activities are related to sensible and well-written answers in a difficult examination? How note taking can serve more effectively writing as a learning tool? The results demonstrated that writing summary notes has an effect on both learning the content knowledge and on the linguistic features of the resulting essays. Yet, several procedural aspects of writing play crucial roles in the learning process. Spontaneous note taking affects learning and writing operations utilising distinct types of mental representations. This depends on the type of notes taken, the nature of the writing tasks, and the writing conditions – such as notes-present or notes-absent. Overall, these results raise the need to pay more attention to the ability to write notes in one's own words, argue purposefully and to monitor the coherence and accuracy of meaning. These skills are especially important in learning by writing.

1   INTRODUCTION

How to study effectively? How to take notes as an authentic writing act, for real purposes, to make a test better? How to take notes so that assist to write good essays? These are questions that puzzle most students, especially in secondary and tertiary education.

If we want to carry out research that will help students develop their study skills, we must look at complex situations and, if possible, use appropriately motivated participants. We need to look at reading, note taking and essay writing in real situations which are, at the same time, reasonably well controlled. Studies on instructional interventions are valuable, and may provide important theoretical and practical insights (*e.g.*, Brown & Palincsar, 1989) but rigorous studies are not easy to conduct, and there is always a trade-off: the more naturalistic the settings, the more difficult it is to maintain control over numerous variables (Shayer, 1994).

Investigations of spontaneous study activities have important practical implications because they may have a stronger effect on learning than do activities that are experimentally induced (*e.g.*, Kardash & Amlund, 1991). The methods of note tak-

V. Slotte, & K. Lonka (2001). Note taking and essay writing. In: G. Rijlaarsdam (Series Ed.) & P. Tynjälä, L. Mason & K. Lonka (Volume Eds), *Studies in Writing, Volume 7, Writing as a Learning tool: Integrating Theory and Practice,* 131 – 143.© 2001 Kluwer Academic Publishers. Printed in the Netherlands.

ing that people use when they study for an examination may be quite different from those adopted in a psychological experiment. Well-controlled experimental situations are usually new for the participants, and normal ways of studying may fail precisely because the material lacks those redundancies on which habits usually rely (van Dijk & Kintsch, 1983). Again, we cannot be sure that the participants in experimental situations are really trying their best (Lonka, 1997; Slotte, 1999). Therefore, we need to test the real learning of real material in real situations (Mayer, 1992).

Finnish university entrance examinations have provided us with ideal settings for this kind of research. The candidates are highly motivated, and the situation is both ecologically valid and reasonably well controlled. Our research project and the so-called Learning-From-Text test (LFT) were developed for entrance examinations to Finnish medical schools (Lonka, Lindblom-Ylänne, & Maury, 1994; Lindblom-Ylänne, Lonka, & Leskinen, 1996; Lahtinen, Lonka, & Lindblom-Ylänne, 1997; Slotte & Lonka, 1999). More recently, we have applied similar ideas to the entrance exams for health-care studies (Slotte & Lonka, 1998, 1999). The purpose of our LFT is to measure deep-level text comprehension skills. It, therefore, widens the scope of traditional entry examinations, which typically measure factual scientific knowledge. The project has the following goals:

1) To develop new ways for assessing cognitive skills of learning from complex texts, namely the LFT based on van Dijk and Kintsch's (1983) model of strategic discourse processing;

2) to study the ways students learn the complex materials, especially the use of spontaneous study strategies and their effects on learning;

3) to conduct follow-up studies in order to see how the LFT predicts success in medical school.

In this chapter we concentrate on the relationship between the quality of note taking during writing and subsequent outcomes – as measured by the content and quality of essay-type answers. During our research project we have studied the notes of more than 1200 students in order to answer the questions: What kinds of note taking activities are related to sensible and well-written answers in a difficult examination? How note taking can serve more effectively writing as a learning tool?

2   NOTE TAKING AND LEARNING: THE THEORETICAL BACKGROUND

Considerable evidence has been presented both for (and some against) the effectiveness of note taking in lectures and from textbooks in terms of the amount recalled in subsequent tests (e.g., Hartley & Davies, 1978; Kiewra, 1988, Kiewra et al., 1991; Bligh, 1998; Wade & Trathen, 1989). The differences may have resulted from the behavioural approach used in many of these studies which aimed to determine the effects of an observable independent measure on an observable dependent measure in an attempt to find out 'how much is learned' (Mayer, 1984).

Written notes seem to have various functions, such as encoding and external storage, and different note taking techniques vary in terms of how much generative effort is included (Kiewra et al., 1991; Lonka, Lindblom-Ylänne, & Maury, 1994).

Generative processing refers to the degree to which the text material to be learned is internally connected to the learner's prior knowledge (Peper & Mayer, 1986). Obviously, the quality and content of notes has an effect on the learning outcome. Note taking may be a generative writing activity to enhance learning, but it may also include mere verbatim copying.

Concept mapping refers to a graphic representation of a text. Usually, concept maps support the retention of main ideas (Rewey, Dansereau, & Peel, 1991), promote meaningful learning (Novak & Gowin, 1984; Okebukola & Jegede, 1988) or enhance summarisation and problem-solving skills (Abbott & Hughes, 1986). Concept mapping may be especially effective in integrating new information with previous knowledge (Mayer, 1984).

Underlining sometimes seems helpful; but in many cases it makes no difference at all, or it may even hold back learning (Hartley, Bartlett, & Branthwaite, 1980; Grabe & Holm, 1992). There is some suggestion that underlining is more effective when difficult texts are involved (Caverly & Orlando, 1991).

Thus the nature of the thought processes that mediate between study activities and learning outcomes is not yet fully understood. It is possible that different kinds of note taking activities may serve different cognitive functions on different occasions (Lonka, 1997; Slotte 1999). Moreover, little is known of those note-taking practices that enhance writing-as-learning, nor is it clear how they affect deep-level learning from text (Kintsch, 1986).

Within the cognitive framework, the active construction of mental representation is the central mediating activity between the learning process and its outcome (*e.g.*, Kintsch & Kintsch, 1996; Lonka, 1997; Mayer, 1984, 1992). And, as in qualitative research, the quality and richness of mental representation is considered more crucial than the mere quantity of knowledge. The manner in which knowledge is represented is thought to determine understanding and to influence problem solving. The active transformation of knowledge – rather than its reproduction – is thought to lead to a deep-level mental representation (Bereiter & Scardamalia, 1987; Chi, Glaser, & Farr, 1988; Glaser & Bassok, 1989; Mannes & Kintsch, 1987).

In our research, our examination candidates use note-taking strategies spontaneously, and they construct all conceptual aids (such as notes, concept maps and underlining) themselves (Lonka, 1997; Slotte, 1999). The qualitative aspects of the learning outcomes are taken into account by comparing subjects' success in various essay-writing tasks that pose qualitatively different demands. The approach to discourse processing is holistic (*e.g.*, Kintsch, 1986; Mandl & Schnotz, 1987). This means that the comprehension process is assumed to be less dependent on the text and more dependent on the construction of a mental model of the phenomenon described in the text.

A holistic, constructively oriented analysis of study strategies, writing, mental representations, and learning outcomes may prove helpful in understanding the process of learning from text. Van Dijk and Kintsch's (1983) model of strategic discourse processing offers conceptual tools for the task, because the model sets up connections between constructivist activities in encoding and the quality of the learning outcomes. The model differentiates between three forms of mental representation that may be constructed while learning from text:

1)   *a surface memory* for actual words and phrases;
2)   *a text base*, in which a coherent representation of the text is formed;
3)   *a situation model*, in which the text content is integrated into the compre-
       hender's knowledge system.

The text base reflects the coherent relations between the propositions in the text and their organisation, whereas the situation model is a mental representation of the situation described by the text. The text base and situation models are not independent of each other, but each has its own characteristics. Kintsch (1986) sees a dichotomy between the two forms of representation, such that remembering or understanding the text depends on the text base, whereas learning from text depends more on the situation model. In an important sense, viewing reading comprehension as memory construction thus provides a framework for taking the quality of the learning into account. This is summarised in Figure 1.

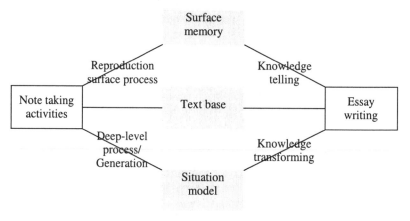

Marton & Säljö, 1976;   Van Dijk & Kintsch, 1983;   Bereiter & Scardamalia
Mayer, 1992; Entwistle &   Lonka *et al.*,1994; Schnotz   1987; Slotte & Lonka 1998.
Waterson, 1988.   1996; Sternberg, 1998.

Figure 1. Theoretical background for note taking and learning from text (Slotte, 1999).

Surface representation may be thought of as related to surface-level processing (Craik & Lockhart, 1972) or to the surface way of approach (Marton & Säljö, 1976, 1984), whereas the text base and the situation model require more deep-level processing. It seems likely that forming a situation model requires more constructive processing and knowledge transforming than does forming a text base (Bereiter & Scardamalia, 1987; Kintsch & Kinstsch, 1996), whereas a coherent representation of a text is sufficient to support telling the text information as such. Situational understanding is the only way to knowledge that will be easily accessed and beneficial later.

However, it should be noted that the learning of details is not necessarily based on surface memory (Lonka, Lindblom-Ylänne, & Maury, 1994). Paying selective attention to details may be a highly meaningful activity. Morris, Bransford, and

Franks (1977) point out that even aspects of the learned material that look superficial may be important, relative to the knowledge possessed by the readers. Again, van Dijk and Kintsch (1983) have shown that the level of the semantic unit in the text base hierarchy determines the likelihood of its recall, and main themes or central ideas are thus easier to learn than are subordinate details. In a recent study, noting information appeared to have little effect on the recall of that information once effects due to the importance of the information were statistically removed (Wade & Trathen, 1989). Previous research also shows that recalling a detail is best enhanced with the help of a meaningful framework or by elaboration (Craik & Lockhart, 1972; Marton & Säljö, 1976). A solid text base offers a frame for recalling meaningful details (van Dijk & Kintsch, 1983), whereas integrating information with prior knowledge may serve to hinder the retention of facts, since the details are changed by the learner (Mayer, 1984).

Mannes and Kintsch (1987) provided empirical evidence to suggest that different test-taking performances depend on different kinds of memory representations. In their experiment students studied an outline providing relevant background knowledge before reading an experimental text. This outline was organised either consistently or inconsistently in relation to the propositional structure of the text. Students with the consistent-outline performed better than students with the inconsistent-outline on cued-recall and recognition tests; they wrote summaries more closely following textual order, and they produced a smaller number of intrusions from the outline material. However, the inconsistent-outline condition did not lead to poorer performance overall. Students in this condition showed superior performance on inference verification tasks as well as on difficult, creative problem-solving tests that required deeper understanding of the material.

Mannes and Kintsch's (1987) study was conducted experimentally, and note-taking activity was not spontaneous. We wanted to find out whether it would be possible to obtain parallel results in more naturalistic settings (Lonka, Lindblom-Ylänne, & Maury, 1994). Therefore, we looked at spontaneous note taking activities in university entrance-exams, especially, using our Learning-From-Text (LFT) test. This test was originally designed by Kirsti Lonka and Sari Lindblom-Ylänne in cooperation with Professor Jaakko Perheentupa and the Faculty of Medicine at the University of Helsinki. Later, we studied similar situations in other medical schools. We have also collected data from health-care students.

3   WHAT IS THE LEARNING-FROM-TEXT TEST?

The Learning-From-Text test (LFT) was originally designed to complement three multiple-choice science tests in biology, chemistry, and physics. Unlike the multiple-choice tests, the LFT tasks were intended to measure the deep-level text comprehension and essay-writing skills of the applicants. The cognitive demands of the LFT have been reported in more details by Lonka *et al.* (1994). The basic idea is that participants read a demanding and a lengthy text in order to answer subsequent essay-type tasks on it. The text to be read is different every year and its content varies from philosophy to statistics and probability theory. The Faculty demands that the content is not known beforehand, so that the applicants cannot prepare themselves for it. As they are reading, the applicants are allowed to make notes on either the text or an attached blank sheet of paper. In most test situations, all of these materials are then collected in and the candidates carry out essay-type tasks without the texts or their notes.

The general design principles of the essay-writing tasks are based on van Dijk and Kintsch's model of strategic discourse processing. One task is usually designed to measure detailed learning, such as defining some concepts from the text. The second task calls not only remembering the text information but also synthesising or pulling together the essentials of the text, designed to measure the formation of a coherent text base. The participants are also required to evaluate critically the text content on the basis of their general knowledge. These tasks are intended to measure the ability to go 'beyond' the text, in other words to formulate a situation model.

Participants are always aware at the beginning of the test session that they given three qualitatively different types of questions. They are also told whether they can use or not their notes during answering the questions. In all, we have analysed the text materials and the notes of 1200 students in terms of their underlining, note taking, and concept mapping on the text paper and on (blank) separate sheets.

Lonka, Lindblom-Ylänne, and Maury (1994) analysed the spontaneous study strategies that applicants used while learning from a text in an entrance examination at the University of Helsinki's medical school. They found that central ideas of the text were learned regardless of overt strategy use, whereas minor details were only learned if they were included in the written notes. Underlining was related to success in a task that required synthesis of the text, whereas concept mapping was related to success in tasks calling for critical review of the materials. However, Lonka *et al.* (1994) did not examine the quality of written notes: they only looked at how many words were written and which concepts were included. Would it make a difference if the notes were written verbatim or were elaborated in the students' own words?

4   THE QUALITY OF WRITTEN NOTES AND CONTENT LEARNING

Lahtinen, Lonka, and Lindblom-Ylänne (1997) distinguished more clearly between different kinds of written notes. They found that half of all participants spontaneously applied some kind of note taking activities during text reading. Slightly more of them wrote verbatim notes following the text order than summarised the text content in their own words. However, the number of students who wrote either verbatim or summary notes was clearly higher among those reading a philosophical text than among those reading a statistics one. Similarly, the number of subjects who drew concept maps while reading a philosophical text was 22%, whereas the corresponding proportion while reading a statistics text was only 7%. Interestingly, underlining was more common among those who read a statistics text than among those who read philosophical text (Lonka, Lahtinen, & Lindblom-Ylänne, 1996).

It is possible that the statistics text required that the main concepts and definitions be appropriately grasped before they could be fully integrated into the readers' knowledge structure, and that this was not necessarily the case with the philosophical one. A knowledge domain of philosophy might instead steer readers towards reasoning at a more general level, so that it is possible to make good use of life experiences (Slotte, 1999). Van Meter *et al.* (1994) presented similar data supporting the idea that different types of materials presented in class may result in different types of notes.

With regard to content learning, it appeared that summarising or concept mapping were superior to verbatim note taking and underlining, which in turn, were superior to reading only (Lahtinen *et al.*, 1997). Both summarising in notes and concept mapping require forming internal connections between idea units and current knowledge. This involves generative processing during writing activity that is thought to determine directly the outcome of learning.

Non-generative activities, on the other hand, aim directly at the reproduction of a text, and include verbatim copying, underlining and simply reading already-generated material (Kiewra *et al.*, 1991). Such study processes may, however, result in forming good enough text bases that enable the reproduction of content knowledge. Non-generative writing help then to reconstruct the text-to-be understood at one hand, and provide memory cues for later use.

Another important question to consider is whether the quality of concept maps plays as important a role as that of note taking. To answer this question, we looked more closely to see whether or not it made any difference if the concept maps were simple or complex. It appeared that students who made more complex and extensive concept maps outperformed those whose maps were less accurate (Slotte & Lonka, 1999). According to these results, it seems likely that the activity of transforming linear text into two-dimensional graphic form requires more cognitive effort in selecting, organising and integrating the main ideas into a compact and efficient representation of the information (Mayer, 1992; Slotte, 1999).

Yet, merely including the relevant concepts of the text in a concept map proved to have only some advantage in defining and explaining those concepts. Moreover, mapping relevant concepts had little effect in inferential reasoning and the application of scientific concepts, whereas omitting the relevant concepts from the maps was related to the inability to apply them. These results were interpreted on the basis of Ausubel's (1968) theoretical model, according to which new concept meanings are not learned in isolation but acquired through assimilation into propositional frameworks (see also Novak, 1990).

5   QUALITY OF WRITTEN EXPRESSION

While our research showed that note taking plays a strong role in content learning (Lonka *et al.*, 1994; Slotte & Lonka, 1999), it was not as clear what that role might be with respect to writing performance. Although it is assumed that summarised and paraphrased notes could act as a first draft, and thus might result in greater coherent and cohesion in essay writing, there is little empirical research to support this contention.

The premise that writing restructures knowledge is a cornerstone in the argument for using writing to facilitate learning (*e.g.*, Greene & Ackerman, 1995). This requires that writing is seen as a thinking tool in the processes of verbalising, constructing and communicating (Björk & Räisänen, 1996; Bereiter & Scardamalia, 1987; Slotte & Lonka, 1998). Writing involves the visualisation of thinking; writers actually see their thoughts on the paper (Olson, 1994). Writing notes in one's own words thus provides an easier and more effective aid for transforming the ideas in a clear and logical manner. The following fragments illustrate spontaneously written notes with reasonable clarity.

> The matter concerned in growth and development basically means that we can get free from the grasp of imagination. The first step in this process is being able to distinguish between imagination and reason. Through efforts and close attention we can achieve the more complete control of rationality. However, the ultimate goal is to work towards the balance of mind which requires self-directed sense.

> Education is dependent on educator's intuition and his or her mental maturity. There are no generally accepted concepts of education → wide concept that depends on one's attitude to life, ideology and knowledge of human nature. Skilful educator is able to direct others to construct themselves to the highest possible level of knowledge. This means that one has to extend her point of view to cover the whole universe → one begins to take much trouble also with others.

The coherent and cohesion notes concentrate on essential text information with some degree of writer's own ideas generated. They often contain arrows to shorten the sentences and logically relate the idea units to a meaningful whole. The author of these kinds of notes also compares the phenomena described in the text to her previous knowledge in order to show similarities and dissimilarities. This does not happen in less cohesion and coherence notes; they are mostly restricted to repeat the text information as such. The following fragments exemplify notes with list of fact copied from the text without any clarification.

- to achieve the completeness → the goal of life

- conatus: efforts that turn out within each individual

-

3 levels: I, II, III → effort to achieve the level III

- strength of life! activity! joy!

The model of completeness → the goal of life

the level of micro and macro
The level of knowledge 1. imagination
-'-   2. one step to liberation
-'-   3. all-inclusive

Conatus effort to maintain own existence, hate/love.

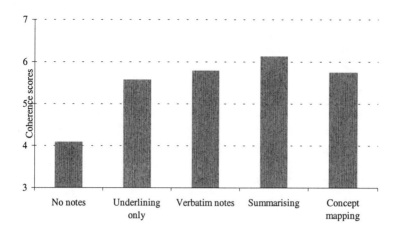

Figure 2. The impact of different note taking activity on the coherence of essay writing.

In writing, novices tend to list information from their memory on paper with minimum transformation, whereas experts tend to apply the so-called knowledge transformation strategy, involving dialectical interaction processes between domain knowledge and the text being written (Bereiter & Scardamalia, 1987; Hildyard, 1996). It is clear that students who have included mostly unessential text information in their notes are more likely to have difficulties in writing coherently. However, expert writers can, at least to some extent, compensate for their lack of clarity in notes by transforming the relationships among the ideas during a written task. Since the transforming process enables learners to use their prior knowledge through inference, it might also enhance learning from text (van Dijk & Kintsch, 1983). A knowledge-based model used by non-expert writers, on the other hand, minimises the need for the planning, construction and problem solving, but it also misses out on the cognitive benefits of writing (Scardamalia & Bereiter, 1991).

In investigating how note taking during lectures influenced writing processes, Benton, Kiewra, Whitfill, and Dennison (1993) found a clear relationship. They showed that the quality and quantity of notes taken produced lengthier, more cohesive and more coherent compare-and-contrast essays. There was, however, no advantage in this relationship unless the notes were later referred to during the essay writing. Our findings on text comprehension were, however, somewhat different from those of lecture listening. (Lahtinen *et al.*, 1997). We found that any type of note taking activity proved superior to not writing notes when coherence was the criterion. This is illustrated in Figure 2.

Two examples of answers below illustrate the notes of different coherence. The scoring method that was used is based on Benton *et al.* (1993) and Wright and Rosenberg (1993). The first one shows a fragment of highly coherent and cohesion answer, whereas the second one exemplifies an answer with complete lack of cohesion and coherence.

> ... In my opinion X's educational views are extremely reasonable, although the writer strongly emphasises the meaning of the 'knowledge' and 'intelligence'. On the other hand, X's views by and large corresponds those of educational psychological at present, X only expresses it in different words. That is, educational psychology also deals with stimulating and raising self-esteem and self-confident ...

> According to X, education affects the whole society. The principal rule is to love the others, only then can we succeed. Therefore, the negative aspects should not be taken into consideration in education, because it only results hostile and bitterness. One's own inner desire is the principal rule of mutual education, which results in pleasure ...

In the latter example, the only connective word 'therefore', does not logically relate the sentences, nor does the content generally concentrate on essential information. Although the writer in some extent expresses her own opinion they remain unrelated without any links to the text information. In contrast, the author in the former text fragment compares the phenomena described in the text to her previous knowledge in order to show similarities and dissimilarities. This kind of argumentative way of writing also continues in the rest of the answer, not quoted here.

No big differences in quality of written expression were found between those who made summary notes or concept maps, and those who copied the text word for word (Lahtinen *et al.*, 1997). These results are similar to those of Benton *et al.* (1993). They elegantly demonstrated that matrix notetakers (viz., notes recorded within the intersecting cells of the matrix) generated cohesive ties as often as conventional notetakers in essay writing. Otherwise, the reason for no benefit of note taking during lecture presumably lies in the different effects of taking notes while reading and while listening to a lecture. While noting from text allows dialectical processes in reading and writing, subjects who take notes during lectures must simultaneously listen, select important ideas and record their notes. Lecture note taking can therefore decrease the degree to which the learner is able actively to generate ideas and organise them into a coherent representation (Kiewra *et al.*, 1991; van Dijk & Kintsch, 1983; Slotte, 1999).

To sum up, it appears that the process of note taking is useful in itself even without the chance to review the notes later. However, at this stage in our research we had constantly to face the problem that all of the participants in our studies had been asked to hand in their notes before writing their answers. We were not able to look at what would happen if the participants could review their notes during writing. Fortunately, a lucky administrative slip offered us a chance to compare a notes-absent and a notes-present condition: in one entrance exam for health-care studies, half of the students were mistakenly told that they could keep their notes after the text materials were collected. This 'accident' provided us with data, the importance of which we instantly realised (Slotte & Lonka, 1998; 1999).

6   IS IT BENEFICIAL TO REVIEW THE NOTES DURING WRITING?

Our results showed that notes-present whilst writing generally resulted in good per-formance in text comprehension (Slotte & Lonka, 1999). However, this effect was mainly limited to tasks calling for detailed learning instead of those requiring the students' to make their own inferences. When only detailed learning was called for, there was more benefit during writing in having the notes-present rather than notes-absent. This was the case even regardless of the note quality. It was thus argued that in tasks only calling for memorisation, the effect of using notes during writing might be more powerful than the activity of mere note taking.

By contrast, when writers were asked to make their own inferences according the text information, the results were the opposite: the writers had more benefit from their coherent and well-written notes-absent than they did when they had the chance to review the note papers during essay-writing. An explanation offered for these findings is that in deep-level text comprehension, the 'copy-paste' strategy, (*i.e.*, text information is copied as such during the reviewing activity) is presumably inade-quate without knowledge transforming and elaborating during the writing process (see also Hidi & Anderson, 1986; Kirby & Pedwell, 1991). Instead, as has been al-ready mentioned, the process of writing coherent notes enhances text comprehen-sion, as it helps writers to clarify the meaning and significance of discourse.

One additional point of interest concerns the relationship between notes-present writing and ongoing higher-order writing processes. Does the notes-present writing enhance or interfere with those processes? Is the nature of the task demands equally important also in written expression? With regard to the quality of essay writing, Slotte and Lonka (1998) demonstrated that, in a task where text-based reproduction of information was needed, notes-present helped the students to write lengthier, more coherent, and cohesive essay-type answers. Again, when a critical review of the text information was required, notes-present did not help the students to improve the quality of their essay-type answers. In this task, the absence of notes enabled the writers to distance themselves from the text material and allowed them to 'go be-yond' the text information that is needed in critical reviewing.

Taken together, the nature of the task demands proved to be essential when re-searching the relations between note taking and essay writing. We may conclude that using notes while essay writing served to remind the writers of what informa-tion they needed to include helping them to produce a well-argued essay. Yet, the mere activity of writing notes also proved to affect essay-writing positively.

7   CONCLUDING SUMMARY

It seems clear that the relationship between note taking and essay-writing is compli-cated. Although it was demonstrated that writing notes has an effect on both learning the content knowledge and on the linguistic features of the resulting essays, several procedural aspects of writing play crucial roles. Spontaneous note taking affects learning and writing operations utilising distinct types of mental representations de-pending on the type of notes taken, the nature of the writing tasks, and the writing conditions – such as notes-present or notes-absent. It is also clear that constructive mental activity is facilitated by note taking activity aiming at transforming knowledge into a coherent whole through deep-level text processing.

It is especially important to establish how different procedural features of writing interact with writing performance. For example, it is likely that the presence of notes during writing particularly affects those who are incline to a surface approach to learning. Kirby and Pedwell (1991) provided evidence for this by showing that students who had access to the text while summarising appeared to 'bring out' a surface approach, which reflects rote learning and extrinsic motivation in those who are prone to it. On the hand, texts-absent summarisation facilitated deeper processing for students who normally adopted a deep approach and who were able to write competent summaries.

In addition to these results, one would expect to find other variables affecting the relationship between note taking and essay-writing. For example, it is quite likely that text complexity, length, genre, and other characteristics of the environment and the writer, all influence the performance. One feature that was looked at in this study was the topic of the text. It was found to be an essential variable in the type of notes taken and suggest that certain strategies are somewhat text-dependent. This finding remind us that we should be rather specific in the generalisation of the results, although in two different topics, the summary notes and concept maps both appeared to be effective learning tools.

8   IMPLICATIONS FOR TEACHING

The fact that the usefulness of essay writing with and without notes differs depending on the nature of the task merits more attention from instructional designers. For example, students should be made aware that various note taking strategies exist. This requires developing metacognitive knowledge about when, and under what conditions, one particular type of note taking activity is more effective than another (Lahtinen et al., 1997). Further, the learning situations should be such that rote learning is not effective.

McKeachie (1994) argues that teachers can have a tremendous impact on how their students can develop a useful repertoire of note taking and other study strategies. One of the most powerful ways of teaching these strategies is through modelling. By using different types of note taking activities in their teaching, teachers can expose students to a wide variety of strategies in different content areas (see also Wilkerson & Irby, 1998). Yet, as has been established here, it is necessary to teach students how to manage on their own when they are studying. It is also clear that students should be provided with opportunities over time to use and perhaps describe their uses of different study strategies. According to McKeachie (1994: 363) guided practice with feedback is one of the most important methods of teaching study strategies. Students need to have opportunities to practice their new study strategies, and to receive feedback so that they can polish their skills.

Given the importance of knowledge transformation during essay-writing (e.g., McNamara, Kintsch, Songer, & Kintsch, 1996; Bereiter & Scardamalia 1987), students should be given many opportunities to write; both with and without their notes and drafts. Further, we agree with McCutchen, Covill, Hoyne, and Mildes (1994) that measurable improvements in the quality of the written expression will most likely result when these activities are embedded in authentic writing situations.

In addition, more attention should be paid to the requirements of essay composition, such as the ability to argue purposefully and to monitor the coherence and accuracy of meaning and language use. These skills are especially important in expository composition processes, as well as in idea generation (Wright & Rosenberg, 1993) for they involve detecting and correcting mismatches between what one considers to be a good text and the text at hand. According to the widely accepted constructivist theories of learning, these reflective dialectical processes, through which knowledge is being transformed and built, also create the necessary conditions for a better quality of expression.

However, particularly in an examination situation, when time is limited and the writer is under pressure, learners may not always notice the importance of the quality of their written expression, and how easily poor quality can create problems between the writer and the reader. Demands for relevant material that answers the question may be overemphasised at the cost of the clarity with which the ideas are expressed (Torrance, Thomas, & Robinson, 1991). Implicit in this view is the novice's belief that producing content for the essay – recalling and relating what one knows about the topic – is a relatively straightforward task (Bereiter & Scardamalia, 1987). Thus when discussing the usefulness of notes, we should ask whether we are referring to the ability to provide content, or to develop a cohesive argument, or to the interplay between them.

PORTFOLIO: INTEGRATING WRITING, LEARNING AND ASSESSMENT

PIRJO LINNAKYLÄ

University of Jyväskylä, Finland

Abstract. This chapter examines portfolio assessment as a tool to support learning by integrating writing in various learning tasks and environments. The author argues that the constructivist and socio-constructivist views of learning necessitate new ideas also in the assessment where the learners have the main role and where the partnership between students and teachers has to be renegotiated. In particular, renegotiation is needed in making decisions on assessment criteria for writing and learning that respect learners' individuality and diversity and empower students with regard to their learning. The learning, assessment and negotiation can take place in various ways and environments. Accordingly, the portfolios can be composed in many forms, including technology-supported and virtual contexts.

1   MULTIFACETED PORTFOLIO

> In my opinion, my pieces dealing with the greenhouse effect, multi-purpose use of forests and hunting are the best ones. I came up with the ideas myself and I have worked completely on my own. In my opinion, my pieces contain important information that everybody should know. I concentrated on these tasks the most and I think they came out nicely (From the 'Forest' project portfolio by a secondary school student, Linnakylä & Pollari, 1997: 203).

For the past six years I have been exploring – in collaboration with a number of my colleagues – the use of portfolios for documenting and assessing students' writing and learning from pre-school to the university and working life. Our prime focus has been on exploring the multiple functions portfolios serve as well as the way portfolios enhance students' learning, particularly their self-assessment, reflection, motivation, and empowerment. In recent years our main interest has been in digital portfolios, more specifically in how they promote authenticity and collaboration in writing and in learning (Linnakylä *et al.*, 1994; Linnakylä, Kankaanranta, & Bopry, 1999; Linnakylä, Kankaanranta, & Arvaja, 2000; Linnakylä & Pollari, 1997; Pollari, Kankaanranta & Linnakylä, 1996).

P. Linnakylä (2001). Portfolio: Integrating writing, learning and assessment. In: G. Rijlaarsdam (Series Ed.) & P. Tynjälä, L. Mason & K. Lonka (Volume Eds), *Studies in Writing, Volume 7, Writing as a Learning tool: Integrating Theory and Practice*, 145 – 160.© 2001 Kluwer Academic Publishers. Printed in the Netherlands.

The main theme of this chapter is to examine portfolio assessment as a tool to support learning by integrating writing in various tasks and environments. I shall argue that the constructivist and socio-constructivist views of learning necessitate new ideas also in the assessment where the learners have the main role and where the partnership between students and teachers has to be renegotiated. In particular, renegotiation is needed in making decisions on such assessment criteria for learning that respect learners' individuality and diversity and empower students with regard to their writing and learning. The learning, assessment and negotiation can take place in various environments. Accordingly, the portfolios can be composed in many ways, including also technology-supported contexts.

Synthesising several definitions, a portfolio can be described as a systematic and purposeful selection of student work composed, collected and selected by students themselves. It demonstrates students' interests and efforts, process and progress as well as achievement in one or more areas over a period of time. In order to enhance learning, the portfolio should also contain the student's own reflection and self-evaluation concerning the rationale in terms of the selected work samples as well as the process of learning. It may also envision future challenges supporting the student's goal-orientation (Belanoff & Dickson, 1991; Linnakylä, 1994; Paulson et al., 1991; Tierney et al., 1991; Valencia, 1990).

Portfolios may serve many different purposes in students' writing and learning, for instance, by providing documentation of individual students' writing and learning process, achievement and progress (Belanoff & Dickson, 1991; Graves, 1992; Mäkinen 1996; Tierney et al. 1991; Valencia, 1990; Valencia & Place, 1994; Wolf, 1989); by illustrating students' personal curricula, authentic learning activities, variety of knowledge and exemplary pieces of work in various subject areas (Graves, 1992, Hansen, 1994; Murphy, 1994; Pollari, 1998); by creating contexts that promote students' self-assessment, reflection, self-regulation and empowerment (Henning-Stout, 1994; Linnakylä, 1998; Milliken, 1992; Pollari, 1998); by building bridges between various writing and learning environments (Freedman, 1993; Kankaanranta, 1998; Kankaanranta & Linnakylä, 1999; Pollari, 1998); by sharing and enriching personal expertise and directing career development and life planning (Hartnell-Young & Morriss, 1999; Kimeldorf, 1994; Tierney et al., 1991; Tillema, 1998); and by promoting enculturation to various learning or working environments (Kankaanranta & Linnakylä, 1999; Linnakylä, 1999).

Altogether, portfolios provide a vehicle for learner-centred assessment that enhances students' writing, learning, motivation, metacognition and self-regulation. They represent a shift toward assessment practices grounded on authentic learning tasks involving various types of writing integrated with different form of learning. In addition, portfolios are also utilised in making school or class curricula as well as teaching, learning and working cultures visible and possible to share and evaluate (Kieffer, Hale, & Templeton, 1998; Linnakylä & Kankaanranta, 1999).

Portfolios can be compiled in the form of notebooks, folders, albums, computer discs, CD-ROMs or web pages, for example. They may include written documents such as notes, memos, journals, reports, essays, as well as other forms of presentation such as pictures, sounds, animation, music etc. However, it is neither the form nor the media that makes a collection of student work a portfolio but self-assessment and reflection on the various stages of producing, composing and selecting the material for the portfolio as well as evaluating the process, outcomes and progress of one's own learning.

2   ASSESSMENT AS A MEANS TO ENHANCE LEARNING

I enclose both these versions in my portfolio, so that you would see the miracle of learning. When I tried to do that metaphor task on my own, the result was lousy. But once we had discussed the task together, something clicked into place. I wanted to try out that task again, when I found that old lousy version. It is just the contrast with the old version that makes the new one look ingenious. Besides, I have already charmed a couple of girls with my original but apt metaphors. (From the 'culture' course portfolio by a secondary school student, Kivelä, 1996: 83)

I am very happy with the result of my work even though the portfolio could have had a bit less of written texts. I could have used more figures, drawings and mind maps so that the portfolio would have been easier to understand. This kind of work suits me very well and I would like to do this kind of work later on as well. In the future, however, I would like us to have less work to be done at home and also more flexible deadlines. The problems with meeting the deadlines were partly my own fault, as I didn't start working properly soon enough. (From the 'Forest' project portfolio by a secondary school student, Linnakylä & Pollari 1997: 204)

If learning is regarded as knowledge construction, the learner's own experiences and activities in creating meaning are crucial. In these activities, previous knowledge and skills, motives and efforts determine the reconstruction process and the quality of learning. The learning process is at its best goal-oriented, constructive, reflective and self-regulated (Brown *et al.*, 1989; Vermunt, 1995). Students are not mere recorders of factual information but also creators and reorganisers of their own unique knowledge structures. To know something entails more than just having received a piece of information. Rather, it means that one has interpreted and related the information to one's prior knowledge. What is important is how students organise, structure, relate, use and judge information and build knowledge in a variety of contexts to solve real-life problems, and also how they communicate the solutions in various forms and to diverse audiences (Dochy & McDowell, 1997; Tynjälä, 1999).

If the learner's active participation in the learning process and its regulation are emphasised, assessment should also focus on these factors and promote their growth. Many earlier studies indicate that the factors being assessed, and the way they are assessed, strongly direct what the students concentrate on in learning (Resnick & Resnick, 1991). On these grounds, the assessment methods should focus on learners' own knowledge construction and production instead of having them take tests that are structured by teachers or external assessors (Moss, 1994).

In order to yield a fuller picture, the elicitation of students' knowledge should be built on their interests, experiences and competencies. The actual products may involve writing tasks illuminating both the process and the outcome of learning. They can be process-related notes, mind-maps, learning logs, diaries or journals, or more finalised outcomes such as essays, project reports, posters, or research papers. They can also include products designed for external purposes like various kinds of artefacts or handicraft items or productions of play, musical theatre, concert, art exhibitions and so forth. These works can be documented by means of photos, slides, videos, CDs, and displayed on the Internet, for example. All these manifold learning documents can be used for assessment, as they can be compiled, showcased and evaluated in the portfolio to illuminate the learners' experiences, responsibilities, strengths, interests and challenges in writing, learning and personal growth. The ultimate goal is, after all, to enhance learning, not to get better in performance monitoring (Stowell & Tierney, 1995; Tynjälä, 1999).

3   INDIVIDUALITY AND DIVERSITY IN ASSESSMENT

I have completed 4 different pieces of work, all having something to do with me and the things I like: music, literature, film, and poetry... Finding oneself, as an individual, is important to all of us and I think that there's something about me captured in this portfolio (From the 'English culture' course portfolio by a secondary school student, Linnakylä & Pollari 1997: 211)

Learning outcomes follow the nature of the learning process. If the learning process is considered individual, then the learning outcomes are individual and diverse as well. Diversity may arise, for example, from students' personal interest areas, content knowledge or the way they present their knowledge, their writing skills, self-esteem, attitudes or self-regulation (Vermunt, 1995). Differences are obvious in outcomes, and the diversity is not only inevitable but also even desirable (Calfee & Perfumo, 1993). Thus the assessment should respect the diversity of experience and creativity of individual learners. Portfolio assessment is based on this ideal of diversity. Only through respect for diversity can creativity and excellence be achieved, since finding excellence involves people working to their own optimal challenge and capacity (Csikszentmihalyi, 1990; Stowell & Tierney, 1995).

Accordingly, instead of using rigid external standards, the learning performance in portfolio should be evaluated by using diverse qualitative criteria that are initiated by the learner and negotiated with the significant partners in the community of learners (Stowell & Tierney, 1995).

Reflection is considered crucial for deepening and enhancing excellence in learning and for the development of metacognition. Reflection demands self-assessment, which can be supported and enhanced by peer- and co-assessment (De Corte, 1993; Longhurst & Norton, 1997). Peer assessment and conferencing with other students, teachers and experts enrich reflection by bringing up diverse viewpoints, experiences and values. Assessment is not considered as a post-control of learning but rather as a means to enrich and deepen both individual and collaborative understanding and to strengthen motivation (Calfee & Perfumo, 1993; Dochy & Moerkerke, 1997; Linnakylä & Pollari, 1997).

From the students' point of view assessment has a positive effect on learning and is found 'fair' (Sambell, McDowell & Brown, 1997, 365) when it:

- relates to authentic tasks;
- represents reasonable demands;
- encourages the students to apply their own knowledge to realistic contexts;

- has long-term benefits;
- rewards genuine effort, rather than 'luck';
- rewards breadth and depth in learning;
- fosters student independence by making expectations and criteria clear;
- provides adequate feedback about students' progress;
- focuses on complex skills and qualities.

These criteria that students experience both as face-valid and as having consequential validity are typical of portfolio assessment (Linnakylä, 1998; Sambell *et al.*, 1997). In addition, portfolio approach could make assessment a valuable learning experience also in longer run in opposition to something students have to take merely for grades or examinations (Birenbaum & Dochy, 1996).

From the validity point of view individuality and diversity in portfolios may be considered a problem. When students have a great deal of freedom in designing their tasks and composing their portfolios, how can we assure the construct validity of assessment? There is a risk of construct under-representation, that is, the assessment method fails to cover all the knowledge and skills it is intended to measure (Messick, 1994). The threat of construct-irrelevant variance is possible as well. The marking may be influenced by irrelevant, unrelated skills, for example, by the quality of printing or handwriting, language or style, by using humour or by the visual means chosen for sample tasks (Linnakylä, 1998; Messick, 1994; Pollari, 1998). On the other hand, highly refined constructs may prove irrelevant for real-life contexts and authentic tasks. In real life, problems tend to be ill-defined and tasks call for combining knowledge and skills from diverse subject areas, and presenting solutions for problems may require high quality of writing and visualisation as well.

Validity and reliability in the evaluation of portfolios have been questioned, especially if portfolios are judged in the traditional psychometric terms as they often are when used for grading or examination purposes (Hamp-Lyons, 1996; Herman, Gearhart & Baker, 1993; Messick, 1994). What are the comparable grading criteria and where they come from? Are they set by the teacher or the external assessor, or are they proposed by each individual student, or are they possibly negotiated in collaboration between these parties? In grading the interrater reliability may drop unacceptably low, since portfolios have to be marked with qualitative and multiple criteria (Moss, 1994). However, several studies also indicate that adequate interrater reliability can be achieved through negotiated and shared criteria as well as through rater training and a well-reasoned marking guide (Linn, 1994; Linnakylä, 1998).

4   PORTFOLIO INTEGRATES WRITING TO LEARNING AND ASSESSMENT

I hereby delight you with my treasure map. The idea crossed my mind when I truly had a feeling like I had been hunting for treasures, as I was browsing the course portfolio. Terrible how many interesting things may escape your notion, if you never return to your old traces... Anyway, I am satisfied with my showcase. I noticed in my course folder that I had not concentrated on small tasks. The picture analysis is now enclosed here fully revised. You see, I began to feel annoyed for how poorly I had done my homework. Of course, it now shows in my work that I've been listening to other peo-

> ple's presentations and your comments – but we were supposed to learn from them, weren't we? I think I learned most when writing the picture analysis. (From the 'Culture' course portfolio by a secondary school student, Kivelä, 1996: 86)

As for the development of a portfolio, it is usually at first a documentary collection containing a variety of pieces of written work that has been composed as learning tasks at school or elsewhere. These written documents may be notes, learning diaries, home assignments or essays, argumentative texts, reports, poems or their drafts. At the end of the course, the project or the term students select a few pieces of work that they evaluate the best or personally the most meaningful ones and state the criteria for the selection in a written rationale. The final showcase portfolio with reflective self-assessment and future envisioning represents students' best work showing their strengths and potentials as well as the competence to reflect on and self-regulate the progress of learning. In this process of documenting, assessing, selecting and reflecting the composer of the portfolio also integrates reading, writing and critical reviewing activities which have proved beneficial for learning (Spivey, 1995, 1997).

Portfolios are thus often based on written documents that students produce in authentic learning situations. Even if the work samples are not produced in written form, at least the introduction, description of the context and process of learning, *e.g.* a learning log or diary, as well as the rationale for the showcase, the reflective self-assessment and envisioning future challenges are written.

The writing tasks related to portfolios vary in terms of the thinking processes they require (cf. Bereiter & Scardamalia, 1987). An introduction or a prologue that describes the author and the learning context as well as the learning journal documenting the process can be classified as *knowledge telling* tasks.

> When I was writing this poem it was night and it was dark outside. I was tired, but I couldn't even imagine of getting sleep before the poem was ready. When I was writing it, I experienced sort of revelations; suddenly I just knew what would come next. The story just came out like by itself. I didn't tear my hair out because of it. I used a dictionary a lot to help me to find as descriptive expressions as possible. And so it was finally finished. Later when I was reading the poem and pondering on its rhymes a clear rhythm and melody began to form in my head. I sang it to myself and so it was born: a little song that springs from a poem that springs from my thoughts and images springing up from a painting by Edelfelt. (From the 'Culture' course portfolio by a secondary school student Pollari, 1998: 182.)

In contrast, the tasks such as the written rationale for the showcase, self-evaluation and reflection require *elaboration or transformation of knowledge*. This includes, for example, giving reasons or grounds for the decisions made and arguing for them, reflection and self-assessment on the selection of the tasks and on one's performance in them as well as discussion about the significance and successfulness of the works displayed.

> Why I chose Misi: The critique about Misi isn't very good, but the songs are the main issue. It was very hard to translate them and still manage to capture the feeling. I never showed them to anybody because they bring out my personality which is very vulnerable. I'm probably afraid they are not good enough because it took quite a long time to get the translation ready. But the best thing was that I learnt new words. (From the 'Culture' course portfolio by a secondary school student, Pollari, 1998)

> When I'm writing I forget everything else when I get into the right mood. I always write with my heart and that's why it is difficult for me to look at my mistakes right in the eye. 'Niio, My Dog Niio' was chosen because I'm hopelessly mad about dogs and the topic is very dear to me. 'Feminism – What Is It?' and 'World Events and Me' I have chosen for about the same reason. In both essays I deal with serious problems of this world. They touch me deeply. (From the 'Writing portfolio' by a lower secondary school student, Linnakylä, 1998: 58)

Writing passages for envisioning future challenges in learning could be defined as *generation of knowledge,* especially if the future visions are constructed on the basis of both self-reflection and evaluation as well as of exploration of possibilities and new horizons in one's personal future (Langer, 1995).

> The portfolio project was quite rewarding. You had to be allowed to take responsibility for what you do. This most certainly benefited the situations we come up with in working life. Also, this course was so different from the usual grinding the book and that was a positive experience. In some parts, actual learning English may have been a bit weak. It really depended on yourself if you learned anything new or not. For my part, I can say that at least my vocabulary and writing in English have improved during the course. Perhaps speaking and listening got a little less attention and in the future you should have pure listening exercises in this course although students might consider it hard in addition to these pieces of work. (From the 'Culture' course portfolio by a secondary school student, Pollari, 1998: 179)

When writing, reading, selecting and reflecting on their works for a portfolio, students face their own learning. Preferably, they start to look at their work more reflectively and critically, which enhances metacognition in writing and in learning. At the same time students' appreciation for their own work, experiences, knowledge, efforts and progress increases. When going through their work samples, the students see the range of the learning tasks, new knowledge and skills that they have personally acquired during the learning process. This may develop awareness of both positive attributions (cf. Weiner, 1986) as well as of future learning challenges and thus advance the development of metacognition and goal-orientation (Herman 1997). While emphasising the best works and potentials of the learner, the portfolio can also enhance the student's confidence and self-esteem in writing and learning.

> The fairy tale certainly isn't any grammatical model performance but making it was an incredible experience. I had never before practised language that way. Listening to the piece gave a nice feeling: I have really created that myself. (From the 'Culture' course portfolio by a secondary school student, Pollari, 1998: 142)

> For myself, this work gave a lot of self-confidence and I began to feel that I could do at least something in English even though my grades are so poor. P.S. Motivation to study grew immensely. (From the 'Culture' course portfolio by a secondary school student Pollari, 1998: 142)

From the assessment and reliability point of view the positive inclination of portfolios – beside their individual nature – can be considered a problem. Some studies claim that portfolios tend to get higher scores than the students' average performance would suggest (Herman *et al.*, 1993). This may well be the case, since students' portfolios display their best work samples. Portfolios may therefore give a more positive image of students' potential than their average performance in traditional tests. But it is also possible that the traditional tests fail to capture parts of students' real capacity and that students perform better when allowed more time and authentic real-life tasks in more meaningful contexts, more encouragement and support in composing their work, including also collaboration with other students and teachers.

5   NEGOTIATING A NEW PARTNERSHIP BETWEEN STUDENTS AND TEACHERS

> The portfolio left a good taste in the mouth. We were given some responsibility. Not all of it, but anyway. Even that was a great victory. We could show that even if not every one of us was able to work independently, at least most of us could. So that the whole class didn't have to abandon their ambitious plans because of a few individuals. The work takes its toll, though. I don't think that I have ever been that stressed. But, however, it was nice. It was challenging, that's why you had the energy and motivation to keep on doing it. (From the 'Culture' course portfolio by a secondary school student, Linnakylä & Pollari, 1997: 204)

Implementing the portfolio assessment will involve more than simply introducing another assessment tool. Implementing portfolios entail some major changes in instruction and student empowerment (Stowell & Tierney, 1995). It calls for negotiation about the goals and quality criteria of learning as well as about the contents and about the tasks to be performed. Moreover, it requires recognition of the importance of a power shift and change in the approach, that is, from top-down to bottom-up and from outside in to inside-out. It also requires acceptance for diversity and individuality in terms of learning processes and learning outcomes alike, and striving for a student-centred approach in order to develop personal or shared criteria for achievement and progress.

In this notion of sharing, a new kind of partnership between the students and the teacher is crucial. Assessment is no longer something done *to* the students, rather it is done *with* the students (Stowell & Tierney, 1995). It means negotiation along several dimensions, including the following:

- various purposes of portfolios;
- goals set on the basis of individual students' progress and future challenges, and partly shared among the learners;
- contents that interest the students and are found significant also in the community of learners;
- task types that suit to the individual students but also widen their writing, learning and metacognition;
- nature and partners of collaboration;
- audience that is significant in assessing and supporting learning;
- evaluation criteria that both the author and the evaluators find appropriate; and
- opportunities for feedback, interaction and future visions.

This negotiation can be expanded to include other communities of learners, parents or other significant partners, experts, administrators, employers depending on the students' age and learning environments.

In the process of negotiation and empowerment, power and resources are not regarded as finite. Learner empowerment does not mean teacher disempowerment, even though the teacher's role may change. Instead, power and resources are something that students and teachers can share, contributing to the growth of power and resources of both parties. The power relationship can be additive and created with others in negotiation and in collaboration (Cummins, 1996).

Renegotiation and gradual release of teacher's responsibility is not an easy transition. It can, however, be grounded and supported by the portfolio composition process, during which the students actually get various opportunities to develop their decision-making ability and to negotiate with their peers and other partners, including the teachers as well (Linnakylä, 1998). Along their portfolio project students encounter various assessment phases and partners that focus on enhancing and developing the students' learning and awareness of different and wider audiences and purposes of their portfolios. Already while producing the writing tasks, the students may work in collaboration with their peers or receive teacher's feedback on their learning process and outcomes. This is usually formative, encouraging and guides the student's learning. While selecting the best work samples for the showcase, students may work collaboratively and assess in pairs or groups each other's works. Co-assessment and feedback from other significant partners and experts may be beneficial for reflection and for self-evaluation. Through peers or other partners the evaluation criteria of the community of learners can be reached and shared for negotiation. The experts may even widen the range of externally valued criteria to be judged and renegotiated.

Through this negotiation process the students get an opportunity to share with the external assessor their previous learning history, interests, and aims – and their own writing curriculum. The portfolio also offers an arena for discussing the assessment criteria (Tierney *et al.*, 1991). Even though experts may have different standards, reflecting their values and beliefs, at least they will start to reconsider the criteria of good writing and learning.

6   RENEGOTIATING ASSESSMENT CRITERIA

> In order to produce a super piece of work, you need extra expertise, long-term planning and organising in producing the piece and diverse forms of work. Extra pieces that originate from your own ideas with your own voice make a portfolio a super portfolio. (From the 'Forest' portfolio by a lower secondary school student, Linnakylä & Pollari, 1997: 205)

Learning is sometimes hindered by circumstances where the evaluation criteria appreciated by the student do not match with those of the teacher. Therefore, when evaluation seeks to support learning, it is essential to renegotiate and agree on shared evaluation criteria in an open and mutually respectful manner. This means that the learner's own criteria are appreciated and adopted as a starting point for the renegotiation. On the other hand, students should learn about what experts of the field think about the assessment criteria. The teacher represents expertise on learning and instruction, and therefore the views of both parties (students and teacher) should be set side by side to form a basis for the negotiation.

In our studies on students' writing portfolios in the lower secondary schools (Linna-kylä, 1998) the following criteria were most often mentioned in students' rationales for selecting the best or most important writing samples:

- personal interest in topic;
- student's own strong voice in style and language;
- meaningfulness of the topics from the students' perspective;
- appreciation of student's own experiences;
- students' ability to handle varied genres and topics;
- sense of humour and ability to arouse excitement;
- imagination and creativity;
- topics true-to-life and close to young people;
- expressing real feelings and sentiments;
- effective strategies in the writing and revising process;
- extensive, well-structured and error-free writing;
- effort, perseverance, boldness and persistence.

Those assessment criteria that were best valued by the students emphasised learners' own interests and topics that they find meaningful. Also personal, characteristic style, one's 'own voice' was appreciated. Awareness of the audience was important as well, but the students seem to put more weight on such aspects as the sense of humour, expression of feelings and arousing excitement than on readability or cor-rectness of style. Students also appreciated the more traditional criteria such as knowledge of genres or effective writing strategies, structuring and error-free writ-ing, but these criteria are regarded as somewhat basic elements rather than as dis-tinctive characteristics making a writing sample particularly good or significant.

In peer assessment, the same criteria were valued. Particularly, imagination and creativity, sense of humour and personal style as well as students' serious interest in the topic were often mentioned. Peer- and co-assessment, however, do not only en-tail that the learners have to understand the meaning of criteria and apply them seri-ously, they also promote important skills having to do with reflection, critical think-ing and self-appraisal (Dochy & McDowell, 1997). Peer- and co-assessment also widen the perspectives of evaluation and diversify mutual negotiation about the evaluation criteria.

The class community can actually (Langer, 1995: 144) offer a 'safe house' to in-teraction and negotiation for students to voice their own ideas, to hear others in ways that enrich their own thinking, to be sensitive to viewpoints not necessarily their own and to communicate clearly. That negotiative approach can give them power – power of voice, control of their growing ideas, and the sense of self that comes from participating in a group of peers who do not always share the same insights or inter-pretations, but who respect one another enough to gain from diversity.

Continuous negotiation and collaboration in composing and assessing a portfolio can be a reliability – or at least a comparability – problem if the portfolio is used for external evaluation for grades or entrance. The evaluators may justifiably ask whose work they are assessing. The question naturally arises because portfolios may con-tain documents that are produced in collaboration with the community of learners. Thus, under an optimal instructional context, the portfolio being assessed is not the result of a single individual but rather of an individual collaborating in a learning context. The more authentic and collaborative the process, the more an individual student's work is likely to have benefited from the work of others (Herman, 1997). If, however, the work is assessed to enhance learning that is authentic, typical to the learning culture and real-life tasks and situations (Brown *et al.*, 1989), collaboration is not a problem but a possibility and an advantage for every party in the community of learners.

7   GAINERS AND CRITICS

> All this time, during this course, I was very interested in this portfolio working, the theme, the arts, was the best possible for me. I was full of different kind of ideas, so it was easy for me to start working. (From the 'Culture' course portfolio by a secondary school student, Pollari, 1998: 180)

> The course was neither very rewarding nor productive for me, which of course was mostly because I'm neither very cultural nor very hardworking. (From the 'Culture' course portfolio by a secondary school student, Pollari, 1998: 198)

Students are individuals also in the way they get motivated and take charge of their learning in portfolio work. Most of the students with whom we have been working have been willing to take an active role in all the stages involved. They have enjoyed the freedom, but also committed themselves to their works, showing such magnificent potential, effort, engagement and creativity that are difficult to trace through traditional tests or examinations.

The greatest gainers were those students who were ready to take the responsibility, to work hard, to collaborate with other students, to exploit teachers' expertise. But above all, they were ready to throw in their own goals, experiences and interests, emotions, sense of humour, and linguistic capabilities to the full. Some of these students flung themselves into their portfolio works with enthusiasm, worked hard, and told later on that they had experienced almost as if a constant flow of learning in their studies.

> First I started to do the portrait of Emily Dickinson. I read her poems and searched information about her. Although it took a lot of time to do this portrait, I think that it was very interesting and meaningful. After getting the first version of the portrait of Dickinson ready, I started to search information about Isadora Duncan. It was easy to make the portrait of her, because there were lots of books, which tell about her, in the library. She has had so unusual life. The third part of my work file consists of the poem/the song that I wrote myself. As a starting point I had a postcard, which has Albert Edelfelt's painting on it. At last I wrote an essay about my hobby, dancing. It came quite easily because I didn't have to search any information. (From the 'Culture' course portfolio by a secondary school student, Pollari, 1998: 180)

> I experienced this portfolio course a very suitable working method for me. It gave me the opportunity for self-directed work and for working methods of my own choice. I could also allot my time myself, considering how much time each work would need. I could choose my topics, so they were topics that really interested me personally. (From the 'Culture' course portfolio by a secondary school student, Pollari, 1998: 182)

Some students, however, set their goals very high exhibiting excellent work with an ambitious attitude, which sometimes turned into perfectionism even, causing anxiety if the goals had been set too high compared to the students' competence. In such cases they felt that constructing a portfolio did not give them adequate support and that the showcase revealed their weaknesses more clearly than traditional tests (Linnakylä, 1998; Pollari, 1998).

But among the students we have been working with we have also found some students reluctant to accept an active role and to take charge of their own learning (Linnakylä, 1998, Pollari, 1998). Some of them openly preferred the traditional way of teacher-directed learning and assessment.

> I have been against this kind of working method from the beginning and I am still against it. This kind of work suits probably those who know English well and who can do their work on time and independently... I still support the ordinary way to work. Many people must have left their work till the last moment and that causes an awfully lot of stress. (From the 'Culture' course portfolio by a secondary school student, Pollari, 1998: 192)

> I did my best, I tried really hard, and here's the result. The teacher can better assess them. I think it is the teacher's duty, not the student's, to assess and to give grades. (From the 'Writing portfolio' by a lower secondary school student, Linnakylä, 1998: 61)

Some students wanted to show that they were better when compared to other students rather than be assessed by their own progress. Some of the reluctant ones just preferred 'easy living' and did not want to invest much time and serious effort in planning their learning and constructing a portfolio and especially in writing a reflective self-assessment, which they found a waste of time.

> Well, there's now some evidence of my work. There's not too much on the bottom line, but it ought to show, at least, that I have felt my responsibility for that the others will receive reasonable basic knowledge about medieval literature. Examining the model of Hell was fun, especially when I tried to place teachers in the right categories. At first I was certain that teachers who make people construct portfolios should find place right beside Judas, but when the others enthusiastically presented portfolios of their own, I decided to let you climb a few steps higher to slightly cooler spheres. In fact, this was indeed more fun than listening to lectures, but to get the full joy out of this would probably call for more time to delve deeper. As it happened, I didn't have that time, or yes I did but it had to be allocated for something else, so it's no use to explain. Anyhow, I think I have worked at least for a seven's worth (on the scale 4 – 10). I believe that the others were able to follow my presentation, as I didn't take it to such philosophical spheres as some people lost in their existential anguish. (From the 'Culture' course portfolio by a secondary school student, Kivelä, 1996: 89)

It is obvious that students represent a range of beliefs as do teachers. We have found teachers willing to accept the notion of involving students in the portfolio assessment process and ready to implement this idea also in practice. Then again, we have also met many teachers who did accept the idea in theory, but were still reluctant to incorporate student involvement in actual practice, especially in setting goals and in defining the criteria for evaluation (Linnakylä, 1998). The majority of both, students and teachers, however, have been willing to renegotiate the new partnership. In general, teachers seem to be in favour of gradual release of freedom and responsibility.

Some students agree with them, but quite a few would also be ready for more radical empowerment.

> I did my best and I can't help if that is not enough. I have wondered how my work will be evaluated but right now it doesn't make any difference. The most important point is that I have succeeded in one-way or another and even if I don't get 10 (the best grade) from this course I am not disappointed. I have already given myself a highest grade from trying and crossing my limits. And the most important point is that I am satisfied with my works and proud of them. (From the 'Culture' course portfolio by a secondary school student, Linnakylä & Pollari 1997: 211)

8   PORTFOLIOS IN TECHNOLOGY SUPPORTED LEARNING CONTEXTS

Today, learning and writing tasks are often technology supported and outcomes are presented in the electronic form. Likewise, a portfolio can be composed in the digital form accessible through computers. Digital portfolios are typically compiled by means of word processing tools or multimedia software (Kieffer *et al.*, 1998; Kankaanranta & Linnakylä, 1999).

We have studied digital web portfolios in the project called CATO (Collaboration and authenticity in open technologically enriched and virtual learning contexts, Linnakylä *et al.*, 2000). Central themes in our studies have included the inquiry on possibilities of digital portfolios in various learning and working environments. We have also sought to construct a prototype model of web portfolio through exploring and evaluating university students' and experts' portfolios on the Internet (Kankaanranta & Linnakylä, 1999; Linnakylä *et al.*, 1999).

Through our exploration many advantages of digital portfolios have been verified. Multimedia portfolios can provide a richer picture of the student or expert than the traditional text-based showcases. By means of multimedia one's learning processes and outcomes can be demonstrated more diversely than before, by exploiting not only written texts but also graphical and visual images, pictures, sounds and video clips. Multimedia can also illustrate the various tools and facilities that have been used in the learning, writing or working processes as well as in presenting the artefacts in the portfolio.

In the hypertext format the knowledge, skills, and competencies can be easily connected by links to various learning or working environments, communities and collaborators involved both in and outside the school (cf. Bergman, 1999). The hypertext features also make it easy to add in new sections, subject or knowledge areas or fields of expertise as well as to reduce the old ones. The longitudinal follow-up of the progress can also be demonstrated by interlinking portfolios of different times. The digital form enables easy and fast data transfers and access, thus facilitating more diverse and broad-based sharing of knowledge and skills. By digital means the students' and experts' competencies can be made visible in a form that is easy to approach, even repeatedly if necessary. Another significant feature is that web portfolios can be added with discussion forums enabling the audience to interact with the author, *e.g.* in the form of questions, comments and feedback. These sites also serve further renegotiation of goals and criteria for assessment and evaluation available to all interested parties.

> This portfolio contains both works ordered by customers and works representing study projects. The works have been made mainly as teamwork, and the contributors and their tasks are specified in conjunction of each work. This gave the impression that the author has good co-operation skills. On the page with descriptions on his projects and works, the author mentions an ongoing project called 'Calliola' (www-page designing). In the introduction the author comments his study path: 'After I realized that my education in social sciences was not enough for me and that I was wasting my creative skills I decided to look for education from digital culture.' This portfolio could be used as an example of how digital and multimedia features can be utilised. Professionalism shows also in there that the pages contain a link to appropriate sites where additional software needed in watching/listening can be downloaded. (An IT student's review on a portfolio by a multimedia student, Linnakylä, 1999: 168)

A digital portfolio is typically structured so that the opening page introduces the author and purpose and outlines the contents of the portfolio. The contents may be organised according to the various subject areas or fields of expertise, or according to the contexts and situations where learning or working has taken place. In some cases more experienced students or experts organise their portfolios according to different tasks and positions they have had, and describe their studies more like a collateral underlying these professional tasks (Kankaanranta & Linnakylä, 1999). The opening page usually has links leading to various parts or sections, paths and levels, highlighting the respective issues of learning process, authentic tasks, collaboration, achievement and progress with related self-assessments and reflections.

The readers or evaluators, of course, make their own choices in selecting the parts and paths of the portfolio to be studied. The composer, however, can influence on their choices, not only by interesting contents but also by attractive links, by narratives describing learning and progress, by argumentative and self-critical reflections, and by future-oriented creative challenges. The layout of the portfolio, utilisation of multimedia, sophisticated use of texts and visual elements also influence on readers' choices.

> The front page of C's portfolio is startling in my opinion. One can make some inferences solely on that basis, already, about C as a student, artist and professional. It tells you what kind of style she represents. As an artist C describes herself through her works of art. This is likely to be the most reliable option compared to the situation where she would try to explain her art and herself as an artist only in writing. Indeed, one picture is worth a thousand words, and everybody can make their own personal interpretations. A written description was also in place, anyhow, and it gave certain depth to the artist's characterisation. (A biology student's review on a portfolio by an art student, Linnakylä, 1999: 164)

As far as texts are concerned, the reviewers usually wish for brief and to the point, yet personal use of writing and language. Interestingly, individuality and personal expression were looked for also with regard to the usage of colours and graphics. It is also considered important that the modes of expression are in line with the contents, both in terms of style and with respect to the purpose of the portfolio.

> The visual impression of the front page is pleasant. The background colour is not too dominant but stylish. B could have reconsidered his choice for the photograph, though, as it is too dark and fuzzy. It is a good solution to have a photo on the front page, however, since a photo gives you some idea about the person involved. (A biology student's review on a portfolio by a literature student, Linnakylä, 1999: 165)

> Technologically the page is simple and sensible. It is not dull, however, although apart from the heading it is just 'in black and white'. Spaces between paragraphs make it easier to read and also help quick browsing. Actual technological utilisation shows only as the list of links inserted on the main page. There is nothing else in this portfolio that would require the electronic form. For example, B can be contacted through e-mail, but her applications and recommendations she will send by post. This is quite funny, as such, since she tells us having attended a number of seminars on Internet environments and also having used the Net and taught its use in her classes. She could have displayed her possible know-how in some way. (A linguistics student's review on a portfolio by a literature student, Linnakylä, 1999: 165)

On the other hand, it is evident that in the use of multimedia, different reviewers prefer different styles and means of expression. Some look for simplicity, textuality and elegance, while some others appreciate innovative graphics, pictures, animations and bright colours. Most people seem to be annoyed, however, by simultaneous use of multiple media, as well as by excessive hyperlinks, which may easily distract, or even distress, the reader. The reviewers have also considered the use of digital means in terms of smooth reading and reader's guidance, but also with regard to composing their own portfolios.

> Simple can be beautiful. Masculine pages, but so is the author. A good-looking man. The picture embedded in the context marvellously. Things can be presented very aptly and briefly, that I learnt from his pages. The colours were strong, but are surely in line with the personality of the author. Yet, the use of colours was not exaggerating but neon green on black background was lively and easy to read. (An education student's review on a portfolio by a multimedia student, Linnakylä, 1999: 166.)

> The portfolio has been published with nice layout without any technical specialities. There were hypertext links to the employer's web site and to pages of study requirements *etc*. This portfolio is easy to distract away from, which is not a good thing for a showcase portfolio. Personally, I would like to ensure reader's access back to the portfolio at will, *e.g.* by using a framed start-up page or by opening all 'outbound' links in a separate browsing window. The material is easy to update when all the text is in the same file. Nevertheless, I might not choose an approach quite as linear as this for text presentation. (An IT student's review on an educational consultant's portfolio, Linnakylä, 1999: 166)

> This one I chose as a warning to myself. Absolutely shocking. The pages were loaded with everything possible and impossible. There were colours and different fonts – sometimes smaller, sometimes bigger – and there were pictures, both photographs and hand-drawn. The pages gave very restless feeling. There was an unreasonable abundance of links so that when I was browsing through the pages, I could not help thinking that now I must get out of here or I will be totally drowned in the depths of the pool of links. (An education student's review on a multimedia expert's portfolio, Linnakylä, 1999: 166)

9   DEVELOPING LEARNER IDENTITY IN COLLABORATIVE, NETWORKED WORLD

> To live, and indeed prosper the Net, we need to know who we are. In the Information Age our lives, and our world, will depend on our capacity to link up the Net and the Self (Manuel Castells, 1999: 1).

New technologies help us build portfolio environments that encourage people to question old conventions and to strengthen experimentation, innovation, and creativity. Although a digital portfolio largely resembles the text and paper-based showcases, it has also many new and novel features (Reinking, McKenna, Labbo, & Kieffer, 1998; Windschitl, 1998).

Construction of a digital portfolio still demands diverse writing skills from the author, as well as mastery of the writing process and effective writing strategies. Among other things, skills related to planning, prewriting, drafting, revising, editing, and publishing of various texts are still called for. But in addition, one needs to be able to apply these skills also to the mode and style of expression in the world of multimedia. This also calls for both traditional and new ways to organise and construct text in the hypertext format so that the text runs in a linear fashion within sections but at the same time the sections are harnessed to serve and highlight the macrostructure of the content. The core elements are picked up to form the main page with an introduction, a list of contents and a purpose statement, while the work samples, written descriptions, journal narratives, argumentative rationales and reflective self-assessments are organised to support and supplement the main purpose and work samples. The author also needs skills of intertextual organisation, as by linking different texts can be combined and engaged in mutual interaction. By the same token, one needs to know various kinds of genres. Moreover, one should also know how to use them side-by-side in the same set of pages with skilful variations in order to serve various functions, situations and readers. As for the language, one still needs to know the potentials and restrictions of written language, but one also needs to be aware of the modes of expression of other media, especially those of visual and auditive language. Actually, in the context of new media literacy including writing skills, one should master the whole range of the multimedia and polystructured virtual language with all its styles and rhetorical potential (cf. Bolter, 1998; Lemke, 1998) to be able to take full advantage of the means technology allows for composing a digital portfolio.

While hypertexts and multimedia provide a diversity of options, only few people can take full advantage of these possibilities as yet (Windschitl, 1998). Taking a look at digital portfolios by experts in the field of multimedia can therefore be quite educational and interesting. Crossing the technological borders in writing, learning and assessment can be fascinating as well (Kankaanranta & Linnakylä, 1999). Digital portfolios make learning and working even more visible and sharable and their evaluation more reflective, interactive and negotiable.

The digital portfolios seem to provide incentives for their authors as well. Indeed, it is a fundamental human need and value *per se* to feel having accomplished something and to see some results of one's work, even if the work were of highly intellectual and immaterial knowledge products (Bruner, 1996; Koski, 1998). In any case, we will need in the future individuals who have a strong identity, and consequently, the skills and courage for making visible, displaying, assessing and sharing their competence both in writing and through the language of multimedia. Courage and openness is needed also in further construction of that identity in interaction with others both within one's own community of learners and in the technologically enhanced, networked world.

NEW TECHNOLOGY, WRITING AND LEARNING

JAMES HARTLEY* & PÄIVI TYNJÄLÄ**

*University of Keele, Staffordshire, UK, ** University of Jyväskylä, Finland

Abstract. The participants involved in most previous studies on writing have written their texts by hand but writing with the aid of a computer is much more prevalent today. This chapter specifically examines the effects of new technology on writing and, by implication, on writing to learn, and presents examples how technology has created new possibilities for using writing for purposes of learning. The chapter is divided into four main parts. Part one briefly introduces the chapter. Part two considers the nature of writing in terms of interactions between planning, writing and editing. Part three examines how computer aided writing changes these processes. Here individual and collaborative writing and learning, electronic mail, the Word Wide Web, computer-conferencing, and voice-activated systems are discussed in turn. Part four considers whether or not writing with computers changes the ways that people write, think and learn. The chapter concludes that writing with computers facilitates writing but that it does not necessarily alter its nature. Writers learn from writing – whether or not it is computer based. However, computers and computer networks provide environments where the writing and learning processes may be supported in ways that are not possible without the technology.

1   INTRODUCTION

In this chapter it is taken as axiomatic that writing involves thinking and learning. This view has been cogently discussed in the previous chapters and we do not wish to dwell on it here. What we do want to do, however, is to discuss the effects of new technology on writing and thus, by implication, on writing to learn.

Many people who write documents today now use personal computers and computer-aided writing programs – and this includes children. But the new technology has invaded more than just the physical act of writing. It is also used in the planning, the researching and the preparation for writing. And it is used in the production of the final output. Indeed, it is remarkable how our methods of writing and reproducing text have changed over the last thirty years or so and, doubtless, will continue to do so.

In this chapter we wish to consider three aspects of this development:
1) We shall discuss the nature of writing, and how different people go about it.
2) We shall discuss the effects of using new technology upon these procedures.

J. Hartley, & P. Tynjälä (2001). New technology, writing and learning. In: G. Rijlaarsdam (Series Ed.) & P. Tynjälä, L. Mason & K. Lonka (Volume Eds), *Studies in Writing, Volume 7, Writing as a Learning tool: Integrating Theory and Practice,* 161 – 182.© 2001 Kluwer Academic Publishers. Printed in the Netherlands.

3) Finally we shall speculate about whether or not using new technologies changes
    the ways that writers think – and learn.
Our theme throughout this chapter is that writing with computers is very different
from writing without them. We shall argue that new technology facilitates many
traditional aspects of writing and thus that writing to learn is made easier with new
technology. But, as we shall point out, we think that it is much less clear whether or
not this new technology actually changes our processes of writing, thinking and
learning.

2   THE NATURE OF WRITING

Many children and adults write a great deal. And the kinds of things that they write
about vary. Some items are dashed off without much thought – letters home, re-
minder-notes, *etc.* Some require more painstaking effort – a love letter, a poem, a
poster for a research presentation, an essay for a study course, or an overview chapter such as this one.
    The authors of books and articles about the nature of writing (*e.g.*, Hayes &
Flower, 1986; Hayes, 1996; Sharples, 1999) typically divide the process of writing
into three overlapping stages as follows:
*   *Planning and collecting* – thinking about the content of the text, its organisation
    and what materials are needed;
*   *Initial drafting leading to more final writing* – putting down one's thoughts on
    paper – or on screen – and
*   *Revising and editing* – re-thinking and re-planning the content, as well as cor-
    recting spelling errors, checking the page-numbers of publications, and the like.
Young children have to think concurrently about writing neatly (if they are writing
by hand); the spelling of particular words; their grammar; the clarity and length of
their sentences; grouping sentences to form paragraphs; and making these paragraphs cohere together to form subsections of the text. With very young children the
physical act of writing interferes with their concentration on the content. For skilled
writers the problems are reversed. Thinking about the content interferes with the
production of the text. Thus skilled writers have the same problems as novices, but
they are more likely to be aware of them in the opposite order. But all writers move
to and fro between these various stages: there is no set order and there is no limit to
the number of times that any one stage might be revisited. And, when producing
anything other than a routine text, many writers are likely to have a selection of materials on their desk or nearby (*e.g.*, books and articles), parts of which might be
incorporated into the final product. Small wonder then that writing is a complex
task.
    Some researchers (*e.g.*, Wason, 1970) have suggested that in order to improve
our writing skills it is helpful to separate out these different aspects of writing. Thus
they suggest that during the *planning* stage we should map out the broad issues that
we wish to cover and the sequence in which we will eventually put them. Often this
is done by sketching in a few sub-headings. During the *writing* stage they suggest
that we should write as quickly as we can, without paying a great deal of attention to

punctuation and to spelling, or even to completing sentences. *Reviewing* and *editing* can follow later, and these stages too can be subdivided. For example, we might review first for content, then for grammar and style, and finally edit the format of the references.

But, of course, different writers write in different ways. In one study the writing styles of 88 highly productive academic psychologists were assessed with a questionnaire (Hartley & Branthwaite, 1989). By using a statistical method called cluster analysis the authors were able to describe different kinds of writers. These were distinguished in terms of (1) their attitudes and (2) their styles of composition. Thus there were 'enthusiastic' or 'anxious' writers, and there were 'doers' (people who got on with it) or 'thinkers' (people who dallied, and wrote multiple drafts). And, as one might expect, productivity was highest with the 'enthusiastic doers'. Productivity and the use of new technology need not necessarily be related but it is of interest to note that Cohen (1996) reported that more productive academics made a greater use of new technologies. Thus, it may be that people who want to be effective and productive are eager to apply new tools in their work.

Torrance, Thomas and Robinson (1994) similarly described three kinds of postgraduate writers in the social sciences. In their research Torrance and his colleagues distinguished between:

- *planners* – those who preferred to have their ideas clear before starting to write, and who produced few drafts;
- *revisers* – those who preferred to start writing first before taking final decisions about content; and
- *mixed* – those who planned but were then forced to change their plans by repeated revising.

Torrance and his colleagues reported that their 'planners' claimed – in self-report questionnaires – to write more text overall in a given time period than did their 'revisers' and the 'mixed' students. Both the 'planners' and the 'revisers' seemed happy with their writing styles, but members of the 'mixed' group reported more difficulties and anxieties.

It is important to note at this point that the individual differences between writers described in many separate studies may not be persistent ones (despite the remarkably consistent results obtained by Levy & Ransdell, 1996). Presumably people's methods and styles of writing vary with the individual and the task in hand. Easy tasks do not require much planning, whereas difficult ones do. So the simple labels that we researchers use to describe different kinds of writers do not in fact do justice to the variety of writing styles that exist. One thing that writers have in common, however, is that they are trying to communicate with their reader. In planning, revising and editing they are involved in learning from what they have written in order to make their meaning clearer.

3   WRITING AND LEARNING WITH COMPUTERS

3.1 Individuals, Word Processors and Computer-Based Writing Environments

When considering individuals writing with computers we find it helpful to think about computer-aided writing programs at four levels of complexity. These four levels are:

Level 1. Early simple programs used for word-processing – making deletions and substitutions, moving paragraphs and sentences about, and printing the text in attractive formats.

Level 2. More modern programs that add to the above – *e.g.*, style, spelling and grammar checkers, and programs that assist with the preparation of indexes and references.

Level 3. More complex programs that aid writing at a higher level – programs that help with the planning and organising of the material. – *e.g.*, outliners, document templates, and 'ideas processors'.

Level 4. Even more modern systems, commonly called 'computer-based writing environments' which assist with a whole suite of programs.

Here we shall describe research conducted at each of these levels.

Level 1 programmes. Much of the early research on computer-aided writing was carried out with programs at this level. The authors of these studies drew attention to:

How much easier (especially for young children) it was to write with a keyboard than with a pen or pencil (after they had learned how to use the keyboard).

How much easier (for all of us) it was to read printed rather than hand-written text.

How much easier it was to make corrections (*e.g.* of spelling) on screen, compared with typing or with writing with pen and paper.

How much easier it was to re-sequence, delete, and re-write sections of text compared with previous methods. Every version looked neat and tidy, unlike edited typed or hand-written text.

How much was *lost* through this process. It was hard (as researchers) to see or understand the processes involved in writing when the crossings out, insertions, and revised sequences didn't appear, and when previous versions were deleted. (Fiormonte, Babini, & Selvaginni (1999) provide an interesting discussion of how useful it is to keep these 'error traces' in studying second-language learning.)

Generally speaking the authors of early articles about simple word-processors predicted that using the new technology at all levels of the educational system would lead to more drafting and revising, longer texts, and texts of better quality. In other words, those word-processors would facilitate writing and learning. There was some evidence to support these claims but much of it was equivocal, particularly that on the effects of revising. Many of the early studies were simply too short, and the participants not practiced enough with word-processing systems for fair comparisons to be made (Wolfe *et al.*, 1996).

Level 2 programs. More modern computer-aided writing programs facilitate the composition of word-processed text as well as just the word-processing of it. Spelling checkers provide a limited example at this level, but grammar and style checkers such as *Grammatik 5* provide more sophisticated examples. Table 1 below lists the kinds of errors that *Grammatik 5* detects. Programs such as these can be run after composing the text, or nowadays concurrently whilst writing it. Our present word-processors, for example, underline spelling errors in red, and grammatical ones in green, as we are writing. We can thus stop and correct as we go, or we can keep going and then edit sections of text at will. During this editing process we can reflect on what we have said, and try to make it clearer. This way we are learning about our writing skills and our thinking contemporaneously.

Table 1. Examples of different types of errors detected by Grammatik 5.

Grammatical errors	Mechanical errors	Stylistic errors
adjective errors	spelling errors	long sentences
adverb errors	capitalisation errors	wordy sentences
article errors	double word	passive tenses
clause errors	ellipsis misuse	end of sentence prepositions
comparative/superlative use	end of sentence punctuation	split infinitives
double negatives	incorrect punctuation	clichés
incomplete sentences	number style errors	colloquialisms
noun phrase errors	question mark errors	Americanisms
object of verb errors	quotation mark misuse	archaic language
possessive misuse	similar words	gender-specific words
preposition errors	split words	jargon
pronoun errors		abbreviation errors
sequence of tense errors		paragraph problems
subject-verb errors		questionable word usage
tense changes		

Early studies of grammar checkers focused on assessing how useful such programs were – particularly for novice writers (*e.g.* see Macdonald, 1983). More recent studies have focused on making comparisons between different programs to see which is the most effective (*e.g.* see Kohut & Gorman, 1995; Nisbet, Spooner, Arther, & Whittaker, 1999). Current studies seem to be concentrating more on highlighting the deficiencies of grammar checkers (*e.g.* see Dale & Douglas, 1996; Sydes & Hartley, 1997). In an earlier paper the first author of this chapter suggested that authors should use both human and computer aids to editing as both have advantages and disadvantages (Hartley, 1984). This is a view that we still hold. However, Pennington (1993) has suggested that grammar checkers should not be used by second-language learners, or by non-proficient writers.

Owston and Wideman (1997) describe the results obtained from a three-year study of children writing with what we have called level one and level two programs. The children with level one programs used their computers relatively infrequently whereas the children with level two programs used their computers on a daily basis. The results showed that the latter group of children significantly improved the quality of their writing with respect to the former – although clearly this could be the result of the increased practice rather than the different levels of program.

Level 3 programs. A number of investigators are currently working on programs that will aid the composing process in an even more sophisticated way. In addition to work, for example, on computer-generated summaries, abstracts and indexes (*e.g.*, see Lehman, 1999; Paice, 1994) and automatic translation (*e.g.*, see A. Hartley & Paris, 1997) researchers and software designers are now writing programs to aid the planning and the organisational sides of writing. Kellogg (1994) for instance discusses three main difficulties that writers experience here:

• attentional overload – having to cope with too many processes all at once;
• idea bankruptcy – a failure to generate usable ideas; and
• anxiety and emotion – which can lead to so-called 'writer's block'.

Kellogg describes a variety of computer programs that help to deal with these fundamental difficulties. 'Funnel' programs channel the writer's attention into only one or two processes at a time. 'Inventor' programs help the writer to form and relate concepts; and 'therapist' programs give feedback and reassurance to the writer. Kellogg describes several computer programs under each heading, as well as programs that combine these different functions, and he gives references to research conducted with them. However, he concludes that these tools are still in their infancy and that they are controversial – so more research is needed (see Nisbet *et al.*, 1999).

Level 4 programs. Sharples and his colleagues provide one example of work on developing suites of sophisticated programs to help people write and learn from their writing. Sharples (1999) describes the development of his programs that he and his colleagues collectively call *The Writer's Assistant.* These programs aim to assist the writer throughout the writing process, from the generation and capture of ideas to the production of a connected piece of prose, combining the effects of a text editor, an 'ideas processor' and an 'outliner' editor' (Sharples, Goodlet, & Pemberton, 1989). Thus, *The Writer's Assistant* not only helps the writer to format the text but to generate new ideas as well.

Another example of a suite of programs designed to enhance students' literacy is what Bransford *et al.* (1996) have called MOST environments (Multi-media environments that Organize and Support Texts). A major goal of these environments is to support children's learning by organising instruction around visually rich and meaningful 'macro contexts' that students and teacher can share and explore. MOST environments emphasise the use of audiovisual media but they also include much literary work. For example, children may create their own books composed of vocabulary they already know. However, characteristic of MOST environments is that they move beyond the traditional text-based curricula and make use of multimedia technologies allowing the interaction between written and oral language with audiovisual information. MOST environments have been successfully used in promoting students' listening comprehension, language acquisition, reading and mental model building. Especially those children who are at risk of school failure have benefited from these environments that integrate 'pure' linguistic activities with audiovisual perception and expression.

Other examples of computer-based writing environments are described in the following section, where we consider group rather than individual writing.

3.2   Writing and Learning Together: Collaboration and Co-Operation

Although it is usual to discuss writing as though it is an individual activity, a great deal of co-operative and/or collaborative writing also takes place. (There is some debate over the different meaning of these two terms that we are using interchangeably here.) In some sense, since most academic writing builds upon the work of others, all such writing can be said to be collaborative – see Nancy Nelson's chapter in this volume, and Sharples (1999). However, what we are dealing with here are writing and learning processes that are intentionally supported by peer collaboration.

What then are the characteristics of collaborative writing, and how might new technology impinge upon them? In this chapter we do not have sufficient space to distinguish between writing in pairs and writing in larger groups, and we shall use the label 'collaborative writing' to describe both paired and group work. Using collaboration in learning to write has been argued for on the basis of the Vygotskian view of the social nature of learning on the one hand, and on the basis of process-based approach to writing on the other hand. The literature in this field (Crook, 1994; Littleton & Light, 1999; Speck, Johnson, Dice, & Heaton, 1999) suggests that collaborative writing can be:

- more efficient – because different aspects of the task can be shared out;
- of better quality – because different individuals can contribute different ideas, and different expertise;
- better thought out – because each individual has to take into account the others' points of view;
- written more quickly – because the less-able contributor is helped by the more-able; or
- written more slowly – because the less-able contributor holds back the more-able ones.

Although collaborative writing is by no means unproblematic (see, for example Neuwirth & Wojahn, 1996), it generally provides a good context for learning to write and writing to learn. But how might new technology affect the process? As with individual writing the new technology itself does not necessarily improve the quality of writing or learning but it creates opportunities for improvements. In this way it may facilitate, or provide a vehicle for better writing and learning. Thus Zeni (1994) illustrated – with transcripts – how two 11-year-olds interacted during a writing assignment using a word-processor. The interactions included talking, typing, and reading back what they had written, as well as non-verbal responses. The extracts showed how oral language and reading back were essential to the development of the texts. Zeni commented, however, that the computers were *not* the key component. Collaboration – and reflection – was seen as much more powerful. Indeed, Sharples (1999) also notes that what distinguishes group from individual computer-aided writing is 'the talk'.

'The talk' – or the interaction between students during the writing process – can also be in a written form, and it too can be facilitated and mediated with computers. This is the case with collaborative writing tools designed to support peer interaction as well as teacher feedback. The PREP Editor (Neuwirth & Wojahn, 1996) is one example of a new type of word processor that allows writers and reviewers communicate throughout the process. While using the PREP Editor the writers and reviewers may create electronic margins or columns in which they can write their texts and comments. For example, a student may write plans in one column, a draft text in another column and provide a third column for comments. In addition to specialised programs of this kind, the new versions of the most widely used word processors also allow readers to add comments into the text.

Neuwirth and Wojahn (1996) have examined the use of the PREP Editor in a university writing course, called *Argumentation*. Based on classroom observation, and interviews with the instructor and some students, the authors identified three primary ways the program was used by the instructor and the students. These were: coaching peer reviews, articulating knowledge about revision, and facilitating communication about writing. First, with the PREP Editor the teacher not only commented on students' drafts but she also used the program to comment on the peer reviews so as to coach students in the reviewing process and to help them to assess the value of the comments in light of their own goals for their texts. The second way the instructor and the students used the program was to help overcome the difficulties students face in revision. For example, the instructor asked students to make columns for comparing the old and new version in relation to comments they had received. If students had not responded to the comment, they were to record why they didn't, and if they did respond, they were asked to write a brief note about how they attempted to address the comment. This way the instructor used the program to support students in making their thinking about revisions more visible or, in other words, she encouraged them to reflect actively on their writing. The third benefit of the PREP Editor experienced by the students and the instructor was fostering more effective communication. For example, with the network-based system students and teachers may communicate and share their ideas without being in the same place or without meeting at a certain time.

So far, we have discussed how new technology may be used in collaboration for learning to write. Now it is time to move on to discuss the collaboration for writing to learn. Collaboration has long been recognized as an important element in learning and therefore much effort in recent years has been put into the design of collaborative learning environments and computer tools for collaborative learning (*e.g.*

Crook, 1994; Dillenbourg, 1999; Koschman 1996; Vosniadou, De Corte, & Mandl, 1994; Vosniadou, De Corte, Glaser, & Mandl, 1996). In most of these learning tools writing in different forms plays an important role.

Table 2. An Example of a CSILE discussion note in a session on biology. (Reproduced with permission from M. Scardamalia & C. Bereiter and Erlbaum Press). Key words: **P** = problem, **MT** = my theory, **INTU** = I need to understand, **NI** = new information. Letters in the initial brackets are the initials of the students contributing to the discussion.

(AR) **P**	How does a cell function?
(AR) **MT**	I think a cell functions by oxygen coming into the cell and then the cell can do its work by breathing.
(JD) **MT**	I agree with your theory but when the cell functions I don't think it is breathing. I think that the oxygen you're breathing is doing it.
(AK) **MT**	I think a cell functions by the 'things' inside itself. (organelles).
(AR) **INTU**	How does the oxygen get into the cell, if the cell really does breathe oxygen? (AK)
MT	I don't think that cells breath oxygen. I just think that the cells need oxygen to do their work. But if the cells do breath oxygen, I think there is some kind of tube in the cell that helps the cell get the oxygen it needs
(AR) **NI**	I found out that the cell takes food and oxygen in through the membrane. This happens regularly. The cell then changes the food and oxygen into energy. It uses the energy to do its work.
(AR) **INTU**	How do the food and oxygen get to the cell's membrane?
(AR) **MT**	I think that there are very small tubes that lead to each cell and that the food and oxygen go down those tubes and into the cell through the cell's membrane.
(AK) **MT**	I disagree with your theory, Andrea. I think that the oxygen and the food go into the cell automatically as a daily process.
(AK) **INTU**	What does the oxygen do when it gets to the cell?
(AR) **MT**	This is what I think the oxygen does when it gets to the cell. I think that the oxygen goes into the cell through the membrane and then it goes to the nucleus where it is turned into energy.

Among the most well-known specialised computer-based learning environments that involve the participants in writing together is the *CSILE* (Computer Supported Intentional Learning Environments) developed by Scardamalia and Bereiter (1996; Scardamalia, Bereiter, & Lamon, 1994). There are also commercial systems available, such as AT&T's *Learning Network*, Apple's *Global Education Network*, Microsoft's *Global Schoolhouse*, and several others (see Bisaillon, Clerc, & Ladouceur, 1999; Fabos & Young, 1999).

The aim of the *CSILE* system – to take just one example – is to prevent students from engaging in surface learning and busywork and to encourage them to take part in more meaningful learning and discussion, the process that Scardamalia and Bereiter call *collaborative knowledge building*. The system runs on networked computers – usually eight to a classroom. As Scardamalia and Bereiter (1996) report:

'It provides a single communal database into which students may enter various kinds of text and graphic notes. They can retrieve notes by others, comment on them (with authors being notified of the comments), link notes to one another, or create group discussion notes (see Table 2). CSILE-mediated discourse can be carried on in any or all academic areas, limited only by the availability of machine time'. (p. 155)

CSILE differs from e-mail in that it is not a person-to-person medium. Notes entered in to communal database are not notes to any specific person – rather they form collective knowledge that is available for everyone.

CSILE is currently being used with a variety of subject matters at all levels, from Grade 1 to University, although it is most widely used in upper-elementary and middle schools. The authors cite studies that show that CSILE students consistently do better on tests of understanding and depths of explanations than do non-CSILE students.

3.3 Electronic-Mail

Many people – including children – now communicate with electronic mail. To some extent e-mail changes the way that people write and some commentators already talk of e-mail as an additional genre for written language. Studies of the language used in e-mail suggest that it lies somewhere between formal written discourse and conversation. Messages in e-mail tend to be short and speech-like, and less care is taken with grammar and spelling (Davis & Brewer, 1997; Eklundh, 1994; Gotcher & Kanervo, 1997; Rice, 1997; Wild, 1999). There is some suggestion that academic e-mails are more distorted than business ones, possibly because greater proportions of business e-mail are sent to multiple recipients rather than to individuals (Gains, 1999).

E-mail can be a useful tool for writing to learn. Some of the advantages are that when a student sends an e-mail he or she is writing to a specific person – not doing an exercise for the teacher – and thus the audience for the communication is better defined. Furthermore this person often replies so that, unlike many writing exercises, a natural dialogue is set up (Britsch & Berkson, 1997). Trenchs (1996) suggests that this can be particularly valuable in second-language learning. Wild (1999) provides examples of where adults (writing in their first language) expressed their thoughts more quickly when using e-mail and, similarly, revised them more quickly in response to the more immediate and informal feedback obtained with e-mail. Wild's examples came from two e-mail lists – where members communicate with each other on specific topics, and individual writing soon merges into group writing. Hammond (1999) lists the benefits of being a member of such an e-mail discussion group as follows:

- an opportunity to articulate ideas on a topic and receive feedback on one's contribution;
- an opportunity to reflect on the ideas and perspectives of others, particularly of one's peers;
- an opportunity to gain help, as and when it is needed; and
- an opportunity to become a member of a social environment that increases motivation and supports learning.

Hammond also includes a useful discussion between the characteristics of what he calls 'communicative learners', 'quiet learners' and 'non-participant learners' in such groups (the latter often being called 'lurkers' in the jargon).

E-mail systems make it also easier to use dialogue journal writing (see Staton, Shuy, Peyton, & Reed, 1998) in schools. Dialogue journal communication is a written conversation between two students (or a student and a teacher) taking place on continuous basis, about topics of mutual interested related to curricular contents. As e-mail communication is perceived as a less formal mode of writing and as journals provide a tool for expressive writing, e-mail mediated journals may provide students with a more pleasant forum for exchanging ideas than that provided by classroom instruction. However, as Fabos and Young (1999) remind us, the informal e-mail writing style can also be considered as an impediment to learning if the writing is sloppy or to goes easily off-task.

Marttunen (1992, 1997) examined e-mail communication compared to traditional teaching on a university sociology of education course. In this comparison the traditional group (without e-mail conversation) achieved better results when measured by traditional examination questions (requiring knowledge telling and reproduction of information as such), but the e-mail group succeeded better in tasks requiring argumentation skills. In a content analysis of students' e-mail messages it was found that the messages' level of argumentation improved during the e-mail course and that it was higher in those messages that included counter-argumentation targeted against other students' standpoints. These results suggest that e-mail communication is useful tool, especially for enhancing students' argumentation skills, and that counter-argumentation can be explicitly encouraged.

Some other case studies are now beginning to appear on the use of e-mail, discussion lists and newsgroups in instruction. Barr (1994), Fabos and Young (1999) and Rudy (1996) provide useful critiques of such studies. It remains to be seen whether or not the informality of e-mail will become more acceptable and will spill over into other more traditional forms of writing.

3.4 The World Wide Web, Hypertexts and Hypermedia

The international use of e-mail and worldwide web (WWW) pages by students and schoolchildren provides a further illustration of how the new technologies can facilitate collaborative writing and writing to learn (*e.g.*, see Barr, 1994; Downing & Brown, 1997; Fabos & Young, 1999; Leng, Shave, Scauer, Muehlbacher, & Aiken, 1999; Multisilta, 1997). Many writers suggest that international telecommunication increases participants' motivation, makes writers more aware of their audience, increases their written output and 'broadens their minds'. Thus the new technology here – like e-mail – is helping in the move away from didactic teaching to more learner-centred instruction – in which writing to learn has a more important role.

Most of the documents in WWW are hypertext documents. Hypertext differs from the regular linear text in that it includes links between different parts of the text and it can be read, consequently, in a non-linear way. Hypertexts can be part of larger hypermedia systems that, in addition to text, may include graphics, animations, sound and video material, and all of these items may be interlinked. Although composing into most current hypermedia systems may be too difficult for some, hypermedia may be used as a resource for writing assignments. For example Spoehr (1994) described how a hypermedia corpus called ACCESS was used in high school history and literature classes to provide material for two types of assignments: 1) preparing for classroom discussions and 2) researching and writing an essay. The findings of the study indicated that the students who had used the ACCESS showed better academic performance than non-ACCESS students and their conceptual representations became better structured and more complete.

Goldman (1996) argues that hypermedia systems can play a transformative role in our thinking and research on text processing and learning. According to her, the very nature of hypermedia supports active and constructive reading and writing and demands greater metacognitive functioning than does linear text. Hypermedia systems also make it possible to scaffold reflective activities by different explicit metacognitive cues.

Bonk, Medury and Reynolds (1994) have suggested that the marriage between collaborative writing and multimedia and hypermedia tools might create a new educational term, *integrated collaborative writing media* or *cooperative hypermedia*, for example. Bonk *et al.* state that through cooperative hypermedia systems, children may more readily realise that knowledge is socially constructed, represented and organised. As a communal database environment the CSILE system described above has several of the characteristics of a hypertext or hypermedia environment of this kind, enabling the students to add comments to someone else's note, to link notes, or to attach graphic notes, and so on. As the students' work continues they jointly produce a complex hypertext or even a hypermedia database in which each entry is a node in a larger web of information. In this way each individual student's work will be visible and available for collective use and students construct their understandings with the help of other students' knowledge productions. Research results on the effects of the CSILE on students' learning have been positive (Scardamalia *et al.*, 1994). For example, compared with problem solving in face-to-face co-operative groups, CSILE students outperformed face-to-face groups. This may be due to the fact that in face-to-face discussions there usually is very much variation between students in the extend to which group members contribute, while in using CSILE students seem to participate more equally. Thus, a computer network system may help silent students participate more actively.

In addition to offering actual tools for writing and learning, the web-based systems, especially the WWW, offer considerable amounts of information for writers and learners. Many university departments have designed home pages from which students may find useful information for preparing their term papers, essays and other assignments. For example, a list of self-help documents on the writing process may be found on page of the University of Illinois at Urbana-Champaign (see, http://www.english.uiuc.edu/cws/wworkshop/). The links include, for example, collections of advice, online sources on documentation styles, and even hypertext guides for writers.

So, just as Tynjälä concluded in her chapter that integrating reading, writing and group discussions seems to provide a promising way of using writing as a learning tool, we may now also conclude that multimedia and hypermedia may provide tools and content for this kind of integration. However, as Fabos and Young (1999) suggest, there does appear to be a good deal of rhetoric rather than evidence in this discussion. Although many publications are devoted to this topic, there are few rigorous studies of the effects of these kinds of new technology on students learning in general and writing to learn in particular.

3.5 Computer Conferencing

Computer-conferencing can be seen as another example of how new technology facilitates faster communication and provides new elements in the learning process. With computer-conferencing people from different parts of the world may join together to exchange views. Although modern technology allows a video and audio connection between the partners, most often computer conferences are still arranged solely in a written format. Harvey (1998), for example, describes how 22 authors collaborated to produce a text on evaluation. She writes:

> 'In order to encourage collaboration between the authors, who were based in universities as far apart as Aberdeen and Auckland the (group) set up a private WWW site and a mailbase discussion group. Once the contributors had contributed their sections(s), each of these was made available for review from the WWW page. Any comments were fed back either directly to the author... or to the whole group. Authors were encouraged to feedback comments on all the sections. In addition to this, it was decided to allocate each of the contributors to a group of three and to ask them to make a more detailed review of the other two author's work'. (p. .3)

In more instructional contexts such facilities can be copied and adapted. The discussions may be more local – involving smaller groups – and more focused. The tutor in charge might set specific topics and readings for discussion and these might – or might not be – available on the WWW. Tutors might ask for, and give comments on, essay plans using e-mail. Teachers might set search tasks requiring the use of the WWW.

Torney-Purta (1996) has described a project called ICONS (International Communications and Negotiations Project) that involves students in international negotiation about political issues. Within ICONS students role-play or pretend to be diplomats from different countries. At the beginning of the course the students receive a lengthy scenario set in the near future that describes the world situation with respect to international and economic issues, including an outline of the countries' position on these issues. Students work in teams that represent certain countries. The course begins with introductory lectures and with each team writing a position paper on foreign policy in the assigned country. After this students begin negotiations in computer conferences concerning issues such as human rights and the global environment. The team members communicate face-to-face about the messages to be sent but all the communication between the teams takes place via e-mail and the computer conference in written format. The students are reminded throughout the course that they are supposed to play real diplomats and make decisions about international problems and that most of the writing produced is primarily for the critique

of peers rather than the approval of the teachers. The role of the teachers is to organise and to support the interaction and to grade some of the assignments.

The ICONS students' communication and learning was examined both at the
level of the discourse community (that is, as collaborative construction of meanings
and as socially shared cognition) and at the level of individual students' conceptual
development. The findings at the level of the discourse communities indicated that
the computer conferencing created an environment similar to the one of reciprocal
teaching (Brown & Campione, 1996; Palincsar & Brown, 1984) in which students
support each other's knowledge construction. Further, the discourse communities
created within the teams represented more authentic ways of learning than in most
social sciences classes because the conferences simulated discourse of real-life international political communities. At the individual level the students' conceptual
development was examined with graphic schema maps, interviews and thinking-
aloud problem solving. On average, the students' answers to the problems were
more complex after the ICONS experience and their schemata had clearly been restructured in the direction of more complexity for the majority of participants. These
findings suggest that writing in the context of computer conferencing enhances both
individual cognition and group interaction. (For other examples of computer conferencing, see Hansen, Dirckinck-Holmfelf, Lewis, & Rugelj, 1999.)

Of particular interest in these studies of computer conferencing and e-mail studying is the role played by assessment in the students' writing (e.g., see Jones, 1999;
Lea, 2000; Rimmershaw, 1999). Lea, for example, compared the different kinds of
writing required in two different computer-conferencing courses run by the Open
University in the UK. She showed that the sorts of writing required during the
course differed as a consequence of the course design, but that this changed when it
came to the end-of-course assessment – where both courses were assessed by a traditional essay-type examination. Assessment issues also come to the fore when there
is debate about plagiarism (which is easier with the new technology) and whether or
not students have 'co-operated' (i.e. worked together) or 'collaborated' (i.e. cheated)
(Wojtas, 1999). Thus new forms of collaborative learning require new thinking
about assessment – as Pirjo Linnakylä indicated in the previous chapter.

Although many optimistic views and accounts of successful experiences of the
use of the Internet tools have been published (e.g. Downing & Brown, 1997; Owston, 1997), there are still many problems, limitations and deficiencies in these tools.
Roschelle and Pea (1999) make this very clear in their critical comment on this issue
(see also Windschitl, 1998). These authors point out that most of the Internet tools
currently available are not robust and simple enough for use in average classrooms,
and that the process of authoring and composing contents to web is not well integrated into web browsers, requiring the kind of mastery of complex technical products that most students do not possess. Furthermore, Roschelle and Pea note that the
web is overrated as a tool for collaboration because creating shared understanding –
a prerequisite for collaboration – seems to be harder in web environment than in
face-to-face interaction (see also Hansen et al., 1999). However, Roschelle and Pea
envisage that in the future these kinds of problems may find their solutions, for example, in systems such as CSILE described above that support collaborative representations and socio-cognitive scaffolding.

In sum, it seems to us that although e-mail, WWW and other Internet tools provide useful tools for writing to learn, they do not replace face-to-face interaction, more traditional type of collaborative writing or indeed 'regular' writing but, rather, bring variation and new forms into them.

3.6 Voice Recognition

Most of the issues discussed in this chapter are, of course, mainly relevant for writers who are starting to work with computer-aided writing programs after many years of experience writing by hand. What the picture will be like with writers who have used the new technology 'from birth', as it were, remains to be seen. One cannot but help think that our children's ways of writing will be different from our own, especially when keyboards are displaced by voice-recognition systems and multimedia forms of the WWW become available on the latest mobile telephone/terminal.

Table 3. Using voice recognition software: an example[1].

Rajik is 9 years old. He has cerebral palsy associated with perceptual difficulties. He finds writing by hand very difficult because of his motor difficulties and he is very slow when using a keyboard. He holds his pen so tightly it exhausts him and makes him tense. In addition he has problems with even the simplest spelling. This is causing frustration because the only way he can get his many interesting ideas down on paper at reasonable speed is to dictate to a scribe. Rajik has clear speech and he reads well, so speech recognition is being considered for him. He has had an initial training session, with promising results, but there are concerns that need to be addressed. Rajik is quite adamant that he does not want to use it in his mainstream primary classroom because of the attention it will draw to him. It is also difficult to see how the system would cope in the classroom either. He is willing to consider using it for homework, and his family has a computer that will run the software. But his parents have concerns about their ability to train him in the system. Rajik has decided to wait until his final year at primary school before trying again.

There are as yet few studies of the effects of using voice recognition systems on writing (but see Gretsch, 1999; Reece & Cumming, 1996). The greatest advances with this technique have come in the field of learning disability. Here voice recognition devices have been developed to help the learning-disabled and the visually and the physically impaired, as well as adults/children with dyslexia. (Examples of this work can be found in Bickley, Carlson, Cudd, Hunnicutt, & Reimers, 1998; Blamires, 1999; Nisbet & Poon, 1998; Nisbet *et al.*, 1999; Scrase, 1998; Wetzel, 1996; Yasuda *et al.*, 1998).

Elliott (1998) describes how, as an adult dyslexic reader, she uses the program *DragonDictate*. As she puts it:

---

[1] *Text reprinted with permission of Sage Publications Ltd from L. Rahamim (1999) Scaling physical barriers. In M. Blamires (Ed.).* Enabling technology for inclusion. *(p. 81). London: Paul Chapman.*

'I talk and *DragonDictate* writes for me; when I need my work read back a software package called *Keystone* will do so. I am now learning in an environment that does not create the obstacles that caused stress and failure for many years' (p. 14)

Table 3 provides another example. These new approaches thus serve, as Seymour Papert once so vividly put it, to 'release trapped intelligence'.

4   COMPUTERS, WRITING AND THINKING

Underlying all of these illustrations of the effects of new technology on writing and learning there is an ongoing debate about whether or not new technology will change the ways that people write, think and learn. Undoubtedly, the new technology has – and will continue to – change the ways in which people write. But is this change only a cosmetic one? Is what we do with new technology basically much the same as what we did with the old technology? Or are the changes more fundamental than this?

Kellogg (1994: 144) expresses one side of this argument clearly: 'I prefer at the outset the straightforward assumption that tool choice fails to affect knowledge use, writing quality, and fluency'. The opposing view is well expressed in many quotations provided in Chandler (1995) and especially in Marshall McLuhan's dictum, 'the medium is the message'. One consequence of accepting Kellogg's position is that the previous research on writing is directly relevant to current research with new technology. However, if we accept the McLuhan view, then not much of the previous research on writing is relevant to how children and adults write today.

These issues become very concrete if we think, for example, of the case of Matthew, a sixteen-year-old acquaintance of the first author of this chapter, who had been forbidden by his history teacher to use his word-processor when writing his history essays. Why? Well, the teacher insisted, Matthew would have to write in longhand when sitting the examination. The teacher argued that the ways of thinking required for writing essays in long-hand under examination conditions were different from those required for writing essays at home with a word-processor.

Was the teacher right? What evidence is there that writing with a word-processor requires different kinds of thinking? We are not sure how we can answer questions such as these. There are several possibilities:

- Writing with a word-processor might not involve any changes in processes or in the resulting products.
- Writing with a word processor might involve some changes in processes, but without any obvious effects on the resulting products.
- Writing with a word-processor might involve some changes in processes, leading to some changes (hopefully improvements) in the resulting products.

It seems to us that more sophisticated computer-aided writing programs at level 3 and 4 described above may indeed alter people's writing processes. But whether or not this changes their products or their ways of thinking and learning is a moot point.

Table 4. The effects of technology on the writing process: accounts of the first author's methods of writing over time.

1980: I wrote my first draft in longhand – very roughly – and then I re-wrote it again in longhand maybe once or twice more. I then gave the manuscript it to my secretary who typed it out double-spaced (on a manual typewriter). I then edited this 'printed' version. This usually entailed moving paragraphs about, or even deleting them, and re-phrasing ideas and sentences. My secretary then re-typed what I had written, and we continued this process until I was satisfied or I dared not give it to my secretary again! Figures 3a and 3b (in Hartley, 1980: 193-196) provide examples.

1990: I wrote my first draft in longhand – very roughly – and then I re-wrote it again more neatly. My secretary word-processed the manuscript and printed it out double-spaced. I then edited the printout fairly drastically by hand. My secretary then made the changes for me on the word-processor and then re-printed the document. This procedure then re-iterated, perhaps several times.

1993: I wrote my first draft in longhand and then I word-processed it, edited it on screen and printed it out double-spaced. I then edited the printout by hand and re-processed it, and so the process continued until I was satisfied. (Often this meant that I found I was eventually changing things back to what they were before I last edited them...)

2000: I currently sketch a few preliminary notes or headings on the back of an envelope or rough sheet of paper, and then compose directly 'on screen'. I word-process the text and edit it as I go along, and again after completing a section, article or chapter. I incorporate ideas from subsequent reading as I am writing. I print out initial versions to help with the editing process, and I keep re-iterating this process of composing on screen, editing, adding information, printing and revising the printouts until I am satisfied. I then send off what I call 'the draft version' to colleagues, often by e-mail attachment, for their comments.

We imagine that many of the different kinds of writers that we described at the beginning of this chapter will have started to write with new technology in much the same way as they did before. However, when they discover what the new technology offers, then their strategies will begin to change. Table 4 documents the experiences of the first author of this chapter in this respect.

Well over one hundred studies must have been reported by now that have examined the effects of new technology on writing. (See the reviews by Bangert-Drowns, 1993; Cochran-Smith, 1991; Haas, 1996; Kellogg, 1994; Reed, 1966; Owston & Wideman, 1997.) Here, for the purpose of illustrating the various techniques used by different investigators, we shall outline the results from four typical enquiries. It can be seen from these examples that there are considerable differences in the approaches used and in the results of these investigators.

Enquiry 1. Kellogg and Mueller (1993) carried out two studies, the first with 16 relative novices and the second with 69 more experienced users of word-processors. In both experiments the participants – college students – were trained to classify their thoughts about their writing processes whilst they were writing and then, when they were asked by an experimenter, to press one of four keys to indicate what they were doing – *planning, writing, revising*, or *some other process*. After training and practice for 30 minutes, the participants composed an essay (within a thirty-minute time limit), half using a simple (level one) word-processor and half writing in longhand. They were interrupted approximately every 30 seconds and they responded each time by pressing one of the four keys. Two judges rated the resulting essays, using various measures of content and style.

The results of the first study showed no significant differences between the essays in terms of content but the hand-written essays were judged superior in style. It appeared with longhand that the three processes of planning, writing and revising required similar amounts of time but that, with the word-processor, *more time* was spent on planning and revising, and less on the actual writing. The results of the second study were very similar, with the more-experienced users of word-processors showing the effects slightly more clearly than the less-experienced ones in the first study. Since the time spent on writing the essays was the same for both studies, Kellogg & Mueller concluded that word-processors (at level one) restructured the process of writing, but failed to improve writing performance. (More recent studies, developing Kellogg's methodology, are described by Piolat, Thierrey, Rousey, Thunin, & Ziegler, 1999.)

Enquiry 2. Haas (1996: 77-115) reported the opposite results from Kellogg and Mueller with university students using a more complex (level 2) word-processing system. Here students spent *less time* planning when using a word-processor than when writing in longhand. In this study Haas examined the notes and the verbal protocols (recordings of what the students said) of 20 students writing with both a word-processor and in longhand. The study showed that the students spent significantly less time planning in the word-processing condition than in the handwriting one, and that this was particularly marked at the initial planning stage. More detailed analyses of the different kinds of planning used by students in this study showed that there was less conceptual planning and more sequential planning with word-processing than with handwriting. Haas commented that a likely explanation for these results was that the students began writing sooner and spent less time planning with the word-processor because making changes was easier with the word-processor. She also claimed that word-processing encouraged an over-preoccupation with tidying and fiddling at a local word or sentence level.

Enquiry 3. Oliver and Kerr (1993) studied the marks obtained by 240 student teachers who submitted essays in either a handwritten, typewritten or word-processed form (level 1). In addition, these students also completed a questionnaire on their writing strategies. The results indicated that the students who used a word-processor obtained higher marks than did those that used a typewriter or wrote their essays in longhand. Subsequent analyses revealed, however, that this was mainly an artefact of the amount of revision that the students did when they were writing their essays. Students who revised more, irrespective of which group they were in, obtained higher marks. But, of course, as word-processors facilitate revision, it is possible that they helped some students to achieve higher marks than they might have obtained without them.

Enquiry 4. Zellermayer, Salomon, Globerson, and Givon (1991) used a more advanced (level 3) writing system in their experiment. They used a specially designed computing tool that they called *The Writing Partner*. This suite of programs was designed on the basis of work carried out by Bereiter and Scardamalia (1987). The programs provided three kinds of help during writing: (a) memory support; (b) guides concerning evaluation and coherence; and (c) guides to remind the writer of rhetorical elements, writing goals, and the writer's audience. All three kinds of help were largely contingent upon the writer's input – that is to say the program 'chose' when to intervene, depending upon what the students wrote.

Zellermayer *et al.* (1991) studied 60 thirteen-fifteen-year-old pupils divided into three groups. Group 1, the control group, wrote five essays with a conventional word-processor. Group 2 wrote five essays using *The Writing Partner*. Group 3 wrote five essays with a version of *The Writing Partner* that provided the same guidance, but this time only at the writer's request.

Two trained judges assessed 'blind' the resulting essays on a single holistic rating scale and on five analytic scales designed to measure: number of ideas, coherence, idea development, cohesion and connectedness, and endings. The results showed that the group who used the original *Writing Partner* (Group 2) produced significantly better essays overall than did both the control group (Group 1) and the group who could solicit the programs when they wished (Group 3).

To test whether or not the computer-aided writing programs had changed writing performance, members of all three groups completed another essay, using pen and paper, two weeks later. The assumption was that if writing performance had been changed then this would show itself on such a post-experimental writing task. The results were very similar to those described above. The essays written by Group 2 were significantly better than the essays written by Groups 1 and 3.

Zellermayer *et al.* (1991) argued that the pupils who had used the original version of *The Writing Partner* had first of all internalised the cognitive writing strategies offered and then, subsequently, made use of them. They offered some support for this conclusion from data collected from a questionnaire about effective writing strategies that the pupils completed just before they wrote their post-test essays.

The results from these four enquiries are thus mixed. There is some evidence that the new technology can facilitate various aspects of writing, but there is little evidence to suggest that the nature of writing itself changes. Much appears to depend upon the participants, the writing tasks, the technology used, and the research methods employed.

At this point it may be instructive to consider some data collected by the first author when he was preparing this chapter. It occurred to him that as he had shifted from writing by hand to writing by computer, then it might be possible to detect changes in his writing over time. He thus analysed seven review chapters such as this one published over a thirty-year period, using the readability tools provided with the standard Microsoft package *'Office, '97'*. The results are shown in Table 5. It can be seen that there is in fact little difference over time. The average sentence lengths, and readability scores remain much the same. The number of passive sentences declines steeply from the first chapter in this genre, but that is really all. There is little evidence here, then, to suggest marked changes in output. Table 5 thus shows an example of where the changes in procedures documented in Table 4 have not lead to changes in the resulting products. It is possible of course that writing in a particular genre ensures that the end result will be much the same, although the ways of getting there may be different. But if ways of thinking as well as ways of writing have changed over time this is certainly not apparent in these data.

Table 5. Readability statistics for review chapters written by the first author over time.

Chapter date	1972	1978	1982	1987	1995	1999	2001[2]	Average
No. of words sampled	1032	978	990	1125	1014	1026	931	1014
No. of sentences	45	45	38	48	42	42	41	43
Average no. of words/ sentence	23	22	26	23	24	24	23	24
% passive sentences	35	13	21	14	21	19	17	20
Flesch index[3]	42	36	39	50	47	44	53	44
Kincaid grade level[4]	12	12	12	11	12	11	10	11

5   CONCLUDING REMARKS

People writing with computers now – with the additional help of e-mail, the WWW and collaborative tools – have much more rapid access to i) the materials that they need; and ii) the comments and assistance of colleagues. Furthermore, they find it easier to revise and edit their texts, and to explore the consequences of doing so. As far as making revisions is concerned a useful motto now seems to be, 'If in doubt, try it out'. Thus the new technology removes much of the effort previously entailed in writing.

In addition, writers using the new technology have much greater control over the appearance of the finished product. Gone are the days when writing involved a chain of separate experts – author – typist – editor – designer – printer – publisher – each contributing his or her own expertise and time to the finished text. Children today (working in groups, for example, to produce a school newspaper) come to appreciate the importance of all these diverse aspects of writing and to learn that writing involves more than just putting down words on paper.

---

[2] *This chapter.*
[3] *Flesch scores range from 0 – 100. The higher the score the more readable the text. But all of the scores here are designated 'difficult' except that of the present chapter and the 1987 one: these are labelled 'fairly difficult' (see Hartley, 1994 for further details).*
[4] *Add five to obtain an approximate reading age.*

Furthermore, this easier drafting allows authors writing lengthy documents over time (such as this chapter) to come to understand and to explain better the topics that they are working with. The process of knowledge transformation taking place in the writer's mind and in the continuously developing text leads to enhanced understanding and even changes in thinking (see, Scardamalia & Bereiter, 1991). It leads, in other words, to learning. This is illustrated in Table 6 that, to give just one example from this text, presents the first version of one of the earlier paragraphs for this chapter. Comparing this version with the final one (on page 162) shows – in a limited way – the effects of writing on thinking, and vice-versa.

Table 6. How writing changes thinking – or thinking changes writing!
The original version of the text shown on page 162 of this book.

Books and articles about the nature of writing typically divide the process of writing into three main, but overlapping stages. These involve:
- *Planning*: thinking about both the content of the text, and its organisation;
- *Writing*: putting down one's thoughts on paper – or on screen;
- *Editing*: re-thinking and re-planning, as well as correcting spelling errors and the like.
Skilled writers move constantly to and fro between these stages. When we are writing we have to think concurrently about writing neatly (if we are writing by hand): the spelling of some particular words; the grammar and the length of the sentences; how to group these sentences to form complete paragraphs; and how to make these paragraphs cohere to form particular sub-sections of the text. Also, when writing academic prose, we are likely to have a selection of materials on our desk or nearby (for example, books, previous articles written by ourselves, and articles by others) parts of which might be incorporated into the final product (see Chapters 2 and 3). Small wonder then that writing is a skilled and complex task!

Normally, of course, the effects of writing on learning are not apparent in the texts we read. We do not see the thinking, writing and learning processes. We do not see the initial drafts and the semi-completed versions. We only read the published versions. These published texts do not show the debates that the authors conduct with themselves (and sometimes with their colleagues) about what they are trying to say. Thus, for example, this present version of this chapter does not show the debates that we conducted with ourselves and with each other – whilst we were writing about it – on whether or not new technology changes the ways that people write and think. This debate eventually lead us to our conclusions reported here, and one of us to even more refined conclusions that have now been developed in a more recent article (Hartley, Howe, & McKeachie, in press).

Although most published papers seem to emphasise positive aspects of new technology we must not forget that there are also many problems in using it. These include hardware and software limitations, user resistance and lack of ability to choose and apply the right tool for a given task (Hansen *et al.*, 1999). Problems of this kind pose considerable challenges to computer and program designers, researchers and educators. In addition, problems related to the writing and learning processes themselves complicate the picture further.

Today research is expanding rapidly in the fields of writing and learning processes, computer assisted instruction (CAI), and computer supported collaborative learning (CSCL). What is needed now – we think – is a strengthening interdisciplinary research and partnerships with program designers, researchers and educators to develop practical tools based on theories of writing and learning processes. The development of the many promising tools described here and in other forums indicates that we can invent and develop even more useful and user-friendly systems for individual and collaborative knowledge construction in the future.

REFERENCES

Abbott, R. D., & Hughes, R. E. (1986, April). *Effects of verbal-graphic note-taking strategies on writing.* Paper presented at the annual meeting of the American Education Research Association, San Francisco, CA.

Ackerman, J. M. (1993). The promise of writing to learn. *Written Communication, 10*, 334-370.

Adnanes, M., & Ronning, W. M. (1998). Computer-networks in education – a better way to learn? *Journal of Computer Assisted Learning, 14,* 2, 148-157.

Albin, M. L., Benton, S. L., & Khramtsova, I. (1996). Individual differences in interest and narrative writing. *Contemporary Educational Psychology, 21*, 305-324.

Allan, J. (1996). Learning outcomes in higher education. *Studies in Higher Education, 21*, 93-108.

American Association for the Advancement of Science (1990). *Science for all Americans Project 2061.* New York: Oxford University Press.

American Association for the Advancement of Science (1993). *Benchmarks for science literacy.* New York: Oxford University Press.

American Association for the Advancement of Science (1998). *Blueprints for reform.* New York: Oxford University Press.

Anderson, D., Benjamin, B., & Paredes-Holt, B. (1998). *Connections. A guide to on-line writing.* Needham Heights, Mass.: Allyn and Bacon.

Anderson, J. R. (1982). Acquisition of cognitive skill. *Psychological Review, 89,* 369-406.

Anderson, J. R. (1987). Skill acquisition: Compilation of weak-method problem solutions. *Psychological Review, 94,* 192-210.

Anson, C. M., & Beach, R. (1995) *Journals in the classroom: writing to learn.* Norwood, MA: Christopher-Gordon Publishers.

Anthony, R. J., Johnson, T. D., & Yore, L. D. (1996). Write-to-learn science strategies. *Catalyst, 39,* 10-16.

Applebee, A. N. (1984). Writing and reasoning. *Review of Educational Research, 54*, 577-596.

Applebee, A. N. (1996). *Curriculum as conversation: Transforming traditions of teaching and learning.* Chicago: University of Chicago Press.

Applebee, A. N., & Langer, J. A. (1983). Instructional scaffolding: Reading and writing as natural language activities. *Language Arts, 60,* 168-175.

Applebee, A. N., Langer, J. A. & Mullis, I. V. S. (1985). *Writing: Trends across the decade, 1974-84* (Report No. 15-W-01). Princeton, NJ: Educational Testing Service.

Askeland, K. (1997, September). *Project organised learning – what is it 'really'?* Paper presented at the International Conference on Project Work in University Studies, Roskilde, Denmark.

Atkins, J. (1995). What should we be assessing? In P. Knight (Ed.), *Assessment for Learning in Higher Education* (pp. 25-33). London: Kogan Page.

Audet, R. H., Hickman, P., & Dobrynina, G. (1996). Learning logs: A classroom practice for enhancing scientific sense making. *Journal of Research in Science Teaching, 33*, 205-222.

Ausubel, D. P. (1968) *The psychology of meaningful verbal learning.* New York: Grune and Stratton.

Ballantyne, R., & Packer, J. (1995). The role of student journals in facilitating reflection at the doctoral level. *Studies in Continuing Education, 17*, 29-45.

Bangert-Drowns, R. L. (1993). The word-processor as an instructional tool: A meta-analysis of word-processing in writing instruction. *Review of Research in Education, 63,* 69-93.

Barr, H. (1994). Social studies by electronic mail. *Social Studies, 85,* 281-284.

Barrett, H. (1999). Strategic questions when planning for electronic portfolios. In P. Linnakylä, M. Kankaanranta, & J. Bopry (Eds.) *Portfolioita verkossa. Portfolios on the web* (pp. 36-53). University of Jyväskylä, Finland: Institute for Educational Research.

Bartlett, F. C. (1932). *Remembering: A study in experimental and social psychology.* Cambridge: Cambridge University Press.

Bartlett, F. C. (1958). *Thinking: An experimental and social study.* New York: Basic Books.

Baynham, M. (1999). Double-voicing and the scholarly 'I': On incorporating the words of others in academic discourse. *Text, 19*, 485-504.

Bazerman, C. (1985). Physicists reading physics: Schema-laden purposes and purpose-laden schema. *Written Commnication, 2,* 3-23.

Bazerman, C. (1988). Shaping written knowledge. Madison, WI: University of Wisconsin Press.

Bean, T. W., & Zulich, J. (1989). Using dialogue journals to foster reflective practice with preservice, content-area teachers. *Teacher Education Quarterly, 16,* 33-40.

Belanoff, P. & Dickson, M. (1991). *Portfolios. Process and products.* Portsmouth, NH: Boynton/Cook.

Benton, S. L., Corkill, A. J., Sharp, J. Downey, R., & Khramtsova, I. (1995). Knowledge, interest, and narrative writing. *Jounal of Educational Psychology, 87,* 66-79.

Benton, S. L., Kiewra, K. A., Whitfill, J. M., & Dennison, R. (1993). Encoding and external-storage effects on writing processes. *Journal of Educational Psychology, 85,* 267-280.

Bereiter, C. (1990). Aspects of an educational learning theory. *Review of Educational Research 60,* 603-624.

Bereiter, C. (1994). Constructivism, socioculturalism, and Popper's World 3. *Educational Researcher,* 23, 21-23.

Bereiter, C. (1995). A dispositional view of transfer. In A. McKeough, J. Lupart, & J. Marini (Eds.), *Teaching to transfer* (pp. 21-34). Mahwah, NJ: Erlbaum.

Bereiter, C. (1997). Situated cognition and how to overcome it. In D. Kirshner & J. A. Whitson (Eds.), *Situated Cognition. Social, Semiotic, and Psychological Perspectives* (pp. 281-300). Mahwah, NJ.: Erlbaum.

Bereiter, C., & Scardamalia, M. (1993). *Surpassing ourselves: An inquiry into the nature of expertise.* Chicago: Open Court.

Bereiter, C., & Scardamalia, M. (1987). *The psychology of written composition.* Hillsdale, NJ: Lawrence Erlbaum.

Bereiter, C., & Scardamalia, M. (1996). Rethinking learning. In D. R. Olson & N. Torrance (Eds.) The handbook of education and human development. New models of learning, teaching and schooling (pp. 485-513). London: Blackwell.

Berger, P. L., & Luckmann, T. (1966). *The social construction of reality.* New York: Doubleday.

Berger, P. L., & Luckmann, T. (1979). *The social construction of reality: a treatise in the sociology of knowledge.* Repr. Harmondsworth: Peregrine Books.

Bergman, T. (1999). Networking for the self-directed learner in the digital age. In P. Linnakylä, M. Kankaanranta, & J. Bopry (Eds.) *Portfolioita verkossa. Portfolios on the web* (pp.16-35). University of Jyväskylä, Finland: Institute for Educational Research.

Berkenkotter, C., Huckin, T. N., & Ackerman, J. (1988). Conventions, conversations, and the writer: Case study of a student in a rhetoric Ph.D. program. *Research in the Teaching of English, 22,* 9-44.

Bernardo, A., (with M.S. Domingo & E.L.F. Pena) (1995). *Cognitive consequences of literacy: Studies on thinking in five Filipino Communities.* Manila:University of the Philippines Education Research Program and Department of Education, Culture and Sports.

Berti, A. E., & Bombi, A.M. (1988). *The child's construction of economics.* Cambridge, England: Cambridge University Press.

Berti, A.E. (1994). Children's understanding of the concept of the state. In M. Carretero & J.F. Voss (Eds.), *Cognitive and instructional processes in history and the social sciences* (pp. 49-75). Hillsdale, NJ: Erlbaum.

Bickley, C., Carlson, R., Cudd, P., Hunnicutt, S., & Reimers, B. (1998). TIDE-ENABL – The first year. In I. P. Porrero & E. Ballabio (Eds.), *Improving the quality of life for the European citizen* (pp. 258-261). Amsterdam: IOS Press.

Biggs, J. (1987). *Student approaches to learning and studying.* Melbourne: Australian Council for Educational Research.

Biggs, J. (1988). Approaches to learning and to essay writing. In R. R. Schmeck (Ed.), *Learning strategies and learning styles* (pp. 185-228). New York: Plenum Press.

Biggs, J. (1996). Enhancing teaching through constructive alignment. *Higher Education, 32,* 347-364.

Birenbaum, M., & Dochy, F. (Eds.) (1996). *Alternatives in assessment of achievement, learning processes and prior knowledge.* Boston: Kluwer.

Bisaillon, J., Clerc, I., & Ladouceur, J. (1999). A computer writing environment for professional writers and students learning to write. *Journal of Technical Writing and Communication, 29,* 185-202.

Bissex, G. (1980). *Gnys at wrk: A child learns to write and read.* Cambridge, MA: Harvard University Press.

Björk, L., & Räisänen, C. (1996). *Academic writing. A university writing course.* Lund, Sweden: Studentlitteratur.

Blamires, M. (Ed.) (1999). *Enabling technology for inclusion.* London: Paul Chapman.

Bligh, D. (1998). *What's the use of lectures?* (5th ed.). Exeter, UK: Intellect.

Blumenfeld, P. C., Soloway, E., Marx, R. W., Krajcik, J. S., Guzdial, M., & Palincsar, A. (1991). Motivating project-based learning: Sustaining the doing, supporting the learning. *Educational Psychologist, 26,* 369-398.

Boekaerts, M. (1997). Self-regulated learning: A new concept embraced by researchers, policy makers, educators, teachers, and students. *Learning and Instruction, 7,* 161-186.

Boice, R. (1993). Writing blocks and tacit knowledge. *Journal of Higher Education, 64,* 19-54.

Bolter, J. D. (1998). Hypertext and the question of visual literacy. In D. Reinking, M. McKenna, L. Labbo, & R. Kieffer (Eds.) *Handbook of literacy and technology. Transformations in a posttypographic world* (pp. 3-14). Mahwah, N.J.: Erlbaum.

Bonk, C. J., Medury, P.V., & Reynolds, T.H. (1994). Cooperative hypermedia: The marriage of collaborative writing and mediated environments. *Computers in the Schools, 10,* 79-124.

Boscolo, P. (1995). The cognitive approach to writing and writing instruction: A contribution to a critical appraisal. *Cahiers de Psychologie Cognitive, 14,* 343-366.

Boscolo, P. (1997). *Psychology of school learning: Cognitive and motivational aspects.* Turin, Italy: UTET [in Italian].

Boud, D. (1995). Assessment and learning: contradictory or complementary? In P. Knight (Ed.), *Assessment for learning in higher education* (pp. 35-48). London: Kogan Page.

Brandt, D. (1998). The sponsors of literacy. *College Composition and Communication, 49,* 165-185.

Brandt, D. (2001). *Literacy in American lives.* New York: Cambridge University Press.

Bransford, J. D., & the Cognition and technology Group at Vanderbilt. (1996). MOST. Environments for accelerating literacy development. In S. Vosniadou, E. De Corte, R. Glaser, & H. Mandl (Eds.), *International perspectives on the design of technology supported learning environments* (pp. 223-255). Mahwah, N.J.: Erlbaum.

Britsch, S. J., & Berkson, K. I. (1997). 'I am that... kid tha acts weird:' Developing e-mail education in the third-grade classroom. *Teaching Education, 8,* 97-104.

Britt, M. A., Rouet, J. F., Georgi, M., & Perfetti, C. A. (1994). Learning from history text: From causal analysis to argument models. In G. Leinhardt, I. L. Beck, & C. Stainton, *Teaching and learning in history* (pp. 47-84). Hillsdale, NJ: Erlbaum.

Britton, J. (1969). Talking to learn. In D. Barnes, J. Britton, & H. Rosen (Eds.), *Language, the learner, and the school* (pp. 79-115). Harmondsworth: Penguin.

Britton, J. (1982). Shaping at the point of utterance. In G. M. Pradl (Ed.), *Prospect and retrospect: Selected essays of James Britton* (pp. 139-145). Montclair, NJ: Boynton/Cook. (Reprinted from A. Freedman, & I. Pringle (Eds.) (1980), Reinventing the rhetorical tradition. Conway, A.R., L. & S. Books, for the Canadian Council of Teachers of English).

Britton, J., Burgess, T., Martin, N., McLeod, A., & Rosen, H. (1975). *The development of writing abilities: 11-18.* London: Macmillan.

Brown, A. L., & Campione, J. C. (1996). Psychological theory and the design of innovative learning environments: On procedures, principles and systems. In L. Schauble & R. Glaser (Eds.), *Innovations in learning. New environments for education* (pp. 289-325). Mahwah, N.J.: Erlbaum.

Brown, A. L., & Day, J. D. (1983). Macrorules for summarizing texts: The development of expertise. *Journal of Verbal Learning and Verbal Behavior, 22,* 1-14.

Brown, A.L., & Palincsar, A.S. (1989). Guided, cooperative learning and individual knowledge acquisition. In L. B. Resnick (Ed.), *Knowing, learning and instruction: Essays in honor of Robert Glaser* (pp. 393-451). Hillsdale, NJ: Erlbaum.

Brown, J. S., Collins, A., & Duguid, P. (1989). Situated cognition and the culture of learning. *Educational Researcher, 18,* 32-42.

Brown, W.S. (1998). Power of self-reflection through epistemic writing. *College Teaching, 46,* 35-38.

Bruffee, K. (1984). Collaborative learning and the 'conversation of mankind'. *College English, 46,* 635-652.

Bruner, J. (1978). The role of dialogue in language acquisition. In A. Sinclair *et al.* (Eds.), *The child's conception of language.* New York: Springer-Verlag.

Bruner, J. (1986). *Actual minds, possible worlds.* Cambridge, MA: Harvard University Press.

Bruner, J. (1987). Life as narrative. *Social Research, 54,* 11-32.

186

Bruner, J. (1990). *Acts of meaning.* Cambridge, Mass: Harvard University Press.

Bruner, J. (1996). *The culture of education.* Cambridge, Ma: Harvard University Press.

Bruner, J., & Feldman, C. F. (1990). Metaphors of consciousness and cognition in the history of psychology. In D. E. Leary (Ed.), *Metaphors in the history of psychology* (pp. 230-238). Cambridge: Cambridge University Press.

Bryan, L. H. (1996). Cooperative writing groups in community college. *Journal of Adolescent and Adult Literacy, 40,* 188-193.

Bush, V. (1945). As we may think. *Atlantic Monthly, 176* (1), 101-108.

Calfee, R., & Perfumo, P. (1993) Student portfolios: Opportunities for a revolution in assessment. *Journal of Reading, 36,* 532-537.

Campbell, J., Smith, D., & Brooker, R. (1998). From conception to performance: How undergraduate students conceptualise and construct essays. *Higher Education, 36,* 449-469.

Camps, A., & Milian, M. (2000). Metalinguistic activity in learning to write: an introduction. In: Rijlaarsdam, G. & Espéret, E. (Serie Eds.) & Camps, A. & Milian, M. (Vol. Eds.) (2000). *Studies in Writing: Vol. 6. Metalinguistic Activity in Learning to Write.* [pp 1-28] *Amsterdam*: Amsterdam University Press.

Carey, S., & Smith, C. (1993). On understanding the nature of scientific knowledge. *Educational Psychologist, 28,* 235-251.

Carretero, M., Jacott, L., Limon, M., Lopez-Manjon, A., & Léon, J.A. (1994). Historical knowledge: Cognitive and instructional implications. In M. Carretero & J. F. Voss (Eds.), *Cognitive and instructional processes in history and the social sciences* (pp. 357-376). Hillsdale, NJ: Erlbaum.

Cassirer, E. (1957). *The philosophy of symbolic forms* (Vol.3). (R. Manheim, trans.). New Haven, CT: Yale University Press.

Castelli, C., Colazzo, L., & Molinari, A. (1998). Cognitive variables and patterns of hypertext performance: Lessons learned for educational hypermedia construction. *Journal of Educational Multimedia and Hypermedia, 7* (2-3), 177-203.

Castells, M. (1999). 'Network society in the information age'. Paper presented in the conference Life Beyond the Information Society conference in Turku, Finland, 16-17 August, 1999.

Caverly, D. C., & Orlando, V. P. (1991). Textbook study strategies. In R. F. Flippo & D. C. Caverly (Eds.), *Teaching reading and study strategies at the college level* (pp. 86-165). Newark, DE: International Reading Association.

Chandler, D. (1995). *The act of writing.* Aberystwyth: University of Wales, UK.

Chi, M. T. H., Glaser, R., & Farr, M. J. (1988). *The nature of expertise.* Hillsdale, NJ: Erlaum.

Chomsky, N. (1980). *Rules and representations.* New York: Columbia University Press.

Cleminson, A. (1990). Establishing an epistemological base for science teaching in the light of contemporary notions of the nature of science and of how children learn science. *Journal of Research in Science Teaching, 27,* 429-445

Cobb, P. (1994). Where is the mind? Constructivist and sociocultural perspectives on mathematical development. *Educational Researcher, 23,* 13-20.

Cobb, P. (1999). Where is the mind? In P. Murphy (Ed.), *Learners, learning & assessment* (pp. 135-150). London: Paul Chapman & The Open University.

Cochran, C. A. (1993). *Rhetorical relevance in reading and writing.* Unpublished doctoral dissertation, Carnegie Mellon University, Pittsburgh, PA.

Cochran-Smith, M. (1991). Word-processing and writing in elementary classrooms: A critical review of related literature. *Review of Educational Research, 61,* 107-155.

Cohen, J. (1996). Computer-mediated communication and publication productivity among faculty. *Internet Research: Electronic Networking Applications and Policy, 6,* 2/3, 41-63.

Collins, J. (1982). Discourse style, classroom interaction and differential treatment. *Journal of Reading Behavior, 14,* 429-437.

Commander, N., & Smith, B.D. (1996). Learning logs: A tool for cognitive monitoring. *Journal of Adolescent & Adult Literacy, 39,* 446-453.

Connolly, P. (1989). Writing and the ecology of learning. In P. Connolly & T. Vilardi (Eds.), *Writing to learn in mathematics and science* (pp. 1-14). New York: Teachers College Press.

Connolly, P., & Vilardi, T. (Eds.) (1989). *Writing to learn in mathematics and science.* New York: Teachers College Press.

Council of Ministers of Education, Canada. (1997). *Common framework of science learning outcomes.* Ottawa, ON: Council of Ministers of Education, Canada.

Craik, F. I. M., & Lockhart, R.S. (1972). Levels of processing: A framework for memory research. *Journal of Verbal Learning and Verbal Behavior, 11*, 671-684.

Craven, J. A, III, Hand, B., & Prain, V. (1999). *Constructing science: Developing the language of science.* Paper presented at the International Conference of the Association for Education Teachers in Science, Austin, TX: January 14-17.

Crook, C. (1994). *Computers and the collaborative experience of learning.* London: Routledge.

Csikszentmihalyi, M. (1990). Flow. *The psychology of optimal experience.* New York: Harper & Row.

Cummins, J. (1996). *Negotiating identities: Education for empowerment in a diverse society.* Ontario, CA: California Association for Bilingual Education.

Curriculum Corporation. (1994). *Science – a curriculum profile for Australian schools.* Carlton, Victoria, Australia: Curriculum Corporation.

Curtin, C. B. (1982). Armadillo. In *McGraw-Hill encyclopedia of science and technology* (Vol. 1, pp. 705-706). New York: McGraw-Hill.

Daiute, C. (1986). Do 1 and 1 make 2? Patterns of influence by collaborative writers. *Written Communication, 3*, 382-408.

Dale, H. (1994). Collaborative writing interactions in one ninth-grade classroom. *Journal of Educational Research, 87*, 334-344.

Dale, R. & Douglas, S. (1996). Two investigations into intelligent text processing. In M. Sharples & T. van der Geest (Eds.), *The new writing environment: Writers at work in a world of technology* (pp.123-146). London: Springer.

Damerow, P. (1999). *The origins of writing as a problem of historical epistemology.* Preprint 114, Max-Planck Institute for the History of Science, Berlin, Germany.

Davis, B., & Brewer, J. (1997). *Electronic discourse.* New York: SUNY Press.

De Corte, E. (1993). *'Learning Theory and Instructional Science.'* Paper presented at St. Gallen, Switzerland, 5-6 March, 1993.

Department of Education. (1995). *Science in the national curriculum.* London, UK: Author.

Dickinson, A. K., & Lee, P.J. (Eds.) (1986). *Historical teaching and historical understanding.* London: Heineman.

Dillenbourg, P. (Ed.). (1999). *Collaborative learning: Cognitive and computational approaches.* Oxford: Pergamon.

DiPardo, A. & Freedman, S. (1988). Peer response groups in the writing classroom: Theoretic foundations and new directions. *Review of Educational Research, 58*, 119-149.

DiVesta, F. J., & Gray, G. S. (1972). Listening and note-taking. *Journal of Educational Psychology, 63*, 8-14.

Dochy, F., & McDowell, L. (1997). Assessment as a tool for learning. *Studies in Educational Evaluation, 23*, 279-298.

Dochy, F., & Moerkerke, G. (1997). Assessment as a major influence on learning and instruction. *International Journal of Educational Research, 27*, 415-432.

Doise, W., & Mugny, G. (1984). *The social development of the intellect.* Oxford: Pergamon.

Doronila, M.L.C. (1996). *Landscapes of literacy.* Paris: UNESCO.

Downing, A., & Brown, I. (1997). Learning by cooperative publishing on the World Wide Web. *Active Learning, 7*, 14-16.

Driver, R., Leach, J., Millar, R., & Scott, P. (1996). *Young people's images of science.* Philadelphia, PA: Open University Press.

Dunn, D. S. (1996). Collaborative writing in a statistics and research methods course. *Teaching of Psychology, 23*, 38-40.

Durkheim, E. (1948). *The elementary forms of religious life.* Glencoe, IL: The Free Press.

Durst, R. K. (1987). Cognitive and linguistic demands of analytic writing. *Research in the Teaching of English, 21*, 347-376.

Dyson, A. (1993). *The social worlds of children learning to write in an urban primary school.* New York: Teachers College Press.

Dyson, A. (1995). Writing children: Reinventing the development of childhood literacy. *Written Communication, 12*, 4-46.

Dyson, A. (1997). *Writing superheroes: Contemporary childhood, popular culture, and classroom literacy.* New York: Teachers College Press.

Dysthe, O. (1996). The multivoiced classroom. Interactions of writing and classroom discourse. *Written Communication, 13*, 385-425.

188

Eklundh, K. S. (1994). Electronic mail as a medium for dialogue. In L. van Waes, E. Wondstra, & P. van den Hoven (Eds.) (1994). *Functional communication quality* (pp. 162-173). Amsterdam: Rodopi B.V.

Elliott, E. (1998). Breaking down the barriers. *Ability, 26* (Autumn), 14-15.

Elwert, G. (in press). Societal literacy. In D. Olson & N. Torrance (Eds.), *On the making of literate societies: Literacy and social development.* Oxford: Blackwell.

Emig, J. (1977). Writing as a mode of learning. *College Composition and Communication, 28,* 122-128.

Engeström, Y., Miettinen, R., & Punamški, R. L. (1999). *Perspectives on activity theory.* Cambridge, UK: Cambridge University Press.

Englebart, D. C. (1963). A conceptual framework for the augmentation of man's intellect. In P. W. Howerton & D. C. Weeks (Eds.), *Vistas in information handling* (vol. 1, pp. 1-29). Washington, DC: Spartan Books.

Entwistle, A., & Entwistle, N.J. (1992). Experiences of understanding in revising for degree examinations. *Learning and Instruction, 2,* 1-22.

Entwistle, N. J. (1995). Frameworks for understanding as experienced in essay writing and in preparing for examinations. *Educational Psychologist, 30,* 47-54.

Entwistle, N. J., & Entwistle, A. (1991). Contrasting forms of understanding for degree examinations: the student experience and its implications. *Higher Education, 22,* 205-227.

Entwistle, N. J., Entwistle, A., & Tait, H. (1993). Academic understanding and contexts to enhance it: A perspective from research on student learning. In T. M. Duffy, J. Lowyck, & D. H. Jonassen (Eds.), *Designing environments for constructive learning* (pp. 331-357). Berlin: Springer.

Entwistle, N., & Waterston, S. (1988). Approaches to studying and levels of processing in university students. *British Journal of Educational Psychology, 58,* 258-265.

Eteläpelto, A. (1993). Metacognition and the expertise of computer program comprehension. *Scandinavian Journal of Educational Research 37,* 243-354.

Eteläpelto, A., & Light, P. (1999). Contextual knowledge in the development of design expertise. In J. Bliss, P. Light, & R. Säljö (Eds.), *Learning sites: social and technological contexts for learning* (pp. 155-164). Oxford: Pergamon/Elsevier.

Eteläpelto, A., & Tourunen, E. (1994, November). *Project learning in the education of systems analysts.* Paper presented at the The 4th International Conference on Experiential Learning, Washington, DC [http://cs.jyu.fi/~eero/eero-pub.html].

Fabos, B., & Young, M. D. (1999). Telecommunication in the classroom.: Rhetoric versus reality. *Review of Research in Education, 69,* 217-259.

Fasulo, A., Girardet, H., & Pontecorvo, C. (1998). Historical practices in school through photographical reconstruction. *Mind, Culture, and Activity, 5,* 253-271.

Fasulo, A., Girardet, H., & Pontecorvo, C. (1999). Representing a different culture: Exercises on point of view. *Language and Education, 13,* 1-21

Fellows, N. (1994). A window into thinking: Using student writing to understand conceptual change in science learning. *Journal of Research in Science Teaching, 31,* 985-1001.

Feltovich, P. J., Spiro, R.J., & Coulson, R.L. (1993). Learning, teaching and testing for complex conceptual understanding. In N. Frederiksen, R. J. Mislevy, & I. I. Bejar (Eds), *Test theory for a new generation of tests* (pp. 181-217). Hillsdale, NJ: Erlbaum.

Ferrari, M., Bouffard, T., & Rainville, L. (1998). What makes a good writer? Differences in good and poor writers' self-regulation of writing. *Instructional Science, 26,* 473-488.

Fiormonte, D., Babini, L., & Selvaggini, L. (1999). The digital variants archive project: A new environment for teaching second-language writing skills. In S. Porter & S. Sutherland (Eds.), *Teaching European literature and culture.* Oxford: CTI Centre for Textual Studies Occasional Series, Number 3, pp.27-31.

Flower, L. (1987). Interpretative acts: Cognition and the construction of discourse. University of California, Berkeley. Carnegie Mellon University, Center for the Study of Writing. Occasional Paper No 1.

Flower, L. (1994). *The construction of negotiated meaning: A social cognitive theory of writing.* Carbondale, IL: Southern Illinois University Press.

Flower, L. S., & Hayes, J. R. (1980). The cognition of discovery: Defining a rhetorical problem. *College Composition and Communication, 31,* 21-32.

Flower, L., Wallace, D. L., Norris, L., & Burnett, R. E. (Eds.). (1994). *Making thinking visible. Writing, collaborative planning, and classroom inquiry.* Urbana, IL: National Council of Teachers of English.

Fodor, J. (1983) *The modularity of mind.* Cambridge, MA: MIT Press.

Forrester, M. A. (1995). Indications of learning processes in a hypertext environment. *Innovations in Education and Training International, 32,* 256-268.

Foucault, M. (1971). Orders of discourse: Inaugural lecture delivered at the College de France. *Social Science Information, 10* (2), 7-30.

Freedman, S. W. (1993). Linking large-scale testing and classroom portfolio assessment of student writing. *Educational Assessment, 1,* 27-52.

Fuller, S. (1991). Disciplinary boundaries and the rhetoric of the social sciences. *Poetics Today, 12,* 300-325.

Furnham, A. (1994). Young people's understanding of politics and economics. In M. Carretero & J.F. Voss (Eds.), *Cognitive and instructional processes in history and the social sciences* (pp. 17-47). Hillsdale, NJ: Erlbaum.

Gains, J. (1999). Electronic mail – a new style of communication or just a new medium? *English for Specific Purposes, 18,* 1, 81-101.

Galbraith, D. (1992). Conditions for discovery through writing. *Instructional Science, 21,* 45-72.

Galbraith, D. (1999). Writing as a knowledge-constituting process. In Rijlaarsdam, G. & Espéret, E. (Serie Eds.) & Torrance, M. & Galbraith, D. (Vol. Eds.) (1999). *Studies in Writing: Vol. 4. Knowing `what to write. Conceptual processes in text production.* [pp 139-160]. Amsterdam: Amsterdam University Press.

Galbraith, D., & Torrance, M. (1999). Conceptual processes in writing: from problem solving to text production. Rijlaarsdam, G. & Espéret, E. (Serie Eds.) & Torrance, M. & Galbraith, D. (Vol. Eds.) (1999). *Studies in Writing: Vol. 4. Knowing what to write. conceptual processes in text production.* (pp 1-12). Amsterdam: Amsterdam University Press.

Gallagher, M., Knapp, P., & Noble, G. (1993). Genre in practice. In B. Cope & M. Kalatzis (Eds.) *The power of literacy: A genre approach to teaching writing,* (pp. 179-202). Pittsburgh: University of Pittsburgh Press.

Gamoran, A., & Nystrand, M. (1991). Background and instructional effects on achievement in eighth-grade English and social studies. *Journal of Research on Adolescence, 1,* 277-300.

Gamoran, A., & Nystrand, M. (1992). Taking students seriously. In F. Newmann (Ed.), *Student engagement and achievement in American secondary schools* (pp. 40-61). New York: Teachers College Press.

Gardner, H. (1993). *Frames of mind: The theory of multiple intelligences.* New York: Basic Books.

Gardner, H., & Wolf, D. (1983). Waves and streams of symbolization: Notes on the development of symbolic capacities in young children. In D. R. Rogers & J. A. Slobada (Eds.), *The acquisition of symbolic skills.* London: Plenum.

Gaskins, I. W., Guthrie, J.T., Satlow, E., Ostertag, J., Six, L., Byrne, J., & Connor, B. (1994). Integrating instruction of science, reading and writing: goals, teacher development, and assessment. *Journal of Research in Science Teaching, 31,* 1039-1056.

Geisler, C. (1991). Toward a sociocognitive model: Constructing mental models in a philosophical conversation. In C. Bazerman & J. Paradis (Eds.), *Textual dynamics and the professions: Historical and contemporary studies of writing in professional communities* (pp. 171-190). Madison: University of Wisconsin Press.

Geisler, C. (1994). *Academic literacy and the nature of expertise: Reading, writing and knowing in academic philosophy.* Hillsdale, NJ: Erlbaum.

Gergen, K. J. (1995). Social construction and the educational process. In L. P. Steffe & J. Gale (Eds), *Constructivism in education* (pp. 17-39). Hillsdale, NJ: Erlbaum.

Glaser, R., & Bassok, M. (1989). Learning theory and the study of instruction. *Annual Review of Psychology, 40,* 631-666.

Goldman, S. R. (1996). Reading, writing, and learning in hypermedia environments. In H. van Oostendorp & J. de Mul (Eds.) *Cognitive aspects of electronic text processing* (pp. 7-42). Norwood, NJ: Ablex.

Goodwin, G. G. (1983). Armadillo. In *Collier's encyclopedia* (Vol. 2, p. 66). New York: Collier's.

Gotcher, J. M., & Kanervo, E. W. (1997). Perceptions and use of electronic mail – a function of rhetorical style. *Social Science Computer Review, 15,* 2, 145-158.

Grabe, M., & Holm, J. (1992, April). An analysis of self-reported study strategies and achievement. Paper presented at the annual meeting of the American Education Research Association, San Francisco, CA.

Grabe, W., & Kaplan, R. (1996). *Theory and practice of writing.* New York: Longman.

Graves, D. H. (1992). Portfolios: Keep a good idea growing. In D. H. Graves & B. S. Sunstein (Eds.), *Portfolio portraits* (pp. 1-12). Portsmouth, NH: Heinemann.

Greene, S. & Ackerman, J. M. (1995) Expanding the constructivist metaphor: A rhetorical perspective on literacy research and practice. *Review of Educational Research, 65,* 383-420.

Greene, S. (1994). Students as authors in the study of history. In G. Leinhardt, I. L. Beck, & C. Stainton (Eds.), *Teaching and learning in history* (pp. 137-170). Hillsdale, NJ: Erlbaum.

Greene, S., & Ackerman, J. M. (1995) Expanding the constructivist metaphor: A rhetorical perspective on literacy research and practice. *Review of Educational Research, 65,* 383-420.

Gretsch, G. (1999). Making meaning in a multi-lingual context: Story reading using an oral wordprocessor. *Goldsmiths Journal of Education, 2,* 32-43.

Gubern, M. (1996). Contextual factors enhancing cognitive and meta-cognitive activity during the process of collaborative writing. In G. Rijlaarsdam, G., H. van den Bergh, & M. Couzijn (Eds), *Effective teaching and learning of writing* (pp. 372-386). Amsterdam: Amsterdam University Press.

Gundlach, R. (1982). Children as writers. In M. Nystrand (Ed.), *What writers know: The language, process, and structure of written discourse* (pp. 129-147). New York: Academic Press.

Haas, C. (1996). *Writing technology: Studies on the materiality of literacy.* Mahwah, N.J.: Erlbaum.

Halldén, O. (1993). Learners' conceptions of the subject matter being taught. A case from learning history. *International Journal of Educational Research, 19,* 317-325.

Halldén, O. (1994). On the paradox of understanding history in an educational setting. In G. Leinhardt, I. L. Beck, & C. Stainton (Eds.), *Teaching and learning in history* (pp. 27-46). Hillsdale, NJ: Erlbaum.

Halldén, O. (1998). Personalization in historical descriptions and explanations. *Learning and Instruction, 8,* 131-139.

Halliday, M. A. K., & Martin, J. R. (1993). *Writing science: Literacy and discursive power.* London: Falmer Press.

Hammond, M. (1999). Issues associated with participation in on line forums – the case of the communicative learner. *Education and Information Technologies, 4,* 4, 353-367.

Hamp-Lyons, L. (1996). Applying ethical standards to portfolio assessment of writing in English as a second language. In M. Milanovic & N. Saville (Eds.), *Performance testing, cognition and assessment: Selected papers from the 15th Language Testing Research Colloquium* (pp. 151-164). Cambridge: Cambridge University Press.

Hand, B., & Keys, C.W. (1999). Inquiry investigation: A new approach to laboratory reports. *The Science Teacher, 66,* 27-29.

Hand, B., Prain, V., Lawrence, C., & Yore, L. (1999). A writing-in-science framework designed to improve science literacy. *International Journal of Science Education, 10,* 1021-1036.

Hansen, J. (1994). Literacy portfolios: windows on potential. In S. H. Valencia, E. H. Hiebert, & P. P. Afflerbach (Eds.), *Authentic reading assessment: Practices and possibilities* (pp. 26-40). Newark: IRA.

Hansen, T., Dirckinck-Holmfelf, L., Lewis, R., & Rugelj, J. (1999). Using telematics for collaborative knowledge construction. In P. Dillenbourg (Ed.), *Collaborative learning: Cognitive and computational approaches* (pp. 169-196). Oxford: Pergamon.

Hanson, N. R. (1958). *Patterns of discovery.* Cambridge, UK: Cambridge University Press.

Hare, V. C., & Borchardt, K.M. (1984). Direct instruction of summarization skills. *Reading Research Quarterly, 20,* 62-78.

Harris, R. (1986). *The origin of writing.* London: Duckworth.

Harrison, B. T. (1996). Using personal diaries and working journals in reflective learning. In G. Rijlaarsdam, H. van den Bergh, & M. Couzijn (Eds.), *Effective teaching and learning of writing* (pp. 70-85). Amsterdam: Amsterdam University Press.

Hartley, A., & Paris, C. (1997). Multilingual document production: From support for translating to support for authoring. *Machine Translation, 12,* 109-129.

Hartley, J. (1984). The role of colleagues and text editing programs in improving text. *I.E.E.E. Transactions on Professional Communication, P-C 27,* 42-44.

Hartley, J. (1992). Writing: A review of the research. In J. Hartley (Ed.), *Technology and writing* (pp. 18-36). London: Jessica Kingsley.

Hartley, J. (1994). *Designing instructional text.* London: Kogan Page.

Hartley, J. (Ed.). (1980). *The psychology of written communication: Selected readings.* London: Kogan Page

Hartley, J., & Branthwaite, A. (1989). The psychologist as wordsmith: A questionnaire study of the writing strategies of productive British psychologists. *Higher Education, 18*, 423-452.

Hartley, J., & Davies, I. K. (1978). Notetaking: A critical review. *Programmed Learning and Educational Technology, 15*, 207-224.

Hartley, J., Bartlett. S., & Branthwaite, A. (1980). Underlining can make a difference sometimes. *The Journal of Educational Research, 13*, 218-224.

Hartley, J., Howe, M. J. A., & McKeachie, W. J. (in press). Writing through time: Longitudinal studies on the effects of new technology and writing. *British Journal of Educational Technology.*

Hartnell-Young, E., & Morriss, M. (1999). Using portfolios as a vehicle for teacher professional development in technology. In P. Linnakylä, M. Kankaanranta, & J. Bopry (Eds.) *Portfolioita verkossa. Portfolios on the web* (pp. 194-208). University of Jyväskylä, Finland: Institute for Educational Research.

Harvey, J. (Ed.). (1998). *Evaluation cookbook.* Heriot-Watt University, Edinburgh, UK: Learning Technology Dissemination Initiative.

Hawley, A. (1986). *Human ecology: A theoretical essay.* Chicago: The University of Chicago Press.

Hay, I., & Delaney, E.J. (1994). 'Who teaches, learns': Writing groups in geographical education. *Journal of Geography in Higher Education, 18*, 317-334.

Hayes, J. R. (1996). A new framework for understanding cognition and affect in writing. In C. M. Levy & S. Randsdell (Eds.), *The science of writing* (pp.1-27). Mahwah, N.J.: Erlbaum.

Hayes, J. R., & Flower, L (1980). Identifying the organisation of writing processes. In L. W. Gregg & E.R. Steinberg (Eds.) *Cognitive processes in writing* (pp. 3-30). Hillsdale, NJ: Erlbaum.

Hayes, J. R., & Flower, L. S. (1986). Writing research and the writer. *American Psychologist, 41*, 1106-1113.

Heath, S. B. (1978). *Teacher talk: Language in the classroom.* Arlington, Va.: Center for Applied Linguistic.

Heath, S. B. (1980, November). *What no bedtime story means: Narrative skills at home and school.* Paper prepared for the Terman Conference, Stanford University, Stanford, CA.

Heath, S. B. (1983). *Ways with words: Language, life, and work in communities and classrooms.* New York: Cambridge University Press.

Hendry, G. D. (1996). Constructivism and educational practice. *Australian Journal of Education, 40*, 19-45.

Henning-Stout, M. (1994) *Responsive assessment: A new way of thinking about learning.* San Francisco: Jossey-Bass.

Herman, J. (1997). Large-scale assessment in support of school reform: lessons in the search for alternative measures. *International Journal of Educational Research, 27*, 395-413.

Herman, J., Gearhart, M. & Baker, E. (1993). Assessing writing portfolios: Issues in the validity and meaning of scores. *Educational Assessment, 1*, 201-224.

Herrington, A., & Moran, C. (Eds.) (1992). *Writing, teaching, and learning in the disciplines.* New York: Modern Language Association.

Hidi, S., & Anderson, V. (1986). Producing written summaries: Task demands, cognitive operations, and implications for instruction. *Review of Educational Research 56*, 473-493.

Hidi, S., & McLaren, J. (1990). The effects of topic and theme interestingness on the production of school expositions. In H. Mandl, E. De Corte, N. Bennett, & H. F. Friedrich (Eds.), *Learning and Instruction: European research in an international context*: Vol. 2.2. *Analysis of complex skills and complex knowledge domains* (pp. 295-308). Oxford, UK: Pergamon.

Hidi, S., & McLaren, J. (1991). Motivational factors in writing: The role of topic interestingness. *European Journal of Psychology of Education, 6*, 187-197.

Hildebrand, G. (1998) Disrupting hegemonic writing practices in school science: Contesting the right way to write. *Journal of Research in Science Teaching, 35*, 345-362.

Hildyard, A. (1996).Writing, learning and instruction of. In: De Corte, E. & Weinert, F. E. (Eds.), *International encyclopedia of developmental and instructional psychology.* (pp. 562-564). Oxford: Elsevier.

Hillocks, G., Jr. (1986). *Research on written communication: New directions for teaching.* Urbana, IL: National Conference on Research in English.

Hofer, B. K., & Pintrich, P.R. (1997). The development of epistemological theories: Beliefs about knowledge and knowing and their relation to learning. *Review of Educational Research, 67*, 88-140.

Holland, J.H., Holyoak, K.J., Nisbett, R.E., & Thagard, P.R. (1986). *Induction: Processes of inference, learning, and discovery.* Cambridge, MA: MIT Press.

Holliday, W.G., Yore, L.D., & Alvermann, D.E. (1994). The reading-science learning-writing connection: Breakthroughs, barriers and promises. *Journal of Research in Science Teaching, 31,* 877-893.

Hounsell, D. (1984). Learning and essay writing. In F. Marton, D. Hounsell, & N. Entwistle (Eds.) *The experience of learning* (pp. 103-123) Edinburgh: Scottish Academic Press.

Howard, V. A., & Barton, J.H. (1986). *Thinking on paper.* New York, NY: Quill.

Järvinen, A. (1990). Development of reflection during high-level professional education. *Proceedings of the 12the European AIR Forum, Lyon, 1990* (pp. 93-109). Utrecht: Lemma.

Johnson-Eilola, J. (1997). *Nostalgic angels: Rearticulating hypertext writing.* Norwood, NJ: Ablex.

Johnson-Laird, P.N. (1988). *The computer and the mind: An introduction to cognitive science.* Cambridge, MA: Harvard University Press.

Jonassen, D. (1991). Evaluating constructive learning. *Educational Technology, 31,* 28-32.

Jones, C. (1999). From the sage on the stage to what exactly? Description and the place of the moderator in co-operative and collaborative learning. *Association for Learning Technology Journal, 7,* 2, 27-36.

Kankaanranta, M. (1998). *Kertomuksia kasvusta ja oppimisesta. Portfoliot siltana päiväkodista kouluun.* [Stories of growth and learning. Portfolios as a bridge from kindergarten to primary school]. University of Jyväskylä: Institute for Educational Research.

Kankaanranta, M., & Linnakylä, P. (1999). Digital portfolios as a means to share and develop expertise. In P. Linnakylä, M. Kankaanranta, & J. Bopry (Eds.), *Portfolioita verkossa. Portfolios on the web* (pp. 210-242). University of Jyväskylä: Institute for Educational Research.

Kardash, C. M., & Amlund, J.T. (1991). Self-reported learning strategies and learning from expository text. *Contemporary Educational Psychology, 16,* 117-138.

Kellogg, R. T. (1994). *The psychology of writing.* New York: Oxford University Press.

Kellogg, R. T., & Mueller, S. (1993). Performance amplification and process restructuring in computer-based writing. *International Journal of Man-Machine Studies, 39,* 33-49.

Kelly, G., & Chen, C. (1999). The sound of music: Constructing science as sociocultural practices through oral and written discourse. *Journal of Research in Science Teaching, 36,* 883-915.

Keys, C. W. (1994). The development of scientific reasoning skills in conjunction with collaborative writing assignments: An interpretive study of six ninth-grade students. *Journal of Research in Science Teaching, 31,* 1003-1022.

Keys, C. W. (1999). Revitalizing instruction in scientific genres: Connecting, knowledge production in the writing to learn in science. *Science Education, 83,* 115-130.

Keys, C. W., Hand, B., Prain, V., & Summers, P. (1998, April). *Rethinking the laboratory report: Writing to learn from investigation.* Paper presented at the annual meeting of the National Association of Research in Science Teaching, San Diego, CA.

Keys, C.W. (1995). An interpretative study of students' use of scientific reasoning during a collaborative report writing intervention in ninth grade general science. *Science Education, 79,* 415-435.

Kieffer, R., Hale, M., & Templeton, A. (1998). Electronic literacy portfolios: technology transformations in a first-grade classroom. In D. Reinking, M. McKenna, L. Labbo, & R. Kieffer (Eds.), *Handbook of literacy and technology. Transformations in a post-typographic world* (pp. 145-163). Mahwah, N.J.: Lawrence Erlbaum.

Kiewra, K. A. (1988). Cognitive aspects of autonomous note taking: Control processes, learning strategies, and prior knowledge. *Educational Psychologist, 23,* 39-56.

Kiewra, K. A., DuBois, N. F., Christian, D., McShane A., Meyerhoffer, M., & Roskelley, D. (1991). Note-taking functions and techniques. *Journal of Educational Psychology, 83,* 240-245.

Kimeldorf, M. (1994). *Creating portfolios for success in school, work, and life.* Minneapolis: Free Spirit.

Kintsch, E., & Kintsch, W. (1996) Learning from text. In E. De Corte & F. E. Weinert (Eds.), *International encyclopedia of developmental and instructional psychology* (pp. 519-524). Oxford: Elsevier.

Kintsch, W. (1986). Learning from text. *Cognition and Instruction, 3,* 87-108.

Kintsch, W., & van Dijk, T. A. (1978). Toward a model of text comprehension and production. *Psychological Review, 85,* 363-394.

Kirby, J. R., & Pedwell, D. (1991). Students' approach to summarisation. *Educational Psychology, 11,* 297-307.

Kivelä, R. (1996). Omia reittejä luokattomassa lukiossa [Own paths in the open secondary school]. In P. Pollari, M. Kankaanranta, & P. Linnakylä (Eds.), *Portfolion monet mahdollisuudet.* [The diverse possibilities of portfolios.] (pp. 81 – 94). University of Jyväskylä: Institute for Educational Research.

Klein, P. D. (1999). Reopening inquiry into cognitive processes in writing-to-learn. *Educational Psychology Review, 11*, 203-270.

Kohut, G. F., & Gorman, K. J. (1995). The effectiveness of leading grammar/style software packages in analyzing business students' writing. *Journal of Business and Technical Communication, 9*, 341-361.

Koschman, T. (Ed.). (1996). *CSCL: Theory and practice of an emerging paradigm.* Mahwah, NJ: Erlbaum.

Koski, J. T. (1998). *Infoähky ja muita kirjoituksia oppimisesta, organisaatioista ja tietoyhteiskunnasta.* [Information overload and other writings on learning, organisations and knowledge society] Jyväskylä: Gummerus.

Kuhn, D. (1989) Children and adults are intuitive scientists. *Psychological Review, 96*, 674- 689.

Kuhn, D., Weinstock, M., & Flaton, R. (1994). Historical reasoning as theory-evidence coordination. In M. Carretero & J. F. Voss (Eds.), *Cognitive and instructional processes in history and the social sciences* (pp. 376-401). Hillsdale, NJ: Erlbaum.

Kuhn, D. (1991). *The skills of argument.* Cambridge, UK: Cambridge University Press.

Kuhn, D. (1993). Science as argument: Implications for teaching and learning scientific thinking. *Science Education, 77*, 319-337.

Kumpulainen, K. (1996). The nature of peer interaction in the social context created by the use of word processors. *Learning and Instruction, 6*, 243-261.

Lahtinen, V., & Lonka, K. (1997, August) The effect of metacognitive awareness on note-taking and learning from text. Paper presented at the 7th European Conference for Research on Learning and Instruction, Athens, Greece.

Lahtinen, V., Lonka, K, & Lindblom-Ylänne, S. (1997). Spontaneous study strategies and the quality of knowledge construction. *British Journal of Educational Psychology, 67*, 13 -24.

Landow, G. P., & Delany, P. (1991). Hypertext, hypermedia, and literary studies: The state of the art. In P. Delany & G. P. Landow (Eds.), *Hypermedia and literary studies* (pp. 3-5). Cambridge, MA: MIT Press.

Langer, J. A. (1992). Discussion as exploration: Literature and the horizon of possibilities. In G. Newell & R. Durst (Eds.), *The role of discussion and writing in the teaching and learning of literature* (pp. 23-24). Norwood, MA: Christopher Gordon Publishers.

Langer, J. A. (1995). *Envisioning literature. Literary understanding and literature instruction.* New York: Techers College Press.

Langer, J. A., & Applebee, A. N. (1987). *How writing shapes thinking: A study of teaching and learning* (Research Report No. 22). Urbana, IL: National Council of Teachers of English.

Langer, J.A. (1986). Learning through writing: Study skills in the content areas. *Journal of Reading, 29*, 400-406.

Latour, B. (1987). *Science in action.* Cambridge, MA: Harvard University Press.

Lave, J., & Wenger, E. (1991). *Situated learning. Legitimate peripheral participation.* Cambridge: Cambridge University Press.

Lawless, K. A., & Brown, S. W. (1997). Multimedia learning environments: Issues of learner control and navigation. *Instructional Science, 25*, 117-131.

Lea, M. R. (2000). Computer conferencing: New possibilities for writing and learning in higher education. In M. R. Lea & B. Stierer (Eds.), *Student writing in higher education: New contexts* (pp.69-85). Buckingham, UK: Open University Press.

Lehman, A. (1999). Text structuration leading to an automatic summary system: RAFI. *Information Processing and Management, 35*, 2, 181-191.

Lehtinen, E., & Repo, S. (1996). Activity, social interaction, and reflective abstraction: Learning advanced mathematical concepts in a computer environment. In S. Vosniadou, E. De Corte, R. Glaser, & H. Mandl (Eds.), *International perspectives on the design of technology-supported learning environments* (pp. 105-128). Mahwah, NJ: Erlbaum.

Leinhardt, G. (1994). History: A time to be mindful. In G. Leinhardt, I. L. Beck, & C. Stainton (Eds.), *Teaching and learning in history* (pp. 209-255). Hillsdale, NJ: Erlbaum.

Leinhardt, G., McCarthy Young, K., & Merriman, J. (1995). Integrating professional knowledge: The theory of practice and the practice of theory. *Learning and Instruction, 5*, 401-408.

Lemke, J. (1998). Metamedia literacy: Transforming meanings and media. In D. Reinking, M. McKenna, L. Labbo, & R. Kieffer (Eds.), *Handbook of literacy and technology. Transformations in a post-typographic world* (pp. 283-302). Mahwah: Lawrence Erlbaum.

Leng, P., Shave, M., Scauer, H., Muehlbacher, J. R, & Aiken, R. (1999). An experiment in multi-national collaborative learning and group work using the Internet. *Education and Information Technologies, 4,* 1, 33-47.

Leont'ev, A. N. (1978). *Activity, consciousness, and personality.* Englewood Cliffs, NJ: Prentice Hall

Leont'ev, A. N. (1981). *Problems of the development of mind.* Moscow: Progress Publishers.

Leu, D. J., & Reinking, D. (1996). Bringing insights from reading research to research on electronic learning environments. In H. van Oostendorp & S. de Mul (Eds.), *Cognitive aspects of electronic text processing* (pp. 43-76). Norwood, N.J.: Ablex.

Levy, C. M., & Ransdell, S. (1996). Writing signatures. In C. M. Levy & S. Ransdell (Eds.). *The science of writing* (pp.149-162). Mahwah, N.J.: Erlbaum.

Levy-Bruhl, L. (1923). *Primitive mentality.* London: George Allen & Unwin.

Lindblom-Ylänne, S., Lonka, K., & Leskinen, E. (1996). Selecting students for medical school: What predicts success during basic science studies? A cognitive approach. *Higher Education, 31,* 507-527.

Linn, R. L. (1995).Performance assessment: Policy promises and technical measurement standards. *Educational Researcher, 23,* 4-14.

Linnakylä, P. (1994). Mikä ihmeen portfolio. [What portfolio?] In P. Linnakylä, P. Pollari & S. Takala (Eds.), *Portfolio arvioinnin ja oppimisen tukena [Portfolio in assessment and learning]* (pp. 9-31). University of Jyväskylä: Institute for Educational Research.

Linnakylä, P. (1998). Individuals in the school picture. Exploring students' writing portfolios. In H. Jokinen & J. Rushton (Eds.), *Changing contexts of school development – the challenges to evaluation and assessment* (pp. 54-64). University of Jyväskylä: Institute for Educational Research.

Linnakylä, P. (1999). Verkkoportfoliot tutkijakoulutuksessa. Mitä toisten portfolioista voi oppia? [Web portfolios in graduate studies. What can you learn by reading academic portfolios?] In P. Linnakylä, M. Kankaanranta & J. Bopry (Eds.), *Portfolioita verkossa. Portfolios on the web* (pp. 142-178). University of Jyväskylä: Institute for Educational Research.

Linnakylä, P., & Pollari, P. (1997). Portfolios – portraits of potential. In J. Frost, A. Sletmo, & F. Tonnessen (Eds.), *Skriften på väggen* [Writings on the wall] (pp. 201-214). Copenhagen: Dansk Psykologisk Forlag.

Linnakylä, P. & Kankaanranta, M. (1999). Digitaaliset portfoliot asiantuntijuuden osoittamisessa ja jakamisessa. [Digital portfolios in showing and sharing expertise] In A. Eteläpelto & P. Tynjälä, (Eds.) *Asiantuntijaksi oppiminen* [Learning to be an expert] (pp. 223-240). Helsinki: WSOY.

Linnakylä, P., Kankaanranta, M., & Arvaja, M. (2000). Collaboration and authenticity in technology supported and virtual learning contexts. In C. Day & D. Veen (Eds.), *Educational Research in Europe.* [EERA Yearbook 2000] (pp. 910103). Leuven: Garant & EERA.

Linnakylä, P., Kankaanranta, M. & Bopry, J. (Eds.) (1999). *Portfolioita verkossa. Portfolios on the web.* University of Jyväskylä: Institute for Educational Research.

Linnakylä, P., Pollari, P., & Takala, S. (Eds.) 1994. *Portfolio arvioinnin ja oppimisen tukena* [Portfolio in assessment and learning]. University of Jyväskylä, Finland: Institute for Educational Research.

Littlejohn, K., & Light, P. (Eds.). (1999). *Learning with computers.* London: Routledge.

Longhurst, N. & Norton, L.S. (1997). Self-assessment in coursework essays. *Studies in Educational Evaluation 23,* 319-330.

Lonka, K. (1997). *Explorations of constructive processes in student learning.* Doctoral dissertation. Helsinki, Finland: University of Helsinki.

Lonka, K., & Ahola, K. (1995). Activating instruction – how to foster study and thinking skills in higher education. *European Journal of Psychology of Education, 10,* 351-368.

Lonka, K., Lahtinen, V., & Lindblom-Ylänne, S. (1996, September) Learning from complex texts: An overview of a research project. Paper presented at the conference on Using Complex Information Systems, Poitiers, France.

Lonka, K., Lindblom-Ylänne, S. & Maury, S. (1994). The effect of study strategies on learning from text. *Learning and Instruction, 4,* 253-271.

Lonka, K., Maury, S., & Heikkilä, A. (1997, August). How do students' thoughts of their writing process relate to their conceptions of learning and knowledge. A paper presented at 7th European Conference of EARLI (European Association of Research on Learning and Instruction). Athens, Greece, August 26 to 30, 1997.

Lukinsky, J. (1990). Reflective withdrawal through journal writing. In J. Mezirow and Associates, *Fostering critical reflection in adulthood. A guide to transformative and emancipatory learning* (pp. 213-234). San Francisco, CA: Jossey Bass.

Lyons, J. (1999). Reflective education for professional practice: Discovering knowledge from experience. *Nurse Education Today, 19*, 29-34.

Macdonald, N. H. (1983). The UNIX Writer's Workbench software: rationale and design. *Bell System Technical Journal, 62*, 1891-1908.

Mäkinen, K. (1996). Using a portfolio in teaching and assessing EFL writing. *Tempus, 8*, 8-9.

Mandl, H., & Schnotz, W. (1987). New directions in text comprehension. In E. De Corte, H. Lodewijks, R. Parmentier, & P. Span (Eds.), *Learning & instruction. European research in an international context* (Vol. 1, pp. 321-338). Oxford: Pergamon.

Mandl, H., Gruber, H., & Renkl, A. (1996). Communities of practice toward expertise: Social foundation of university instruction. In P. B. Baltes & U. M. Staudinger (Eds.), *Interactive minds. Life-span perspectives on the social foundation of cognition* (pp. 394-412). Cambridge: Cambridge University Press.

Mann, W. C., & Thompson, S. A. (1988). Rhetorical structure theory. *Text, 8*, 243-281.

Mannes, S. M., & Kintsch, W. (1987). Knowledge organization and text organization. *Cognition and Instruction, 4*, 91-115.

Many, J. E., Fyfe, R., Lewis, G., & Mitchell, E. (1996). Transversing the topical landscape: Exploring students' self-directed reading-writing-research processes. *Reading Research Quarterly, 31*, 12-35.

Martin, N., D'Arcy, P., Newton, B., & Parker, R. (1976). *Writing and learning across the curriculum: 11-16: Schools council project*. Montclair, NJ: Boynton/Cook.

Marton, F. (1988). Phenomenography: Exploring different conceptions of reality. In D.M. Fetterman (Ed.), *Qualitative approaches to evaluation in education. The silent scientific revolution.* (pp. 176-205). New York: Praeger.

Marton, F., & Säljö, R. (1976). On qualitative differences in learning – I. Process and outcome. *British Journal of Educational Psychology, 46*, 4-11.

Marton, F., & Säljö, R. (1984). Approaches to learning. In F. Marton, D. J. Hounsell, & N. J. Entwistle (Eds.), *The experience of learning* (pp. 36-55). Edinburgh, UK: Scottish Academic Press.

Marttunen, M. (1992). Commenting on written arguments as a part of argumentation skills – comparison between students engaged in traditional vs. on-line study. *Scandinavian Journal of Educational Research, 36*, 289-302.

Marttunen, M. (1997). Electronic mail as a pedagogical delivery system: an analysis of the learning of argumentation. *Research in Higher Education, 38*, 345-363.

Mason, L. (1998). Sharing cognition to construct scientific knowledge in school context: The role of oral and written discourse. *Instructional Science, 25*, 359-389.

Mason, L. (in press). Introducing talk and writing for conceptual change: A classroom study. In L. Mason (Ed.), Instructional practices for conceptual change in science domains [Special issue]. *Learning and Instruction*.

Mason, L., & Boscolo, P. (2000). Writing and conceptual change. What changes? *Instructional Science, 28*, 199-226.

Mathison, M. A. (1998). Students as critics of disciplinary texts. In N. Nelson & R. C. Calfee (Eds.), *The reading-writing connection: 97th yearbook of the National Society for the Study of Education* (pp. 249-265). Chicago: University of Chicago Press for NSSE.

Mayer, R. E. (1984). Aids to text comprehension. *Educational Psychologist, 19*, 30-42.

Mayer, R. E. (1992). Cognition and instruction: Their historic meeting within educational psychology. *Journal of Educational Psychology, 84*, 405-412.

McCarthey, S. J. (1992). *The influence of classroom discourse on student texts: The case of Ella.* Research Report 92-3. East Lansing, MI: National Center for Research on Teacher Learning.

McComas W. F., & Olson, J.K. (1998). The nature of science in international science education standards documents. In W. F. McComas (Ed.), *The nature of science in science education rationales and strategies* (pp. 41-52). Boston, MA: Kluwer.

McComas, W. F. (1998). The principal elements of the nature of science: Dispelling the myths. In W. F. McComas (Ed.), *The nature of science in science education rationales and strategies* (pp. 53-70). Boston, MA: Kluwer.

McCrindle, A. R., & Christensen, C.A. (1995). The impact of learning journals on metacognitive and cognitive processes and learning performance. *Learning and Instruction, 5*, 167-185.

McCutchen, D., Covill, A., Hoyne, S. H., & Mildes, K. (1994). Individual differences in writing: Implications of translating fluency. *Journal of Educational Psychology, 86*, 256-266.

196

McGinley, W. (1992). The role of reading and writing while composing from sources. *Reading Research Quarterly, 2*, 227-248.

McInnis, R. G. (1996). Introduction: Defining discourse synthesis. *Social Epistemology, 10*, 1-25.

McKeachie, W. J. (1994). *Teaching tips. Strategies, research, and theory for college and university teachers* (9th ed). Lexington, MA: Heath.

McNamara, D. S., Kintsch, E., Songer, N. B., & Kintsch, W. (1996). Are good texts always better? Interactions of text coherence, background knowledge, and levels of understanding in learning from text. Cognition and Instruction, *1*, 1-43.

Mehan, H. (1979). *Learning lessons.* Cambridge, MA: Harvard University Press.

Messick, S. 1994. The interplay of evidence and consequences in the validation of performance assessments. *Educational Researcher, 23*, 13-23.

Meyer, B. J. F. (1985). Prose analysis: Purposes, procedures, and problems. In B. K. Britton & J. K. Black (Eds.), *Understanding expository text* (pp. 11-64). Hillsdale, NJ: Erlbaum.

Milliken, M. (1992). A fifth-grade class uses portfolios. In D. Graves & B. Sunstein (Eds.), *Portfolio portraits* (pp. 34-44). Portsmouth, N.H.: Heinemann.

Ministry of Education. (1993). *Science in the New Zealand curriculum.* Wellington, NZ: Learning Media.

Moore, R. (1993). Does writing about science improve learning about science? *Journal of College Science Teaching, 22*, 212-217.

Morris, C. D., Bransford, J. D., & Franks, J. J. (1977). Levels of processing versus transfer appropriate processing. *Journal of Verbal Learning and Verbal Behavior, 16*, 519-533.

Morrison, K. (1996). Developing reflective practice in higher degree students through a learning journal. *Studies in Higher Education, 21*, 317-332.

Moss, P. (1994). Can there be validity without reliability? *Educational Researcher 23*, 5-12.

Multisilta, J. (1997). Learning environments on the World Wide Web: Experiences from Astronomy On-Line. *Education and Information Technologies, 2*, 171-177.

Murphy, S. (1994). Portfolios and curriculum reform: Patterns in practice. *Assessing writing, 1*, 175-206.

National Assessment of Educational Progress. (1979). *Reading/literature released exercise set, 1979-80 assessment.* No. 11-RL-25. Princeton, N.J.: Educational Testing Service.

National Council of Teachers of English and International Reading Association (1996). *Standards for the English language arts.* Urbana, IL: National Council of Teachers of English.

National Education Association. (1894). *Report of the Committee of Ten on secondary school subjects.* New York: American Book Company for NEA.

National Research Council (1996). *National science education standards.* Washington, DC: National Academy Press.

Nelson, N. (1998). Reading and writing contextualized. In N. Nelson & R. C. Calfee (Eds.), *The reading-writing connection: 97th yearbook of the National Society for the Study of Education* (pp. 266-285). Chicago: University of Chicago Press for NSSE.

Nelson, N. (in press). Discourse synthesis: Process and product. In R. McInnis (Ed.), *Discourse synthesis: Studies in historical and contemporary social epistemology.* Westport, CN: Praeger.

Nelson, T. (1967). Getting it out of our system. In G. Schecter (Ed.), *Information retrieval: A critical review* (pp. 191-210). Washington, DC: Thompson.

Nelson, T. (1981). *Literary machines: The report on, and of, Project Xanadu concerning word processing, electronic publishing, hypertext, thinkertoys, tomorrow's intellectual revolution, and certain other topics including knowledge, education, and freedom* (3rd. ed). Swarthmore, PA: T. Nelson.

Neuwirth, C.M., & Wojahn, P.G. (1996). Learning to write: Computer support for a cooperative process. In T. Koschman (Ed.), *CSCL: Theory and practice of an emerging paradigm* (pp.147-170.) Mahwah, NJ: Erlbaum.

Newell, G. E. (1984). Learning from writing in two content areas: A case study/protocol analysis. *Research in the Teaching of English, 18*, 265-287.

Newell, G. E., & Winograd, P. (1989). The effects of writing on learning from expository text. *Written Communication, 6*, 196-217.

Niguidula, D. (1997). Picturing performance with digital portfolio. *Educational Leadership, 11*, 26-29.

Nisbet, P., & Poon, P. (1998). *Special access technology.* University of Edinburgh, UK: Communication Aids for Language and Learning Centre.

Nisbet, P., Spooner, R., Arther, E. & Whittaker, P. (1999). *Supportive writing technology.* University of Edinburgh, UK: Communication Aids for Language and Learning Centre.

Norris, C. (1997). *Against relativism: Philosophy of science, deconstruction and critical theory.* Malden, MA: Blackwell Publishers.

Novak, J. D. (1990). Concept mapping: A useful tool for science education. *Journal of Research in Science Teaching, 10,* 937-949.

Novak, J. D., & Govin, D.B. (1984). *Learning how to learn.* Cambridge, MA: Cambridge University Press.

November, P. (1996). Journals for the journey into deep learning: A framework. *Higher Education Research and Development, 15,* 115-127.

Nussbaum, J. (1989). Classroom conceptual change: A philosophical perspective. *International Journal of Science Education, 11,* 530-540.

Nystrand, M. (1982). The structure of textual space. In M. Nystrand (Ed.), *What writers know: The language, process, and structure of written discourse* (pp. 75-86). New York and London: Academic Press.

Nystrand, M. (1986a). Where do the spaces go? The development of word segmentation in the Bissex texts. In M. Nystrand, *The structure of written communication: Studies in reciprocity between writers and readers* (pp. 159-178). Orlando and London: Academic Press.

Nystrand, M. (1986b). Learning to write by talking about writing: A summary of research on intensive peer review at the University of Wisconsin-Madison. In M. Nystrand (Ed.), *The structure of written communication: Studies in reciprocity between writers and readers* (pp. 179-212). Orlando and London: Academic Press.

Nystrand, M. (1986c). *The structure of written communication: studies in reciprocity between writers and readers.* Orlando and London: Academic Press.

Nystrand, M. (1989). Social-interactive model of writing. *Written Communication, 6,* 66-85.

Nystrand, M. (1990a). CLASS 2.0 *user's manual: A laptop-computer system for the in-class analysis of classroom discourse.* With Craig Weinhold. Madison, WI: Wisconsin Center for Education Research.

Nystrand, M. (1990b). Sharing words: The effects of readers on developing writers. *Written Communication, 7,* 3-24.

Nystrand, M. (1991, April). *On the negotiation of understanding between students and teachers: Towards a social-interactionist model of school learning.* Paper presented at the annual meeting of the American Educational Research Association, Chicago, IL.

Nystrand, M. (1997). *Opening dialogue: Understanding the dynamics of language and learning in the English classroom.* With Adam Gamoran, Robert Kachur, and Catherine Prendergast. New York: Teachers College Press.

Nystrand, M., & Brandt, D. (1989). Response to writing as a context for learning to write. In C. Anson (Ed.), *Writing and response: Theory, practice, and research* (pp. 209-230). Urbana, IL: National Council of Teachers of English.

Nystrand, M., & Gamoran, A. (1991). Instructional discourse, student engagement, and literature achievement. *Research in the Teaching of English, 25,* 261-290.

Nystrand, M., & Gamoran, A. (1996, April). *The effects of classroom discourse on writing development.* Paper presented at the annual meeting of the American Educational Research Association, New York.

Nystrand, M., & Graff, N. (2000). Report in argument's clothing: An ecological perspective on writing instruction. Report Series 13007. Albany: National Research Center on English Learning and Achievement.

Nystrand, M., Cohen, A., & Dowling, N. (1993, January). Addressing reliability problems in the portfolio assessment of college writing. *Educational Assessment, 1,* 53-70.

Nystrand, M., Gamoran, A., & Carbonaro, W. (1998). Towards ecology of learning: the case of classroom discourse and its effects on writing in high school English and social studies. National Research Center of English Learning and Achievement, Albany, NY. Report Series 2.34.

Nystrand, M., Greene, S., & Wiemelt, J. (1993). Where did composition studies come from? *Written Communication, 10,* 267-333.

Okebukola, P. A., & Jegede, O. J. (1988). Cognitive preference and learning mode as determinants of meaningful learning through concept mapping. *Science Education, 72,* 489-500.

Oliver, R., & Kerr, T. (1993). The impact of word processing on the preparation and submission of written essays in a tertiary course of study. *Higher Education, 26,* 2, 217-226.

Olson, D. (1994). *The world on paper: The conceptual and cognitive implications of writing and reading.* Cambridge: Cambridge University Press.

Owston, R. D. (1997). The World Wide Web: A technology to enhance teaching and learning? *Educational Researcher, 26*, 27-33.

Owston, R. D., & Wideman, H. H. (1997). Word processors and children's writing in a high-computer access setting. *Journal of Research on Computing in Education, 30*, 2, 202-221.

Paice, C. (1994). Automatic abstracting. In A. Kent (Ed.), *Encyclopaedia of library and information science* (Vol. 3, Supplement, 16) (pp. 16-27). New York: Dekker Inc.

Pajares, F., & Johnson, M. J. (1994). Confidence and competence in writing: The role of self-efficacy, outcome expectancy, and apprehension. *Research in the Teaching of English, 28*, 313-331.

Pajares, F., & Johnson, M. J. (1996). Role of self-efficacy beliefs in the writing of high school students: A path analysis. *Psychology in the Schools, 33*, 163-175.

Palincsar, A.S., & Brown, A.L. (1984). Reciprocal teaching of comprehension-fostering and monitoring activies. *Cognition and Instruction, 1*, 117-175.

Paulson, F. L., Paulson, P. R., & Meyer, C. A. (1991). What makes a portfolio a portfolio? *Educational Leadership, 48*, 60-63.

Pennington, M. C. (1993). Computer-assisted writing on a principled basis: The case against computer-assisted text analysis for non-proficient writers. *Language and Education, 7*, 43-59.

Penrose, A. M. (1992). To write or not to write. Effects of task and task interpretation on learning through writing. *Written communication, 9*, 465-500.

Peper, R. J., & Mayer, R. E. (1986). Generative effects of note-taking during science lectures. *Journal of Educational Psychology, 78*, 34-38.

Perfetti, C. A., Britt, M. A., Rouet, J. F., Georgi, M. C., & Mason, R. A. (1994). In M. Carretero & J. F. Voss (Eds.), *Cognitive and instructional processes in history and the social sciences* (pp. 257-283). Hillsdale, NJ: Erlbaum.

Petraglia, J. (1995). *Reconceiving writing, rethinking writing instruction* (pp. 51-77). Mahwah, NJ: Erlbaum.

Piaget, J. (1929). *The child's conception of the world.* London: Kegan Paul. (Originally published in French in 1926).

Piaget, J. (1932). *The language and thought of the child* (M. Gabain, Trans.). New York: Harcourt Brace. (Original work published in French 1923)

Piaget, J. (1963). *Psychology of intelligence.* Paterson, NJ: Littlefield, Adams & Co.

Piolat, A., Thierrey, O., Rousey, J-Y., Thunin, O., & Ziegler, J. C. (1999). SCRIPTKELL: A tool for measuring cognitive effort and time processing in writing and other complex activities. *Behavior Research Methods, Instruments and Computers, 31*, 1, 113-121.

Poell, R. F., Van der Krogt, F.J., & Warmerdam, J.H. M. (1998). Project-based learning in professional organizations. *Adult Education Quarterly, 49*, 28-42.

Pollari, P., Kankaannranta, M. & Linnakylä, P. (1996). *Portfolion monet mahdollisuudet* [The diverse possibilities of portfolios]. University of Jyväskylä, Finland: Institute for Educational Research.

Pollari. P. (1998). *'This is my portfolio'. Portfolio as a vehicle for students' empowerment in their upper secondary school English studies.* An unpublished licentiate thesis. University of Jyväskylä. Department of English.

Popper, K. R., & Eccles, J.C. (1977). *The self and its brain.* Berlin: Springer-Verlag.

Prain, V., Hand, B. (1996). Writing for learning in the junior secondary science classroom: Issues arising from a case study. *International Journal of Science Education, 18*, 117-128.

Prain, V., & Hand, B. (1996). Writing for learning in secondary science: Rethinking practices. *Teaching and Teacher Education, 12*, 609-626.

Prain, V., & Hand, B. (1996a). Writing for learning in secondary science: Rethinking practices. *Teaching and Teacher Education, 12*, 609-626.

Prain, V., & Hand, B. (1996b). Writing for learning in the junior secondary science classroom: Issues arising from a case study. *International Journal of Science Education, 18*, 117-128.

Prain, V., & Hand, B. (1999). Students' perceptions of writing for learning in secondary school science. *Science Education, 83*, 151-162.

Prosser, M., & Webb, C. (1994). Relating the process of undergraduate writing to the finished product. *Studies in Higher Education, 19*, 125-138.

Quinn, K.B. (1995). Teaching reading and writing as modes of learning in college: A glance at the past; a view to the future. *Reading Research and Instruction, 34*, 295-314.

Radmacher, S. A., & Latosi-Sawin, E. (1995). Summary writing: a tool to improve student comprehension and writing in psychology. *Teaching in Psychology, 22*, 113-115.

Rahamim, L. (1999). Scaling physical barriers. In M. Blamires (Ed.), *Enabling technology for inclusion* (pp. 75-82). London: Paul Chapman.

Reece, J. E., & Cumming, G. (1996). Evaluating speech-based composition methods: Planning, dictating and the listening word processor. In C. M. Levy & S. Ransdell (Eds.), *The science of writing* (pp. 361-282). Mahwah, N.J.: Erlbaum.

Reed, W. M. (1996). Assessing the impact of computer-based writing instruction. *Journal of Research on Computing in Education, 28,* 4, 418-437.

Reich, R. B. (1992). *The work of nations.* New York: Vintage Books.

Reinking, D., McKenna, M., Labbo, L. & Kieffer, R. (Eds.) (1998) *Handbook of literacy and technology. Transformations in a post-typographic world.* Mahwah, N.J.: Lawrence Erlbaum.

Reither, J. A., & Vipond, D. (1989). Writing as collaboration. *College English, 51,* 855-867.

Resnick, L. B. (1987). Learning in school and out. *Educational Researcher, 16,* 13-20.

Resnick, L., & Resnick, D. (1991). Assessing the thinking curriculum: New tools for educational reform. In B. R. Gifford & M. C. O'Connor (Eds.), *Changing assessment: Alternative views of aptitude, achievement and instruction.* Boston: Kluwer.

Rewey, K. L., Dansereau, D. F., & Peel, J. L. (1991). Knowledge maps and information processing strategies. *Contemporary Educational Psychology, 16,* 203-214.

Rice, R. E. (1998). Scientific writing: A course to improve the writing of science students. *Journal of College Science Teaching, 27,* 267-272.

Rice, R. P. (1997). An analysis of stylistic variations in electronic mail. *Journal of Business and Technical Communication, 11,* 1, 5-23.

Rimmershaw, R. (1999). Using conferencing to support a culture of collaborative study. *Journal of Computer Assisted Learning, 15,* 189-200.

Rivard, L. P. (1994). A review of writing to learn in science: Implications for practice and research. *Journal of Research in Science Teaching, 31,* 969-983.

Rogoff, B. (1990). Apprenticeship in thinking: Cognitive development in social context. Oxford: Oxford University Press.

Rogoff, B. (1999). Cognitive development through social interaction: Vygotsky and Piaget. In P. Murphy (Ed.) *Learners, learning & assessment* (pp. 69-82). London: Paul Chapman Publishing in association with The Open University.

Rogoff, B., Matusov, E., & White, C. (1996). Models of teaching and learning: Participation in a community of learners. In D. R. Olson & N. Torrance (Eds.) *The handbook of education and human development* (pp.388-414). London: Blackwell.

Rosaen, C. (1989). Writing in the content areas: Reaching its potential in the learning process. In J. Brophy (Ed.), *Advances in research on teaching* (pp. 153-189), vol. 1. Greenwich, CT: JAI Press.

Roschelle, J., & Pea, R. (1999). Trajectories from today's WWW to a powerful educational infrastructure. *Educational Researcher, 28,* 22-25, and p. 43.

Roth, K. J., & Rosaen, C. L. (1991, April). *Writing activities in a conceptual change science learning community: Two perspectives.* Paper presented at the annual meeting of the National Association for Research in Science Teaching, Lake Geneva, WI.

Roth, W-M., & Roychoudhury, A. (1994). Physics students' epistemologies and views about knowing and learning. *Journal of Research in Science Teaching, 31,* 5-30.

Rouet, J. F., Favart, M., Gaonac'h, D., & N. Lacroix (1996). Writing from multiple documents: Argumentation strategies in novice and expert history students. In G. Rijlaarsdam, H. van den Bergh, & M. Couzijn (Eds.), *Theories, models and methodology in writing research* (pp. 44- 60). Amsterdam: Amsterdam University Press.

Rowell, P. A. (1997). Learning in school science: The promises and practices of writing. *Studies in Science Education, 30,* 19-56.

Rubin, D. L. (1988). Introduction: Four dimensions of social construction in written communication. In B. A. Rafoth & D. L. Rubin (Eds.), *The social construction of written communication* (pp. 1-33). Norwood, NJ: Ablex.

Rudy, I. A. (1996). A critical review of research on electronic mail. *European Journal of Information Systems, 4,* 198-213.

Ruscio, K. P. (1986). Bridging specializations: Reflections from biology and political science. *The Review of Higher Education, 10,* 29-45.

Russell, D. (1995). Activity theory and its implications for writing instruction. In J. Petraglia (Ed.), *Reconceiving writing, rethinking writing instruction* (pp. 51.77). Mahwah, NJ: Erlbaum.

Russell, D. (1997). Writing and genre in higher education and workplaces: A review of studies that use cultural-historical activity theory. *Mind, Culture, and Activity, 4*, 224-237.

Russell, D. R. (1990). Writing across the curriculum in historical perspective: Toward a social interpretation. *College English, 52*, 52-73.

Sambell, K., McDowell, L. & Brown, S. (1997). 'But is it fair?': An exploratory study of student perceptions of the consequential validity of assessment. *Studies in Educational Evaluation, 23*, 349-371.

Sanders, T. J., Spooren, W. P., & Noordman, L. G. (1992). Toward a taxonomy of coherence relations. *Discourse Processes, 15*, 1-35.

Sawyer, R. J., Graham, S., & Harris, H.R. (1992). Direct teaching, strategy instruction, and strategy instruction with explicit self-regulation: Effects on composition skills and self-efficacy of students with learning disabilities. *Journal of Educational Psychology, 84*, 340-352.

Scardamalia, B., Bereiter, C., McLean, R.S., Swallow, J., & Woodruff, E. (1989). Computer-supported learning environments. *Journal of Educational Computing Research, 5*, 51-68.

Scardamalia, M., & Bereiter, C. (1986). Helping students become better writers. *School Administrator, 42*(4), 16 & 26.

Scardamalia, M., & Bereiter, C. (1991). Literate expertise. In K. A. Anderson & J. Smith (Eds.) *Toward a general theory of expertise. Prospects and limits* (pp. 172-194). Cambridge: Cambridge University Press.

Scardamalia, M., & Bereiter, C. (1996). *Adaptation and understanding: A case for new cultures of schooling.* In S. Vosniadou, E. De Corte, R. Glaser, & H. Mandl (Eds.), *International perspectives on the design of technology supported learning environments* (pp.149-163). Mahwah, N.J.: Erlbaum.

Scardamalia, M., & Bereiter, C. (1996). Computer support for knowledge-building communities. In T. Koschmann (Ed.), *CSCL: Theory and Practice of an emerging paradigm* (pp. 249-268). Mahwah, NJ.: Erlbaum.

Scardamalia, M., Bereiter, C., & Lamon, M. (1994). The CSILE Project: Trying to bring the classroom into World 3. In K. McGilly (Ed.), *Classroom lessons. Integrating cognitive theory and classroom practice* (pp. 201-228). Cambridge, MA: Bradford/ MIT Press.

Schnotz, W. (1996). Reading comprehension, learning of. In E. De Corte & F. E. Weinert (Eds.), *International encyclopedia of developmental and instructional psychology* (pp. 562-564). Oxford: Elsevier.

Schumacher, G., & Gradwohl Nash, J. (1991). Conceptualizing and measuring knowledge change due to writing. *Research in the Teaching of English, 25*, 67-96.

Schutz, A. (1967). *Collected papers, vol. 1: The problem of social reality.* The Hague: Martinus Nijhoff.

Scollon, R. & Scollon, S. B. (1980). *The literate two-year old: The fictionalization of self.* Typescript, Center for Cross-Cultural Studies, University of Alaska.

Scollon, R. (1994). As a matter of fact: The changing ideology of authorship and responsibility in discourse. *World Englishes, 13*, 33-46.

Scouller, K. (1998). The influence of assessment method on students' learning approaches: Multiple choice question examination versus assignment essay. *Higher Education, 35*, 453-472.

Scrase, R. (1998). An evaluation of a multi-sensory speaking-computer based system (Starcross-IDL) designed to teach the literacy skills of reading and spelling. *British Journal of Educational Technology, 29*, 3, 211-224.

Scribner, S. & Cole, M. (1981). *The psychology of literacy.* Cambridge, MA: Harvard University Press.

Sharples, M. (1999). *How we write.* London: Routledge.

Sharples, M. (Ed.). (1993). *Computer supported collaborative writing.* London: Springer-Verlag.

Sharples, M., Goodlet, J., & Pemberton, L. (1989). Developing a Writer's Assistant. In N. Williams & P. Holt (Eds.), *Computers and writing* (pp. 22-37). Norwood, N.J.: Ablex.

Shayer, M. (1994). Problems and issues in intervention studies. In A. Demetriou, M. Shayer, & A. Efklides (Eds.), *Neo-Piagetian theories of cognitive development* (pp. 107-121). London and New York: Routledge.

Sheridan, J. (1995). An overview and some observations. In J. Sheridan (Ed.) *Writing-Across-the-Curriculum and the academic library. A guide for librarians, instructors, and writing program directors* (pp. 3-22). Westport, CT: Greenwood Press.

Slotte, V. (1999). *Spontaneous study strategies promoting knowledge construction.* Doctoral dissertation. Helsinki, Finland: University of Helsinki.

Slotte, V., & Lonka, K. (1998). Using notes during essay-writing: is it always helpful? *Educational Psychology, 4*, 445-459.

Slotte, V., & Lonka, K. (1999). Review and process effects of spontaneous note-taking on text comprehension. *Contemporary Educational Psychology*, 24, 1-20.

Songer, N. B., & Linn, M.C. (1991). How do students' views of science influence knowledge integration? *Journal of Research in Science Teaching, 28*, 761-684.

Speck, B. W., Johnson, T. R., Dice, C. P., & Heaton, L. B. (1999). *Collaborative writing: An annotated bibliography.* New York: Greenwood.

Sperling, M. (1995). Uncovering the Role of Role in Writing and Learning to Write: One Day in an Inner-City Classroom. *Written Communication, 12*, 93-132.

Sperling, M. (1996). Revisiting the writing-speaking connection: Challenges for research on writing and writing instruction. *Review of Educational Research, 66*, 53-86.

Spiro, R.J., Feltovich, P.J., Jacobson, M.J., & Coulson, R.L. (1995). Cognitive flexibility, constructivism, and hypertext: Random access instruction for advance knowledge acquisition in ill-structured domains. In L. P. Steffe & J. Gale (Eds.), *Constructivism in education* (pp. 85-108). Hillsdale, NJ: Erlbaum.

Spivey, N. N. (1984). *Discourse synthesis: Constructing texts in reading and writing* (Monograph). Newark, DE: International Reading Association.

Spivey, N. N. (1990). Transforming texts: Constructive processes in reading and writing. *Written Communication, 7*, 256-287.

Spivey, N. N. (1991). The shaping of meaning: Options in writing the comparison. *Research in the Teaching of English, 25*, 390-418.

Spivey, N. N. (1995). Written discourse: a constructivist perspective. In P. Steffe & J. Gale (Eds.), *Constructivism in education* (pp. 313-329). Hillsdale, NJ: Lawrence Erlbaum.

Spivey, N. N. (1997). Reading, writing and the making of meaning. The constructivist metaphor. San Diego, CA: Academic Press.

Spivey, N. N. (1997). *The constructivist metaphor. Reading, writing and the making the meaning.* San Diego, Ca: Academic Press.

Spivey, N. N., & Greene, S. (1989). *Aufgabe* in writing and learning from sources. Paper presented at the annual meeting of the American Educational Research Association, San Francisco.

Spivey, N. N., & King, J. R. (1989). Readers as writers composing from sources. *Reading Research Quarterly, 24*, 7-26.

Spivey, N. N., & Mathison, M. A. (1997). Development of authoring identity. In N. N. Spivey, *The constructivist metaphor: Reading, writing, and the making of meaning* (pp. 223-234). San Diego, CA: Academic Press.

Spoehr, K. T. (1994). Enhancing the acquisition of conceptual structures through hypermedia. In K. McGilly (Ed.), Classroom lessons. Integrating cognitive theory and classroom practice (pp. 75-101). London: The MIT Press.

Staton, J., Shuy, R.W., Peyton, J.K., & Reed, L. (1988). *Dialogue journal communication: Classroom, linguistic, social and cognitive views.* Norwood, NJ: Ablex.

Steffe, L. P., & Gale, J. (Eds.). (1995). *Constructivism in education.* Hillsdale, NJ: Erlbaum.

Stengel, B. (1997). 'Academic discipline' and 'school subject': Contestable curricular concepts. *Journal of Curriculum Studies, 29*, 585-602.

Sternberg, R. J. (1998). Abilities are forms of developing expertise. *Educational Researcher, 27*, 11-20.

Stevens, G., & Cho, J. H. (1985). Socioeconomic indexes and the new 1980 census occupational classification scheme. *Social Science Research, 14*, 142-168.

Stowell, L. P., & Tierney, R. J. (1995). Portfolios in the classroom: What happens when teachers and students negotiate assessment? In R. Allington, & S. A. Walmsley (Eds.), *No quick fix. Rethinking literacy programs in America's elementary schools* (pp. 78-94). New York: Columbia University. Teachers College Press.

Street, B. (1984). *Literacy in theory and practice.* Cambridge: Cambridge University Press.

Sweigart, W. (1991). Classroom talk, knowledge development, and writing. *Research in the Teaching of English, 25*, 497-509.

Sydes, M., & Hartley, J. (1997). A thorn in the Flesch: observations on the unreliability of computer-based readability formulae. *British Journal of Educational Technology, 28*, 143-145.

Tate, G. H. H. (1982). Armadillo. In *Encyclopedia Americana* (Vol. 2, pp. 328-329). Danbury, CT: Grolier.

Tchudi, S. N., & Huerta, M.C. (1983). *Teaching writing in the content areas: Middle school/junior high.* Washington, DC: National Education Association.

Teale, W. & Sulzby, E. (Eds.). (1986). *Emergent literacy: Writing and reading*. Norwood, NJ: Ablex.

Thomas, P. R., & Bain, J.D. (1984). Contextual dependence of learning approaches: the effects of assessments. *Human Learning, 3*, 227-240.

Thurstone, L. L. (1938). Primary mental abilities. *Psychometric Monographs*, No. 1.

Tierney, R. J., O'Flahavan, J.F., & McGinley, W. (1989). The effects of reading and writing upon thinking critically. *Reading Research Quarterly, 24*, 134-173.

Tierney, R., Carter, M., & Desai, L. (1991). *Portfolio assessment in the reading-writing classroom*. Norwood, MA: Cristopher-Gordon Publishers.

Tillema, H. H. (1998). Design and validity of a portfolio instrument for professional training. *Studies in Educational Evaluation, 24*, 263-278.

Torney-Purta, J. (1996). Conceptual change among adolescents using computer networks and peer collaboration in studying international political issues. In S. Vosniadou, E. De Corte, R. Glaser, & H. Mandl (Eds.), *International perspectives on the design of technology-supported learning environments* (pp. 203-219). Mahwah, NJ: Erlbaum.

Torney-Puta, J. (1994). Dimensions of adolescents' reasoning about political and historical issues: Ontological switches, developmental processes, and situated learning. In M. Carretero & J. F. Voss (Eds.), *Cognitive and instructional processes in history and the social sciences* (pp. 103-122). Hillsdale, NJ: Erlbaum.

Torrance, M., & Jeffery, G. (1999). Writing processes and cognitive demands. In: Rijlaarsdam, G. & Espéret, E. (Serie Eds.) & Torrance, M. & Jeffery, G. (Vol. Eds.) (1999). *Studies in writing: Vol. 3. The cognitive demands of writing*, pp. 1-12. Amsterdam: Amsterdam University Press.

Torrance, M., Thomas, G. V., & Robinson, E. J. (1991). Strategies for answering examination essay questions: Is it helpful to write a plan? *British Journal of Educational Psychology, 61*, 46-54.

Torrance, M., Thomas, G.V., & Robinson, E.J. (1994). The writing strategies of graduate research students in the social sciences. *Higher Education, 27*, 379-392.

Tourunen, E. (1996, July). *How to support reflection in project-based learning using learning portfolios and information technology?* Paper presented at the 5th International Conference on Experiential Learning, Cape Town, South Africa [http://cs.jyu.fi/~eero/eero-pub.html].

Trenchs, M. (1996). Writing strategies in a second language: Three case studies of learners using electronic mail. *Canadian Modern Languages Review, 52*, 464-497.

Tucknott, J. M. (1998). The effects of writing activities on children's understanding of science. Unpublished M.Ed. project. Victoria, BC: University of Victoria.

Tucknott, J. M., & Yore, L. D. (1999). *The effects of writing activities on Grade 4 children's understanding of simple machines, inventions, and inventors*. Paper presented at the annual meeting of the National Association for Research in Science Teaching, Boston, MA, March 27-31.

Tynjälä, P. (1998). Writing as a tool for constructive learning: Students' learning experiences during an experiment. *Higher Education, 36*, 209-230.

Tynjälä, P. (1998a). Traditional studying for examination versus constructivist learning tasks: Do learning outcomes differ? *Studies in Higher Education, 23*, 173-189.

Tynjälä, P. (1998b). Writing as a tool for constructive learning: Students' learning experiences during an experiment. *Higher Education, 36*, 209-230.

Tynjälä, P. (1999). Towards expert knowledge? A comparison between a constructivist and a traditional learning environment in the university. *International Journal of Educational Research, 31*, 355-442.

Tynjälä, P., & Laurinen, L. (2000, September). *Promoting learning from text through collaborative writing tasks*. Paper presented at the EARLI SIG Writing Conference, Verona, Italy.

Valencia, S. H. (1990) A portfolio approach to classroom reading assessment: The whys, whats, and hows. *The Reading Teacher, 43*, 338-340.

Valencia, S.H. & Place, N. (1994). Portfolios: A process for enhancing teaching and learning. *The Reading Teacher 47*, 666-669.

Van den Bergh, H., & Rijlaarsdam, G. (1999). The dynamics of idea generation during writing: An online study. In G. Rijlaarsdam & E. Espéret (Series Eds.) & M. Torrance & D. Galbraith (Vol. Eds.), *Knowing what to write: Conceptual processes in text production* (pp. 99-120). Amsterdam: Amsterdam University Press.

Van Dijk, T. A. (1980). *Macrostructures: An interdisciplinary study of global structures in discourse, interaction, and cognition*. Hillsdale, NJ: Erlbaum.

Van Dijk, T. A., & Kintsch, W. (1983). *Strategies for discourse comprehension*. New York: Academic Press.

Van Meter, P., Yokoi, L., & Pressley, M. (1994). College students' theory of note-taking derived from their perceptions of note-taking. *Journal of Educational Psychology, 86*, 323-338.

Van Nostrand, A. D. (1979). Writing and the generation of knowledge. *Social Education, 43*, 178-180.

Van Wijk, C., & Sanders, T. (1999). Identifying writing strategies through text analysis. *Written Communication, 16*, 51-75

Venable, T. L. (1998). Errors as teaching tools – the mass media mistake. Engendering in students a healthy skepticism for the printed word. *Journal of College Science Teaching, 28*, 33-37.

Vermunt, J. (1995). Process-oriented instruction in learning and thinking strategies. *European Journal of Psychology of Education, 10*, 325-349.

Vermunt, J. (1998). The regulation of constructive learning processes. *British Journal of Educational Psychology, 68*, 149-171.

von Glasersfeld, E. (1984). An introduction to radical constructivism. In P. Watzlawick (Ed.) *The invented reality. How do we know what we believe to know. Contributions to constructivism* (pp. 17-40). New York: Norton.

von Glasersfeld, E. (1995). A constructivist approach to teaching. In P. Steffe & J. Gale (Eds.) *Constructivism in education* (pp. 3-15). Hillsdale, NJ: Erlbaum.

von Wright, J. (1992). Reflections on reflection. *Learning and Instruction, 2*, 59-68.

Vosniadou, S. (1994). Capturing and modeling the process of conceptual change. *Learning and Instruction, 4*, 45-69.

Vosniadou, S., de Corte, E., & Mand, H. (Eds.). (1994). *Technology-based learning environments. Psychological and educational foundations.* Berlin: Springer.

Vosniadou, S., de Corte, E., Glaser, R., & Mandl, H. (Eds.) (1996). *International perspectives on the design of technology-supported learning environments.* Mahwah, NJ: Erlbaum.

Voss, J. F., & Wiley J. (1997). Conceptual understanding in history. *European Journal of Psychology of Education* [Special issue], *12*, 147-158.

Vygotsky, L. S. (1962). *Thought and language* (E. Hanfmann & G. Vakar, Trans.). Cambridge, MA: MIT Press.

Vygotsky, L.S. (1978). *Mind and society: The development of higher psychological processes.* Cambridge, MA: Harward University Press.

Wade, S. E., & Thrathen, W. (1989). Effect of self-selected study methods on learning. *Journal of Educational Psychology, 81*, 40-47.

Wade, S. E., Thrathen, W., & Schraw, G. (1990). An analysis of spontaneous study strategies, *Reading Research Quarterly, 25*, 148-166.

Wason, P. C. (1970). On writing scientific papers. *Physics Bulletin, 23*, 407-408. Reprinted in J. Hartley (Ed.), *The psychology of written communication* (pp. 258-251). London: Kogan Page.

Weiner, B. (1986). *An attributional theory of motivation and emotion.* New York: Springer.

Wertsch, J. V., & Hickmann, M. (1987). Problem solving in social interaction: A microgenetic analysis. In M. Hickmann (Ed.), *Social and functional approaches to language and thought* (pp. 251-266). New York: Academic Press.

Wetzel, K. (1996). Speech-recognizing computers: A written-communication tool for students with learning disabilities? *Journal of Learning Disabilities, 29*, 371-380.

Wild, M. (1999). A tale of two mailing lists. *Education and Information Technologies, 4*, 4, 369-389.

Wiley, J. & Voss, J.F. (1996). The effects of 'playing historian' on learning in history. *Applied Cognitive Psychology, 10* (Special issue), S63-S72.

Wilkerson, L., & Irby, D. M. (1998). Strategies for improving teaching practices: A comprehensive approach to faculty development. *Academic Medicine, 73*, 387-396.

Windschitl, M. (1998). The WWW and classroom research: What path should we take? *Educational Researcher, 27*, 28-33.

Wineburg, S. (1991a). Historical problem solving: A study of the cognitive processes used in the evaluation of documentary and pictorial evidence. *Journal of Educational Psychology, 83*, 73-87.

Wineburg, S. (1991b). On the reading of historical texts: Notes on the breach between school and academy. *American Educational Research Journal, 28*, 495-519.

Wineburg, S. (1994). The cognitive representation of historical texts. In G. Leinhardt, I. L. Beck, & C. Stainton (Eds.), *Teaching and learning in history* (pp. 85-135). Hillsdale, NJ: Erlbaum.

Wojtas, O. (1999). Accused students claim they 'cooperated' not collaborated. *Times Higher Educational Supplement,* August 27th, p. 36.

Wolf, D. P. (1989). Portfolio assessment: Sampling student work. *Educational Leadership, 46*, 35-39.

204

Wolfe, C. R. (1995). Homespun hypertext: Student-constructed hypertext as a tool for teaching critical thinking. *Teaching of Psychology, 22,* 29-33.

Wolfe, E. W., Bolton, S., Feltovich, B., & Bangert, A. (1996). A study of word-processing experience and its effect on essay writing. *Journal of Educational Computing Research, 14,* 3, 269-283.

Wray, D., & Lewis, M. (1997). Teaching factual writing: Purpose and structure. *Australian Journal of Language and Literacy, 20,* 131-139.

Wright, R. E., & Rosenberg, S. (1993). Knowledge of text coherence and expository writing: A developmental study. *Journal of Educational Psychology, 85,* 152-158.

Yasuda, S., Okamoto, A., Hasegawa, H., Mekada, Y., Kasuga, M., & Kamata, K. (1998). Communication system for people with physical disability using voice recognizer. *IEICE Transactions on Fundamentals of Electronics Communications and Computer Sciences, E81A,* 6, 1097-1104.

Yore, L.D., (1992). Plausible reasoning in elementary and middle school science: Abduction, induction, deduction, and hypothetico-deduction. *B.C. Catalyst, 35,* 14-21.

Yore, L.D. (1993). Comment on 'Hypothetico-deductive reasoning skills and concept acquisition: Testing a constructivist hypothesis'. *Journal of Research in Science Teaching, 30,* 607-611.

Yore, L. D., & Shymansky, J. A. (1997, September). *Constructivism: Implications for teaching, teacher education and research—breakthroughs, barriers and promises.* Paper presented at the National Science Council ROC Workshop for Science Educators, Taipei, Taiwan.

Yore, L. D., Hand, B., & Prain, V. (1999, January). *Writing-to-learn science: Breakthroughs, barriers, and promises.* Paper presented at the International Conference of the Association for Educating Teachers in Science, Austin, TX.

Young, A., & Fulwiler, T. (Eds.) (1986). *Writing across the disciplines. Research into practice.* Upper Montclair, NJ: Boynton/Cook.

Zellermayer, M., Salomon, G., Globerson, T., & Givon, H. (1991). Enhancing writing related metacognitions through a computerized writing partner. *American Educational Research Journal, 28,* 373-391.

Zeni, J. (1994). Oral collaboration, computers and revision. In S. B. Reagan, T. Fox, & D. Bleich (Eds.), *Writing with. New directions in collaborative teaching, learning and research* (pp. 213-226). Albany: SUNY Press.

Zinsser, W. (1988). *Writing to learn.* New York: Harper & Row.

NAME INDEX

SUBJECT INDEX

214

constructivist epistemology, 40; 83
content analysis, 70; 77; 78; 171
content knowledge, 111; 112; 131;
    137; 141; 148
content problem, 10
co-operation skill, 53
copy-paste strategy, 141
counter-argumentation, 171
creative process, 12
creative synthesis, 35
creative writing, 80
creativity, 148; 154; 155; 160
critical review, 10; 15; 136; 141; 186;
    191; 196; 199
critical thinking, 47; 51; 54; 78; 154;
    204
CSILE, 169; 170; 172; 174; 200
cultural discourse, 14
cultural practices, 12; 14; 16; 42; 112
curricular landscapes, 57; 81

deduction, 110
deductive reasoning, 110
deep approach, 43
deep approach strategy, 43; 47; 142
deep learner, 47
deep-level processing, 134
dialogism, 50
dialogue journal, 48
dialogue journal writing, 171
digital portfolio, 157
disciplinary enculturation, 33
discourse community, 11; 35; 36; 174
discourse knowledge, 111
discourse processing, 132; 133; 136
discourse synthesis, 28; 30; 32; 35;
    44; 46; 196
discursive convention, 8
dispositional dialectic, 45
domain-content learning, 7; 8; 12; 16;
    37; 50; 54; 55
domain-specific skill, 39; 53
Duncan SEI scale, 67

editing, 9; 21; 49; 69; 70; 72; 73; 77;
    78; 81; 114; 160; 161; 162; 163; 165;
    177; 190
elaborateness of argumentation, 67
e-mail communication, 171
emergent literacy, 57; 58; 60
emotional disposition, 106
empowerment, 145; 146; 152; 157;
    187; 198
epistemological beliefs, 20; 86; 92;
    97; 101; 108
epistemological roles, 62
epistemological understanding, 106
essay writing, 44
essay-writing skill, 135
expert knowledge, 38
explicit instruction, 112; 114

forward search hypothesis, 15
free writing, 10; 14; 16; 154

generating ideas, 9; 10; 87; 112
generation of knowledge, 151; 203
generative processing, 133
generative study strategies, 21
generative writing, 133; 137
generic academic skill, 38
genre, 4; 10; 11; 15; 106; 111; 112;
    113; 114; 115; 119; 127; 142; 170;
    180; 200
genre hypothesis, 15
genre schemata, 10
goal-orientation, 146; 151
grammar checkers, 164; 165
Grammatik 5, 165
guided practice, 142

habits of mind, 105; 106; 125
higher order thinking, 84
higher-order thinking, 43; 44; 83;
    101; 114; 119
history curriculum, 83; 87
history learning, 85
horizontal collaboration, 49
hypermedia, 171; 172; 173; 185; 186;
    189; 193; 201

216

modelling, 91; 142
multidimensionality, 41
multimedia, 157; 158; 159; 160; 167;
    172; 173; 175
multimedia portfolio, 157
multimedia technology, 167
multivoiced classroom, 14; 187
multivoicedness, 50

negotiation, 40; 41; 53; 119; 145;
    146; 152; 153; 154; 173; 197
new media literacy, 160
Non-generative activities, 137
note taking, 116; 117; 131; 132; 133;
    134; 136; 137; 139; 140; 141; 142;
    192
note taking strategies, 142
note-taking strategies, 133; 183

objectivist epistemology, 21; 40
oral competence, 2
organizational transformation, 23; 25;
    28; 29; 35; 79

patterns of argumentation, 106; 111;
    114
peer assessment, 42; 148; 154
peer interaction, 168; 193
peer-response groups, 59
personal literacy, 4
portfolio, 21; 42; 43; 56; 145; 146;
    149; 150; 151; 152; 153; 154; 156;
    157; 158; 159; 160; 183; 186; 190;
    191; 192; 194; 196; 198; 202
portfolio assessment, 145; 146; 149;
    152; 156; 189; 190; 197
PREP Editor, 168
prior knowledge, 62; 85; 86; 91; 109;
    110; 133; 135; 139; 147; 184; 192
procedural facilitation, 14
procedural knowledge, 39
process of building knowledge, 23
process of making meaning, 23
process writing, 7; 52; 53
process-oriented approach, 19

project-based learning, 52; 53; 54;
    185; 202

quality of reasoning, 126

rationale of authenticity, 19
rationale of authority, 19
rationalism, 110
reasoning, 3; 16; 20; 44; 50; 83; 84;
    85; 88; 91; 95; 98; 100; 102; 105;
    107; 108; 109; 115; 118; 119; 125;
    126; 128; 137; 183; 192; 193; 202
reasoning processes, 114
reflection, 9; 10; 11; 14; 18; 19; 20;
    21; 39; 47; 48; 53; 55; 67; 68; 79;
    106; 114; 117; 119; 126; 145; 146;
    147; 148; 150; 151; 153; 154; 168;
    183; 185; 192; 194; 202; 203
reflective skill, 39; 48; 55
reflective texts, 97
reliability, 68; 69; 70; 149; 151; 154;
    196; 197
renegotiation, 153
report writing, 37; 52; 192
resources management, 54
revising, 9; 10; 15; 45; 49; 58; 61; 69;
    70; 72; 78; 81; 112; 114; 154; 160;
    163; 164; 177; 178; 188
revising skills, 58
revision, 9; 10; 11; 14; 19; 45; 58; 69;
    73; 77; 78; 79; 91; 168; 178; 204
rhetorical problem, 10; 188

scaffolding, 61; 64; 115; 126; 183
science communication, 106
science curriculum, 83; 90; 91; 98;
    101
science literacy, 105; 106; 108; 110;
    126; 127; 128; 183; 190
science understanding, 106
science writing heuristics, 115
Science Writing Heuristics, 20
science writing strategies, 111
scientific epistemology, 105; 106
scientific inquiry, 105; 106; 107; 108;
    112; 118; 119; 125

LIST OF CONTRIBUTORS

Pietro Boscolo, Professor of Educational Psychology at the University of Padova, Italy. boscolo@psico.unipd.it

William Carbonaro, Assistant professor of sociology at the University of Notre Dame in South Bend, Indiana, USA.

Adam Gamoran, Professor at the Department of Sociology of the University of Wisconsin-Madison, USA, Gamoran@ssc.wisc.edu.

Brian Hand, Associate professor in Science Education at Iowa State University, Ames, Iowa, USA. bhand@iastate.edu.

James Hartley, Research professor of psychology at the University of Keele, Staffordshire, UK. j.hartley@keele.ac.uk.

Pirjo Linnakylä, Research professor at the Institute for Educational Research, University of Jyväskylä, Finland. linnakyl@jyu.fi.

Kirsti Lonka, Director of the Development and Research Unit, Learning Centre, Faculty of Medicine, University of Helsinki, Finland. kirsti.lonka@helsinki.fi.

Lucia Mason, Associate Professor of Developmental and Educational Psychology at the University of Lecce, Italy. lmason@ilenic.unile.it.

Nancy Nelson, Professor at the College of Education of Louisiana State University, Louisiana, USA. nnelson@lsu.edu.

Martin Nystrand, Professor in the Department of English at the University of Wisconsin-Madison, USA. nystrand@ssc.wisc.edu.

David R. Olson, Professor at the Centre for Applied Cognitive Science, at the Ontario Institute for Studies in Education of the University of Toronto, Canada. dolson@oise.utoronto.ca.

Vaughan Prain, Associate professor in the School of Arts and Education, La Trobe University, Bendigo, Australia. v.prain@bendigo.latrobe.edu.au.

Virpi Slotte, Researcher at the Nokia Learning Center China. Ext-virpi.slotte@nokia.com.

Päivi Tynjälä, Senior researcher at the Institute for Educational Research, University of Jyväskylä, Finland. ptynjala@cc.jyu.fi.

Larry D. Yore, Professor of Science Education in the Department of Curriculum and Instruction, University of Victoria, Canada. lyore@pop.uvic.ca.

Studies in Writing

7. P. Tynjälä et al. (eds.): *Writing as a Learning Tool*. 2001
    ISBN HB 0-7923-6877-0; PB 0-7923-6914-9

For Volumes 1 – 6 please contact Amsterdam University Press, at www.aup.nl

KLUWER ACADEMIC PUBLISHERS – DORDRECHT / BOSTON / LONDON

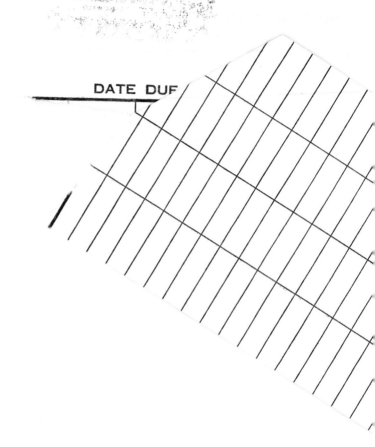

DATE DUE